T0304239

Industrial Relations in Europe

First published in 1985 *Industrial Relations in Europe* examines the development of trade unions and their relations with the employers and employers' organisations in a number of Western European countries in the 1980s. The shared characteristics of these systems are common heritage of political democracy, market economies, the right of employers to manage the business for which they are responsible and the right of employees to belong to unions which are free to bargain and to seek political goals which will advance the interests of their members. With case studies from Denmark, Germany, France, Great Britain, Norway etc. the volume showcases the major structural changes brought about by technological, economic and social factors which had significant implications for trade unions and traditional patterns of industrial relations. A major response was the erosion of centralized processes of decision making and a return to the individual, local initiative and an increased interest in entrepreneurship. This book is a must read for scholars of political economy, industrial economy and economics in general.

Industrial Relations in Europe

The Imperatives of Change

Edited by B.C. Roberts

Routledge
Taylor & Francis Group

First published in 1985
by Croom Helm

This edition first published in 2022 by Routledge
4 Park Square, Milton Park, Abingdon, Oxon, OX14 4RN

and by Routledge
605 Third Avenue, New York, NY 10017

Routledge is an imprint of the Taylor & Francis Group, an informa business

© 1985 The Swedish Employers' Confederation (SAF)

Publisher's Note
The publisher has gone to great lengths to ensure the quality of this reprint but points out that some imperfections in the original copies may be apparent.

Disclaimer
The publisher has made every effort to trace copyright holders and welcomes correspondence from those they have been unable to contact.

A Library of Congress record exists under ISBN: 0709942125

ISBN: 978-1-032-37093-4 (hbk)
ISBN: 978-1-003-33529-0 (ebk)
ISBN: 978-1-032-37094-1 (pbk)

Book DOI 10.4324/9781003335290

INDUSTRIAL RELATIONS IN EUROPE

The Imperatives of Change

Edited by
B.C. ROBERTS

CROOM HELM
London ● Sydney ● Dover, New Hampshire

© 1985 The Swedish Employers' Confederation (SAF)
S–10330, Stockholm, Sweden
Croom Helm Ltd, Provident House. Burrell Row,
Beckenham, Kent BR3 1AT
Croom Helm Australia Pty Ltd, First Floor, 139 King Street,
Sydney, NSW 2001, Australia

British Library Cataloguing in Publication Data

Industrial Relations in Europe: The Imperatives of Change.
   1. Trade-unions—Europe
   I. Roberts, B.C.
   331.88'094   HD6657

   ISBN 0–7099–4212–5

Croom Helm, 51 Washington Street,
Dover, New Hampshire 03820, USA

Library of Congress Cataloging in Publication Data
Main entry under title:

Industrial relations in Europe.

   Includes index.
   1. Industrial relations—Europe—Addresses, essays,
   lectures.   2. Trade-unions—Europe—Political
   activity—Addresses, essays, lectures.
   I. Roberts, B.C. (Benjamin Charles), 1917–
   HD8376.5.154   1985   331'.094   85-21321

ISBN 0-7099-4212-5

CONTENTS

Foreword

Introduction: The SAF Project   1

1. Denmark *Aage Tarp*   5

2. France *J. Nousbaum*   45

3. Federal Republic of Germany *H. Müller-Vogg*   75

4. Great Britain *B.C. Roberts*   100

5. Italy *Federico Butera*   137

6. The Netherlands *A.F. van Zweeden*   159

7. Norway *Einar Thorsrud*   180

8. Sweden *Anders Leion*   204

9. Trade Union Trends in Western Europe:
   A European Perspective *Roland Tavitian*   222

10. Trade Union Trends in Western Europe:
    An American Perspective *Malcolm R. Lovell Jr*   242

A Summary Conclusion   262

Notes on Contributors   271

Index   273

FOREWORD

Important structural and social changes are taking place throughout the industrial world. In the countries of Western Europe trade unions and employers' organisations have an important role to play in this context. They are free to define their own targets and methods, their organisation and relationships with governments and political parties. How they respond to the fundamental changes occurring in the 1980s and beyond is of vital importance to the prosperity of all sections of every society.

Sweden is no exception. In view of this fact, the Swedish Employers' Confederation (SAF) considers it important to broaden its frame of reference. We believe that a development of our future industrial relations would be helped by an international perspective. Discussions on industrial relations have been based on a rather narrow perspective or—at international gatherings—on short-term or specific issues.

In the light of this situation, SAF decided in 1983 to set up a project group. The following were appointed members:

Lennart Grafström, Director, SAF, (Chairman of the group)

Gunnar Högberg, Director General, Swedish Shipowners Association

Lennart Hörnlund, Director General, Swedish Forest Industry Association

Janerik Larsson, Editor-in-Chief, SAF-Tidningen (SAF-Weekly Newspaper)

Gösta Rönn, Director, SAF

Anders Röttorp, Director and Head of Employer Training, SAF

Björn Ström, Director and Head of Personnel Abroad, SAF

Göran Trogen, Executive Director, Swedish Employers' Confederation, General Group

Svante af Winklerfelt, Director General, Swedish Textile and Clothing Industry Association

The Secretary was Tommy Wahlström, SAF (now with the Philips Organisation in Sweden).

In the early phases, Christian Bratt (now Labour Attache in

London) and Annika Sandström (now Rector of the Wallenberg Institute) also participated.

The project group agreed on the following programme:

(1) Qualified and independent reporters from a number of West European countries would be employed to describe conditions in their own country. In addition to this, a European and an American perspective would be added.

(2) The reporters were to be given a common reference framework in the form of a memorandum which the project group drew up.

(3) The reports would be long term in character. The Group emphasised that the views about the future should not be anything in the nature of misty visions but a more concrete look at the five to ten-year perspective.

The SAF study was published in Swedish in the Spring of 1985 under the title 'Western Europe in 1990. The Need to Renew the Organizations on the Labour Market'. It has led to an intense debate in Sweden.

In the course of the project we have met a gratifying interest from various circles in other countries. This reaction has led to an agreement with Croom Helm Ltd to publish the reports in English.

After some introductory comments and the country reports this book concludes with three international analyses, one from the EEC point of view, one from the US angle and a summary conclusion by the Editor, Professor Benjamin Roberts. Each author is responsible for his own contribution.

One person has made this book eminently more readable than it otherwise might have been: Professor Roberts, who has also written the National report about Great Britain and the Summary Conclusions. I wish to thank him sincerely for his enthusiastic and highly competent work.

A fundamental idea behind the SAF project is to initiate and stimulate constructive discussion in Sweden regarding the future role of labour market organisations – both trade unions and employers. It is our hope that this version in English can serve the same purpose in other countries and in the international context.

Olof Ljunggren
Director General
The Swedish Employers' Confederation

INTRODUCTION: The SAF Project

B. C. Roberts

The aim of this project, launched by the Swedish Employers' Confederation (SAF), is to examine the contemporary development of trade unions and their relations with employers and employers' organisations in a number of West European countries with a common heritage of political democracy, market economies and industrial relations systems. The shared characteristics of these systems are: the right of employers to manage the business for which they are responsible; and the right of their employees to belong to unions which are free to bargain and to seek political goals which will advance the interests of their members.

In a period of great technological, economic and social change the SAF believes it to be necessary to investigate, first, the possible future impact of union policies on the conditions under which private enterprise may be required to operate and, second, the effect that these policies might have on the ability of firms to be efficient, profitable and to provide their employees with secure and well-rewarded employment. Along with employers in other West European countries, the SAF is deeply concerned that union power may be used to induce political change inimical to the maintenance of pluralism and a free market economy.

Swedish employers are particularly interested in developments in other countries *vis-à-vis* the degree of centralisation in bargaining structures and processes; attitudes to corporate ownership; employee participation on boards of directors and participation in capital funds; the influence of unions on political parties and government policies; the role of union officials and rank-and-file members in union decisions and activities; and the direction of union ideology—is it shifting towards a greater degree of consensus with employers, or in the opposite direction towards more radical and conflict-orientated policies?

Individual authors were free to develop their analysis of the trends as they saw them, taking account, as far as they thought necessary, of the particular concerns identified by the SAF. Their studies show that in every country major structural changes brought about by technological, economic and social factors have had significant implications for trade unions and traditional

1

patterns of industrial relations. A major response to these changes has been the erosion of centralised processes of decision-making and a return to the individual, local initiative, a revaluation of the importance of private enterprise and an increased interest in entrepreneurship. Trends towards decentralisation exist in countries with socialist governments such as France, as well as in countries with non-socialist governments such as Great Britain.

Unemployment has not led to major revolts from the left and there has been no great upsurge of Marxist radicalism. Rather, this situation has led to closer co-operation between managers and workers within firms and increased efforts to meet competition and create new enterprises. Closer direct relations between management and workers is on the ascendant at plant level. At times this rapprochement involves union representatives and changes in the patterns of collective bargaining, but not infrequently it is achieved through new organisational developments such as quality circles and briefing groups.

At the national level the course of socio-political events in Great Britain, Denmark and the Netherlands show that during the past five years there have been major realignments which have brought about changes so fundamental as to be unlikely to be completely reversed even on a change of government. Such major shifts have been influenced by political and corporate leadership responding, through political parties and business organisations, to the challenges with which they were confronted.

In these respects, Western Europe seems to be following trends already established in the USA and Japan where managements and unions share a greater degree of mutual understanding and concern to resolve problems in their common interest. Whilst it is unlikely that there will be a complete convergence, it would be surprising if the European countries were not to continue to move closer to these nations with their less centralised free market economies.

Industrial relations continue to pose significant problems in all countries, but as the studies show solutions are unlikely to be found by a return to bureaucratic corporatism. Governments have a major role to play in maintaining the social and economic conditions that foster a stable climate of industrial relations, but the evidence suggests that in the context of highly competitive markets employers and unions are being compelled to recognise that they cannot escape responsibility for restructuring their organisations and conducting a dialogue that will enable them to reconcile conflicting interests with the need to achieve the most efficient use of resources.

The new patterns of industrial relations which are emerging inevitably reflect the dominant imperatives which have surfaced under the influence of long-term economic, social and technological changes. These developments, which are analysed in the following chapters, raise many questions, but they also point to answers which are likely to be the basis of new models of industrial relations in the Europe of the next decade.

1 DENMARK

Aage Tarp

Population	5,000,000
Per capita GNP, 1982	US$ 11,000
Exports as per cent of GNP, 1982	27
Number of large companies (among the 500 largest outside the USA)	1 with 13,000 employees

Governments		
	1945	National coalition—all parties except the Farmers and Nazis but including representatives of the Resistance movement
	1945–7	Democratic Liberals-Conservative-Liberals
	1947–50	Social Democrats
	1950–3	Non-Socialist coalition Democratic Liberal-Conservative Parties
	1953–7	Social Democrats
	1957–60	Social Democrats in coalition with Single taxers and Liberals—both non-Socialist parties
	1960–2	Social Democrats in coalition with Liberals
	1962–8	Social Democrats
	1968–71	Coalition of Conservative-Liberal-Democratic Liberal Parties
	1971–3	Social Democrats
	1973–5	Democratic Liberal minority government
	1975–8	Social Democrats
	1978–9	Social Democrats in coalition with Democratic Liberals
	1979–82	Social Democrats
	1982–	Non-Socialist four-party coalition, Conservative-Centre Democrats-Liberals-Christian People's Party

6 Denmark

Public sector (share of GNP, 1982, including transfers)	61 per cent
Trade union membership	around 80 per cent
Trade unions	Landsorganisationen De Samvirkende Fagförbund is the dominating organisation with around 1,300,000 members (around 25 per cent are salaried employees) Faellesrådet för Danske Tjenstemands-og Funktionaer-organisationer (FTF) has 270,000 members.
Employers' organisations	The Danish Employers' Confederation (DA) is the largest with some 22,000 affiliated firms with 480,000 employees.

The Background

The roots and the present structure of the Danish trade union movement date back more than 100 years. Already before the turn of the century, today's system of trade unions and employers' federations and their central organisations was established with strong, representative, well-organised and responsible bodies.

The Danish trade unions, from the outset, have always had and still have broader objectives than just the protection of wages and working conditions. Culture, education and vocational training, as well as social security for workers—above all, unemployment insurance—have been important preoccupations. Characteristic features of the Danish system still include the perception of vocational training as a tripartite task, and the maintenance of an unemployment insurance scheme operated by unemployment funds that are closely linked with the individual trade unions. Such provisions are considered an integral part of the trade union movement.

There is no legislation on trade unions and employers' federations in Denmark. The right of freedom of association is embodied in the Constitution and is practised without any registration or approval of organisations and their collective agreements. Neither has Denmark legislation regulating the industrial relations system. The legal basis of the entire industrial relations framework is, apart from a few exceptions, the system of basic agreements between the two central labour and employers' organisations. The first Main Agreement was signed in 1899. It sets out all the rules of mutual recognition, work stoppages, industrial peace, the employer's right to manage, etc. This agreement has been amended a few times, and it is complemented with the Agreement on Co-operation and Co-operation Committees (1946) and its annexe on Technological Innovation (1981). The main principles of the 1899 agreement stand unchanged, however, and its role as the legal basis of the Danish industrial relations system has never been challenged.

Article 5 of the Main Agreement states the employer's right to demand that supervisors and other employees representing the employer are excluded from membership of any workers' organisation. This means that associations of supervisors and other managerial employees cannot be affiliated with the Federation of Danish Trade Unions (Landsorganisationen i Danmark: LO). Hence it follows that workers' unions and their central organisation can only organise certain well-defined categories of employees, at least in the private sector. Supervisory and salaried employees have their own central organisation parallel to the LO.

The organisational structure of the Danish trade unions is based on the vocational skills of workers who have received apprentice training. In most trades all male workers without such training are members of the big General and Transport Workers' Union (Specialarbejderforbundet i Danmark: SID), and female workers are members of the General Female Workers' Union (Kvindeligt Arbejderforbund i Danmark: KAD). Only a few trades are covered by industrial unions. In a later section the attempts to change this outdated structure and to replace it with industrial unions will be described and evaluated.

The central LO and its affiliated unions form the Danish trade union movement, which is one of the three wings of the Danish labour movement. The other two wings are the Social Democratic Party and Labour's Co-operative Movement, which comprises mainly consumer and building co-operatives. What is the significance of the close ideological, political and organisational ties between the unions, the Social Democratic Party and the co-operatives? Are there tensions within this close alliance? These are the questions examined in the following pages.

In the Danish industrial relations system co-determination and co-operation are embodied in the basic agreements between the central organisations. Employers and workers have thus themselves negotiated the conditions, extent and limits of workers' influence on management. The only exception to this is the provision in the Company Act which gives all employees in a limited company employing more than 50 persons the right, irrespective of union membership and without union intervention, to elect from among themselves three of the members of the board of directors, who will, however, always be a minority. This approach to co-determination was, after some hesitation, welcomed by the employers.

Danish labour market organisations have gone through three stages since they were founded. Up to 1899 they were hostile organisations fighting each other. From then and up to the late 1940s, they had as their primary aim the defence of opposing interests within an industrial relations system formed and operated by themselves. Since then and at least up to the late 1960s, they extended their fields of activity to include collaboration, promotion of mutual worker–employer interests, good human relations, worker participation, quality of life at the workplace, etc. The unions, however, never gave up their belief in and pursuit of conflicting interests. An extensive and ever-increasing member service in many fields forms an important part of the activities of the organisations on both sides of industry.

Whether the third stage has been continued or abandoned during the 1970s and the beginning of the 1980s, as well as an analysis of the prospects for a continuance of the dual aims of the unions, are among the fundamental subjects of this chapter.

The Trade Unions under Full Employment and the Creation of the Welfare Society

With the rapid economic growth from 1958 and its concomitants of full employment and the creation of the modern welfare society, the Danish trade union movement faced a hitherto unexperienced situation. Within a few years the unions had reached most of their traditional goals, which they had been fighting for over the decades since their inception: rapidly increasing real wages, full employment, improved job and social security, improved vocational training, participation, etc. The socialist ideology that had been abandoned many decades before as unattainable was, however, not reactivated at this stage. The optimal and ideal society was now a welfare state based on the mixed economy. Private enterprise and a market economic system, controlled and monitored by a Social Democratic government in close collaboration with the trade unions, as well as positive employer –worker relations at enterprise level, came to be considered the best basis for continued increases of real wages and increased worker and trade union influence. The terms socialism and socialist policy were conspicuous by their absence.

It was soon proved that this strategy had both positive and unexpected negative effects on the influence and functioning of the trade unions. Difficulties were experienced in achieving the major part of wage increases through collective bargaining. Labour shortage, better relations and mutual understanding at the shopfloor level between workers and management, as well as better systems of incentive payment, bonus schemes, etc., caused locally obtained wage increases, statistically registered as wage drift, which soon superseded what the unions could get through the normal bargaining-rounds. Difficulties in maintaining rank-and-file loyalty, interest in and support for the unions emerged. A good many of the union leaders felt that the traditional worker solidarity, represented by and embodied in the trade unions, was gradually being endangered. The threat had three sources: partly it came from the improved mutual management–worker understanding at plant level; partly from the fact that the individual worker under full employment obviously did not feel the need for and importance of trade union protection of his or her working conditions; and partly it was due to the individual worker's interest in acquiring and using all the modern status symbols—some of them inducing a capitalist mode of thought—at the cost of spending less time and effort on trade union activity and solidarity.

The first small indications of cleavage in the well-known solidarity and unity shown by the trade unions also appeared as negative after-effects of the solidarity wage policy. This approach, at the demand of unions representing the lowest-paid, was pursued at the bargaining-rounds from the early 1960s until 1979, and resulted in centralised wage negotiations, special increases to the lowest-paid and hence narrowed wage-differentials, as well as a stronger position for the central organisations. The skilled and higher-paid workers and their unions were not enthusiastic, but they did not officially object and criticise this policy as long as their members could use wage drift to catch up with the increases secured by the low-paid.

Centralised negotiations were also a serious problem for many union leaders in that the process curtailed their role and possibilities to demonstrate their ability to obtain special improvements and wage increases for their members.

Having reached practically all their goals the trade unions soon found themselves in a kind of political, and maybe even an ideological, vacuum. Without new and generally accepted goals and demands it was difficult to maintain the support and enthusiasm of the rank and file and to unify them in a common front. It was soon obvious that the trade union leaders urgently needed new goals to unify and to cement the existence and survival of the trade union movement. This need for new goals was soon exacerbated by the dangerous infiltration of new, very left-wing, activists in many unions' local organisations; something new was needed to counteract their influence.

The increased intervention of Parliament and government in price formation, resource allocation, etc., in the private sector, was the inevitable consequence of the modern mixed economy, as well as the ever-higher level of public service and efforts to even out the distribution of income, through tax policy and many new kinds of social benefits and transfers to the active population. This implied that the trade unions were faced with new tasks and challenges as well as new negotiation partners, i.e. political and public authorities. It is often asserted that the LO during the late 1960s initiated a secret campaign to gain more power and influence, and aimed at extending its area of activity to important fields of government authority and at participation in the decision-making of the political bodies.

A closer investigation of this subject does not lead to a rational and reliable confirmation of this assertion. There does not seem to be any stated or hidden change of the LO ideology and objectives during this period. A careful examination of the traditional trade union aims and responsibilities to their members proves, on the contrary, that very high priority has always been given to efforts to improve the income and thus the material living standards of their rank and file. Hitherto this had been achieved by using just one instrument, namely wage negotiations to increase nominal and real wages. Hence, the only and natural partners were the private employers and their federations. However, the extension of the mixed economy towards *dirigisme* and the simultaneous creation of the welfare society meant that the material living standard was no longer determined almost exclusively by the gross wage. New and important elements were government influence on, and often distortion of, the price structure in the private sector; housing and rent policy; a profusion of free public services; new tax systems; a higher tax burden; new basic principles for the social security system; and social transfers. It does not appear illogical that the LO in its pursuance of its traditional obligations tried to influence these new factors which, to an ever-greater extent, were determining the living standards of workers. Increasingly the LO had to focus on real disposable income, and the nominal wage was only one of its determinants.

Since the negotiating partners in these matters were government and Parliament, it is not surprising that the institutional links between the trade union movement and the Social Democratic Party, as well as Social Democratic members of government, were strengthened. However, this also implied that the traditional distribution of tasks and thus the demarcation line between these two wings of the labour movement became less evident and distinct, and indeed ran the risk of fading away entirely.

To the uncritical observer, it looked as if the LO had intruded into the provinces of the Social Democratic Party and the arena of political democracy; at the same time, the LO's traditional policy in the wage and industrial relations fields had been influenced by the Social Democratic policy in Parliament. This identification of LO policy with Social Democratic policy and vice versa, and thus an apparent lack of an autonomous and objective trade union policy in many fields has, as described in a later section, caused serious problems.

The increasingly exacting government and other public interference in a growing number of smaller sections of economic life and production had an important consequence: public authorities were obliged to consult those affected and interested, for, as only they had the necessary detailed knowledge, the implementation of public regulations inevitably required their involvement in planning, decision-making, administration, etc. The organisations of both sides of industry and the trade organisations were accorded hitherto unparalleled influence on the management of society (war periods excepted). This was not because they wanted more power, but as a necessary instrument of a corporate economic and social welfare system. It was possible to use the term 'democratic' instead of '*dirigiste*' to characterise the system, as the trade unions had never before been so involved in policy implementation and decision-making at so many levels; they gained a great deal of new experience and knowledge of the functioning and management of the public sector, as well as knowledge of monitoring and controlling private enterprises.

This development came gradually and did not seem to have been planned in advance. Closer trade union contacts with the Social Democratic government on economic policy and its implementation began in 1963, when, following the failure of wage negotiations, the government enacted the first comprehensive incomes policy scheme which included renewal of collective agreements by law. This happened after confidential deliberations with the LO about eonomic policy and new social security measures for workers had taken place. The traditional division of tasks, responsibility and autonomy between the three wings of the labour movement was, however, maintained in principle, although government–LO contacts appeared to have become more frequent. At this early stage, their talks seem to have been confined to social security questions, active manpower policy and efforts to train unskilled groups. These were new fields of policy, but the employers were at this stage soon consulted by government, and many new tripartite working groups and commissions were established and entrusted with the preparation of new reforms. Government often started this work at the LO's request.

Many of the LO initiatives also led to closer contacts with and influence on central and local administration. At this stage employer representatives were still invited to participate on the many newly established bodies, so it was a period characterised by tripartite involvement in more and new fields of direct and indirect bearing on social security and employment conditions—both of which had significant implications for labour costs.

The trade unions also became more active at the local, and not least at the regional levels, during this period. They were above all interested in regional development in order to eradicate the remaining pockets of unemployment.

Aftermath of Full Employment: New Trade Union Policy, Targets and Ideology—Trade Union Solidarity Problems

Towards the end of the 1960s the rapid increase of real wages evened out. Higher wages only resulted in higher prices. The inflationary trend became very marked in Denmark. The tax burden on a normal wage income got heavier because of the costs of the welfare society. Industry's investments were increasingly concentrated on labour-saving equipment due to higher labour costs and shortage of manpower. There were frequent economic policy changes—'stop–go'—to cope with more and more serious balance-of-payments problems. Mutual union jealousy occasioned by differences in wage increases became common. The trade union organisational structure, and hence the structure of the system of collective wage agreements, was criticised and accused of hampering industry's flexibility and adaptability to new technology and production. There was a good deal of frustration and lack of satisfaction in spite of the rapid increase of wage-earners' money income. Small but efficient left-wing groups became active at the shopfloor level, and not without success. They won support for extreme wage demands, started illegal—'wild cat'—strikes and spread dissatisfaction with the unions and their Social Democratic leaders at all levels for being too moderate, non-socialist and for supporting employers. It was obvious that the LO and the unions were in crisis, although this was never admitted openly. As could be expected, the unions reacted partly by changing course in some of the institutional arrangements, partly by proposing a re-volutionary new policy aiming at a complete structural change of influence and distribution of income and ownership in the private sector, and thus a structural change of the existing pattern of society. The proposal was the creation of the central wage-earner fund; in the Danish LO terminology, 'economic democracy'.

These serious problems coincided with the retirement, after more than 25 years, of an LO president who had been highly esteemed in all circles. The election of the new president was rather sensational, as the LO Congress did not elect the candidate nominated by the Executive Committee. Their new president was a strong personality. He had a firm and extrovert nature, often taking the lead and running ahead of his troops. The new president found it necessary to concentrate more power within the LO at the cost of the autonomy of the member unions. This course of action was intended to strengthen the trade union front in relations with employers, left-wing groups inside and outside the unions, political parties, the then Liberal coalition government and public administration.

A centralisation of influence and target-setting was also necessary to solve internal rivalry between some of the unions and between members employed in the private and the public sectors. It was equally necessary to have a better co-ordination of policies, targets and activities of all the affiliated unions. In this context, both real and formal power in Denmark had traditionally rested with the individual union, a fundamentally autonomous and independent body. Collaboration within the LO framework and a joint trade union policy could only be established by consensus between member unions, who often have divergent, even opposite, interests. The LO has no formal means or authority to enforce a joint policy. To a large extent, therefore, the LO strength depends on the personality and ability of its president and his officials to make the members co-operate and act jointly. The 1967 LO Congress was convinced that the trade union movement, in the situation prevailing at that time, needed a strong and forceful personality and a dedicated Social Democrat as president, someone who could unite as well as formulate and implement new policies, set new targets and solve external and internal problems.

After 1967 the new LO leader started to rearrange the policies and targets of the trade union movement. As the interdependence between, on the one hand, working conditions and wages and, on the other, important economic and social factors became more obvious, the LO staff of professionals, economists, lawyers, etc., was expanded. This was soon reflected in much better and more factually argued LO proposals and policy.

Soon the LO claims became more far-reaching. The LO leaders and their experts realised that the wage-policy instrument could not continue to give higher real wages. Further improvement of workers' incomes and living standards had to be acquired by new means. It soon became evident that the trade unions had become more determined and militant, demanding more power and influence on the management of private enterprises, as well as a greater influence on the government's economic, social and income distribution policies. During the years up to 1974 this new style was mainly manifested in the following ways.

The Main Agreement was denounced. The LO demanded, in

addition to co-determination, considerable restrictions on the employer's right to direct. Renegotiation of the Agreement on Co-operation and Co-operation Committees was also demanded, with the purpose of extending representative industrial democracy at the enterprise level to higher-management fields. These two agreements, seen by employers as the real basis of the Danish industrial relations system, were, however, renewed without changes to their basic principles. This may be taken as an interesting indication that the LO, despite its intensive campaigns and many words, did not aim at sudden, radical changes in the industrial relations system and hence of the economic and political system of society. Neither did the LO at this stage wish to limit the autonomy of the central organisations to determine themselves the industrial relations system and working conditions.

However, in spite of factional discretion the formal and real trade union attitude *vis-à-vis* the employers—not least at the plant level—became also less and less co-operative and, in some cases, militant. Some trade unions, especially those with many members in the lower-wage brackets, were having to deal with an increasing number of successful activities from left-wing groups (e.g. 'wild cat' strikes in key areas). The general impression was that many union leaders and the LO were reluctant to suppress these activities too severely, for even though they constituted clear violations of the agreements, suppression ran the risk of splitting some unions and of establishing left-wing dominance in others, with the result that the Social Democratic leaders and the LO would lose control over a considerable part of the union movement. The LO tactics were therefore partly a certain turn to the left to maintain control over as many unions as possible, partly a more militant policy *vis-à-vis* the employers, and partly a rather aggressive public stance which stressed opposing interests more than had been the case for many years. In some cases, illegal work stoppages and other actions violating the agreements were given indirect and moral support.

Also there was a change in the LO attitude and action at the bargaining level. Wage and other demands became bigger and more rigorous. The centralisation of negotiations became more insistent because of the higher priority given to the solidarity wage policy, and hence to what appeared to be special increases for the lower-paid groups. This did not, however, contribute to stronger and better trade union unity. The unions of the skilled and better-paid workers were sceptical and reluctant to support efforts to narrow wage-differentials further, but as long as they could catch up with increases for the low-paid through wage drift, they did not oppose the low-wage policy too much. However, the tensions were beginning to show.

A new challenge to the LO in this period was the wage relations between the traditional LO members in the private sector and the rapidly increasing number of public employees, of which many were organised in LO-affiliated unions. In particular, it proved to be a delicate problem to continue the tradition of regulating wages in the public sector, with its very moderate productivity increases, in accordance with the wage development in the new private sector, which had high productivity improvements. And many of the new, rather left-orientated, big groups of public employees demanded an autonomous wage regulation when negotiations in the private sector had come to an end.

The LO membership was fast becoming more heterogeneous than before and this by itself provided a source of further tension, which soon proved serious and added new dimensions to the solidarity wage policy dilemma.

During this period the trade union movement also took the first decisive steps towards a policy focusing as much on the real disposable income as on the nominal wage. This manifested itself in the formulation of demands relating to tax policy, housing and rent policy, price control and social security policy. Some of the central LO proposals were for a further graduated income tax system, as well as improved sickness and unemployment benefits, reduced workers' and increased employers' and government contributions to these social insurance schemes, improved public pension funds for workers and radical improvements to the occupational safety system.

With a Social Democratic government again in office from 1971, the ties between the LO and the government were rapidly re-established. From now on, the government consulted the LO on most important policy issues. The LO had direct access to government, and could thus initiate new legislation and threaten employers with enactment of its demands to pre-empt the employers rejecting them at the LO–employer negotiations. The traditional and well-established Danish tripartite system came under threat and began to vanish. The employers' federations were virtually defenceless, as most of the LO-government contacts were informal and took place behind closed doors.

Because of the increasing LO influence on political decisions, it became more and more difficult to distinguish the LO policy from that of the Social Democratic government.

The traditional division of tasks between the three wings of the labour movement crumbled. The LO policy no longer concentrated only on workers' interests, mainly *vis-à-vis* the employers, but developed a much wider scope—one identical with Social Democratic policy. However, this was not acceptable to all the LO rank and file, partly because of changes in the membership of the unions. The number of trade union members began to increase considerably after 1973, largely as a result of a growing labour force and the stronger desire of an increasing number of employees to be covered by unemployment insurance. For the categories of employees organised by LO-affiliated unions, this is practically, although not formally, possible only if they also join a union which administers the actual unemployment insurance fund. This is one of the main reasons why the number of members in LO-affiliated unions increased from 900,000 in 1971 to 1.3 million in 1981. In 1970, 71 per cent of all workers and 50 per cent of all salaried employees and civil servants were unionised. In 1981 the figures were 87 per cent and 79 per cent, respectively. In this context it should be recalled that 400,000 salaried and civil servants at the lower levels are members of LO-affiliated unions. Not all union members are Social Democrats and, above all, a very considerable number of these new members—research says the majority of them—were not. So the seeds were sown for a comprehensive and very serious discontent with the close relations between the LO and the Social Democratic Party.

The most radical LO action was the central wage-earner fund proposal, so-called economic democracy. There were many reasons behind this scheme, officially submitted in 1971. One of the reasons was the trade union belief that the owners and management of private enterprises have a substantial and real power in society, not least over their employees. In the union view, efforts to obtain more and real worker influence and co-determination did not sufficiently restrict this power, and neither did government control, since a substantial part of real power in a mixed economy was the economic power founded on ownership of production resources. So trade unions could fulfil their obligation to improve the conditions of workers only by securing for the unions co-ownership and thereby power over private enterprises.

The other main reason behind the proposal appeared to be the acknowledgement that the functional distribution of incomes could not be changed further in favour of lower wage earners without very adverse effects. The fiscal and social transfer instruments had reached their limits to even out the distribution of disposable incomes. The only solution to the problem of improving workers' incomes and living standards, therefore, was to procure a new source of income, namely income from capital ownership. At the same time, the LO considered it had a natural right to extend the system of democratic control prevailing in most other parts of society to this new area, and thereby create more equality and democracy in society.

However, individual ownership was not acceptable as this could result in new groups of workers feeling and acting as private capitalists, a consequence hostile to the needed increase in worker solidarity. Neither would it meet the requirement of generating greater worker adherence to the unions and thus cementing the foundation and survival of the trade union movement. The LO solution was the logical one of collective ownership through a system of trade-union-managed central wage-earner funds. The formal exercise of the power and rights stemming from this collective ownership should not, however, be totally centralised; on the contrary, most of the formal power should be exercised by the employees at the individual enterprise, and the remainder by the board of the central fund.

There were other, and to a large extent contradictory, interpretations and explanations of the system within union and Social Democratic circles. These ranged from seeing it as heralding the creation of a new type of socialist society, to those views which understood it to mean the maintenance of the existing market economic system based on private ownership only with the modification that the distribution of power, influence, wealth, income and capital should be more equal and democratic than before. A close investigation and assessment of the whole scheme pointed mainly at the latter interpretation, not least when considering that the working group behind the proposal had a majority of well-known, traditional, solid, right-wing Social Democrats and trade union leaders.

It was, however, evident to employers and even to many in the trade unions that the proposed economic democracy was, by its very nature, likely to be inconsistent with a market economy and with the maintenance of a pluralistic and democratic political system.

The proposal caused a wave of protests and opposition from private business, the non-socialist parties and most of the associations of civil servants and salaried employees. Neither was the proposal met with enthusiasm and support from the trade unions' rank and file or the Social Democratic voters. It was, on the contrary, received with considerable hesitance and scepticism in these circles. And in spite of intensive information and propaganda campaigns over the 1970s, there has been no noticeable increase of worker acceptance of the scheme. To judge from dozens of polls, less than 30–5 per cent of the LO rank and file and Social Democrats are in favour of even a moderated version. For the population as a whole, the percentage is much lower.

The economic democracy scheme could only be carried through by law. In 1973 the then Social Democratic government introduced a Bill to the Folketing (Parliament) based on the LO proposal. It was met with a massive majority protest from the opposition and many Social Democratic MPs were silent or lukewarm. The Bill had only a first reading; since then the wage-earner fund proposal has never again been reintroduced in the Folketing, in spite of the constant LO campaign. The reason for not reintroducing the proposal may be both the lack of support from LO members and the threat from the non-socialist parties to force a referendum should a law on economic democracy be passed—which would entail its rejection.

The wage-earner fund case is also interesting and extraordinary in that the trade union and Social Democratic leaders have not had the sympathy or support of the overwhelming majority of their rank and file and voters. Why the union leaders have not been able to win the support they need and the implications of this situation will be explained later.

Private business—mainly represented by the Federation of Danish Industry and the Danish Employers' Confederation—was critical when they realised the extent of the LO–government co-operation and the LO influence. It was, however, difficult to find effective counter-measures. The strongest reaction came in 1973 from the Danish Employers' Confederation (DA). During the central negotiations, it became evident that the LO and the government had arranged strategy and tactics as regards alternative solutions, but also as regards subjects that were normally dealt with by the tripartite bodies which had formerly given the two parties equal influence on government and legislation. Now it was evident that the tripartite system was only a formality, and the DA was deprived of its normal influence. The DA's protests had no effect, but during negotiations the DA refused to approve the draft settlement unless the LO promised to revert to the normal tripartite procedure, giving the LO and DA equal terms and influence. To this end, the DA demanded the insertion of a protocol in the final settlement on this matter. The LO was reluctant to agree to this demand, but the DA stood firm. This matter was one of the factors which provoked strikes and lock-outs and the loss of 3.6 million working days in 1973. The employers had the protocol inserted, although this did not change the real state of affairs. The LO–government collaboration continued, albeit only within the formal, long-existing framework for co-operation and contacts between the different wings of the labour movement in Denmark.

Private business and its organisations also reacted strongly against the economic democracy proposal. Through the mass media and at thousands of meetings it was criticised. The DA and the Federation of Danish Industry published booklets with alternative proposals. As it became evident that the LO proposal had no chance of being enacted, they stopped their research for better solutions as well as the counter-campaigns. This also implied the abandonment of efforts to find necessary, new, durable and constructive solutions to the income and wealth distribution problems, solutions consistent with maintenance of full employment and economic stability in a pluralist democracy.

Trade Union Policy and Reactions to Political and Structural Crisis since 1974

The development in Denmark since the oil price shock in 1973 has been greatly influenced by the LO and the trade union movement. There appears to have been a noteworthy change in trade union attitudes and policy as from 1980–1, a change which has sown the seed for future problems of trade union development and unity.

The open Danish economy is very vulnerable to international recessions, as it depends totally on imported raw materials, including energy, and on exports. Having already in 1973 a serious internal structural crisis, the recession hit Denmark twice as hard. The delicate task for Parliament, government and the labour market parties was to find a formula and relevant instruments for sharing out the 3–4 per cent decrease in wealth caused by the recession. Another serious problem was to isolate the imported inflation and prevent it from being passed on to domestic prices and costs of production in a country where all wages and salaries, and many other economic factors, were automatically index-regulated.

In addition to these economic problems, Denmark has suffered unstable conditions in Parliament from late 1973 to the present day. New political protest parties gained many seats from both the Social Democrats and the Liberal Parties. The old parties reacted by being very suspicious and much less co-operative. A conspicuous polarisation was the inevitable result, and Parliament became less and less able to agree on a relevant policy to solve the nation's increasingly serious actual and structural problems.

On top of this came internal problems in the big Social Democratic Party. Loyalty and internal discipline had been characteristic of this party, but a serious split on the Executive Committee was now compounded by another split between a right, centre and dynamic left wing, that weakened the party's vigour, determination and long-term thinking. The LO and the trade unions therefore became the real stable and vigorous part of the labour movement, and consequently they felt obliged to take initiatives and act on behalf of the labour movement. In practice, the LO to a large extent decided the policy of the Social Democratic government. It was striking to observe cabinet members' frequent visits to the LO headquarters. Before that time, the LO leaders had always come to the ministers.

The LO, and in particular, some of the big unions, as well as the Social Democratic government, were loath to acknowledge the necessity of immediate action to restructure the Danish economy and to implement measures to ensure stabilisation of the wage development and a general reduction of living standards, exempting only small, socially weak groups. During the first years of the recession, the unions considered it a temporary problem that ought not to influence the solidarity wage policy and other main targets. The economic situation was therefore aggravated to such an extent that, at a later stage, drastic—and for the labour movement, unacceptable—steps were necessary. Inaction allowed the problems to grow even bigger.

It should be admitted that the LO top leaders and their advisers were in a delicate and difficult situation. Under heavy pressure from the large and militant General and Transport Workers' Union (SID) and many public employees, they had to pursue efforts to improve real wages for these groups and the solidarity wage policy. The wage-differentials were thus further eroded, because the higher-paid workers could no longer re-establish the earlier differentials through wage drift. So tensions between the higher- and lower-paid workers were exacerbated. This policy also caused increased unemployment among the less qualified and added to the complexity of wage negotiations.

The employers' reaction to this policy was firm opposition, because it impaired their already weakened competitive strength. The old, relatively friendly and positive mutual understanding and co-operative spirit between the central organisations and most of the member organisations suffered. Many trade union representatives had the impression—rightly or not—that the employers took advantage of the high unemployment in their wage policy. The LO's constant wage-earner fund threat also contributed to less cordial, often hostile attitudes, but at most workplaces the good relations remained unchanged. Workers understood the problems of the enterprise very well, and preferred continued employment to higher nominal wages; the distance between the bottom and the top of the trade union hierarchy increased. There was also a certain discrepancy between the official union wage policy and the understanding of wage restraint among many responsible workers at the shopfloor level. The DA demanded the cancellation of the automatic wage-indexation clause in collective agreements. This was definitively rejected by the LO and the government after strong pressure from SID and public employees.

From the mid-1970s the gap between the union demands and the DA's offers widened to such an extent that it could no longer be bridged through the central bargaining-rounds. In order to avoid imminent big strikes in sectors that had previously been exempted from strike actions, comprehensive lock-outs and political unrest, the collective agreements were renewed by legislation in 1975, 1977 and 1979. It was a widespread and uncontested impression that the LO had previous arrangements with the government to guarantee the renewal of the collective agreements by law, including the LO demands if they were rejected by the employers.

The LO leaders were, on the other hand, in an extremely

difficult situation. Already at a relatively early stage they were aware of the adverse effects of their actual wage policy, and they tried in cautious terms to propose moderations, but without success. It would also be a delicate and difficult task to try to force through a new policy that was contrary to the policy which the very same leaders had promoted so strongly for many years. It could at the same time cause a split in the trade union movement and a massive negative reaction. The internal tensions were already strong. There was also a fear of giving the extremist left-wing activists any opportunity to initiate actions that the trade union leaders could not control. Thus there was very little positive understanding and response when the LO president, in 1975, warned about the necessary 'narrow path' for future wage policy.

A close examination of the LO policy and collaboration with the government during the years 1975–80 proves that the LO top leadership was, after all, well aware of the adverse effects of its own policy, but that a formal and real revision was found impossible. The LO tried, therefore, to find ways and means, in co-operation with government and responsible union leaders, to compensate for and neutralise the adverse effects on employment, economic stability, etc., of its own wage policy. If it could also thereby promote other union targets, it would at the same time imply a needed strengthening of the LO position.

Accordingly, in his report to the 1979 LO Congress, the LO president stated that the LO had deliberately moved into fields other than the traditional industrial relations and labour market tasks. The motivation for this was partly that workers' living standards and conditions of life were to an increasing extent determined by factors other than just their wages, partly that under the prevailing political crisis and instability in Parliament it was up to the trade union movement to shape the course for the future development of society, and partly that the LO, instead of pursuing what it considered a moderate wage policy, was compelled to safeguard workers' interests by other means, i.e. legislation in a great many and new fields. The LO had in this context tried to make Parliament implement a less restrictive incomes policy, without success. Nor had the LO succeeded in establishing a moderate version of economic democracy, nor was there in Parliament support for the LO tax reform proposal. The LO president also stressed that the solidarity policy was the main foundation for all LO activities and policies, and that it should be respected unconditionally.

The LO intensified its already considerable international activity, in particular at the Nordic and West European levels. The staff of international experts was expanded, and the LO as well as many affiliated unions became very active within West European trade union organisations. The LO has not least been interested in a better co-ordination of economic and employment policies within the EEC.

Internal Reactions to the LO Policy, Reconsiderations, First Signs of Internal Discord and of Revision of the Policies of the Trade Union Movement

The joint LO–government policy—that to a large extent was formulated and forced through by the LO—did not result in the intended effects on unemployment, lower inflationary rate, reduced balance-of-payments deficits, etc. The Social Democratic Party and the government had to face growing problems, both internally and in Parliament. The question asked within the party, by other political parties and by the general public was: who governs Denmark? Was it the LO, above all its president, or the government and Parliament who had the real power? According to a 1980 opinion poll, the general public felt that the LO had considerably more influence than government and Parliament. Many found it a matter for growing concern that the LO took so many political initiatives, and that so many government policy proposals came from joint LO–government working groups and were introduced in Parliament only after LO endorsement. The influence of the LO was made evident by the fact that so many LO–government meetings took place in the LO headquarters, and that the LO tried more or less openly to dictate to the prime minister when to resign, when to appeal to the country and with whom to collaborate. For these reasons and because of a difference of opinion on political goals and measures, the relations between the LO president and government soon became strained. The considerable tension between the LO president and the prime minister rapidly degenerated into open hostility.

There was considerable disagreement between the LO president and government as regards the priority to be accorded to the economic democracy proposal as opposed to other urgent legislation. A moderated proposal was now introduced as a profit-sharing scheme. The LO presented a new argument for the scheme, namely that the wage-restraint policy needed to promote employment would lead to an extraordinary increase of profits. Wage restraint was therefore acceptable only if workers got their share of the increased profits in return. The LO president strongly urged the government to include the new economic democracy scheme as an integral part of the economic crisis package introduced to Parliament in December 1979. Other important ingredients were deletion of the next cost-of-living allowances, a 3–4 months' wage and price freeze and a new depreciation of the Danish Krone. The government knew that Parliament would reject the whole package if the wage-earner fund was included as an inseparable element, but the LO president insisted on its remaining. When the government did not include it, the LO president proclaimed this as a serious violation of what he and the prime minister had agreed on.

There was, however, no unanimous support in the trade unions for this unconditional insistence on economic democracy, nor for its inclusion in the package. On the whole, leading union representatives and the rank and file were becoming more openly and more deeply divided on the question of the wage-earner fund and its priority.

There was also a growing discontent with the concentration of influence and power within the LO and its president. This was without precedent and many felt the traditional autonomy and independence of the individual unions to be at risk. Many union leaders and the rank and file began to consider if it was really possible, in the long run, to maintain the united wage-earner front. The solidarity policy of the past 15–20 years was not a complete success and had had many negative effects, while the famous Scandinavian welfare model had proved to be a costly failure in many respects.

When examining the actions and reactions of wage-earners and union leaders in the critical years 1979–80, it appears that there was widespread scepticism about the idea of centralisation of influence and power at both the national and labour market levels. The possibilities of reintroducing a freer and more decentralised system, and much less integration of wage policy with general economic policy, became a focus of debate. A more decentralised wage policy and the market economy, although in a moderated and monitored version, should be given higher priority. These considerations coincided with an extraordinarily steep increase in unemployment, so that the core of highly qualified, steady, hard-working workers was now severely hit. To these workers the link between the level of employment and cost of production, not least wage costs, was evident. Such considerations were not, and will most probably never be, admitted by union leaders—at least not until they retire. In their official speeches and Congress resolutions they adhered to the traditional solidarity policy.

As from 1980–1 there was a significant departure from the bargaining behaviour and other activities of the previous two decades. This new course was manifested not least in the 1980 Agreement on Negotiation Procedure. This agreement is re-negotiated every second year before the start of the bargaining-round. In 1980 it was, contrary to the previous 20 years, agreed to start with decentralised negotiations and, as far as possible, avoid central or government intervention. It was thus left to the direct parties to negotiate without binding central demands. The central organisations should take over only if some of the direct parties failed to reach agreement. This procedure was a success in 1980.

The same procedure was followed in 1982–3, but not with the same positive results. The SID found the possibilities of getting special increases for its members endangered and preferred central negotiations and the traditional solidarity line, for which it had always been the most outspoken supporter. This union therefore blocked the decentralised negotiations, with the result that the 1982–3 round was a mix of centralised and decentralised bargaining, causing a good deal of ill-will among the unions that preferred the decentralised procedure. The parties subsequently agreed that the 1984–5 negotiation round should revert to central procedures. The agreement is, however, rather loose in its wording and subject to a good deal of interpretation. It was, after all, surprising that the DA—a long-term advocate of de-centralised negotiations and a decentralised wage policy—should have given in to the LO demand for this procedure. It caused protests from member federations. Neither was there a general acceptance from all LO unions. It appeared as if the LO had to give in to very strong demands for central negotiations from SID in order to avoid an explosion of the deep unrest and tensions within the trade union movement. It would, however, not be surprising in the future to see a very untraditional combination of centralised and decentralised demands and negotiations, with the main stress on the latter. This is favoured by powerful forces on both sides.

Even before the 1984–5 agreement the subject of bargaining procedure had already provided a focus for the negative tensions between unions representing skilled workers and SID. Matters of controversy were wage-differentials, the scope and principle of solidarity, systems of vocational training and, not least, the organisational structure of the trade union movement. It appears that within a few years it will be a necessary if delicate task to redefine, on the one hand, the subjects of common interest and hence solidarity policy and joint action, and, on the other hand, the areas of special interest which are thus subject to special, decentralised negotiations.

This whole complex of problems and tensions became even more delicate when the LO Congress resolved that trade union policies should give much higher priority to the achievement of full employment and the restoration of the competitive strength of Danish industry. Wage claims had therefore to be moderated in favour of new investment and the creation of more jobs in the private sector. This implied that due consideration had to be given to the special conditions of the individual industries and trades. Hence, it followed logically that high priority to full employment and job creation and high priority to solidarity wage policy are inevitably mutually exclusive.

The reorientation towards employment and the acknowledge-ment of the employment–wage cost interdependence was already manifested in the trade unions' factual wage policy at this stage. Both in the 1980–1 and in particular in the 1982–3 negotiations, wage demands were considerably moderated, and the negotiations were, in comparison with the previous ten years, straightforward and concluded without government intervention. It was also quite extraordinary that the unions—apart from relatively few 'wild cat' strikes beyond their responsibility, and with relatively moderate protests—abided with the new non-socialist government's inter-vention in the already existing agreements, even though this inter-vention dictated some months' wage freeze and the cancellation of the automatic wage-indexation clauses over a two-year period. Under Social Democratic governments, the trade unions had always declared the existing agreements sacred and taboo to the legislator. It was as remarkable that the LO and most of the unions, official arguments aside, in practice respected government's recommendation to keep the annual wage increases, including wage drift, within a 4 per cent limit over the next two-year period, and that they accepted new temporary clauses in the minimum-wage agreements giving the central employer organisations a hitherto unknown right to monitor and intervene to ensure that the proclaimed wage-restraint targets were observed.

The moderation of most unions' and workers' demands and actions was also reflected in a fall in the number of legal and illegal strikes in the private sector. It appears that most union leaders strengthened their measures against the attempts of left-wing groups to provoke unrest and 'wild cat' strikes. The only exceptions were SID and certain unions of public employees. They moved in the opposite direction, thus intensifying tensions within the trade unions. The role and behaviour of SID and its president during the bus drivers' strikes and blockades in April and May 1984 disclosed a notable lack of leadership and capability to maintain internal discipline and make members respect existing rules. SID has, on the contrary, given moral and other support to members on illegal strikes. The Labour Court fined SID 20 million Danish Krone.

The attentive observer could also register an interesting change in the trade union attitude to technological development and innovation. The original stance of some union representatives had been that a considerable part of unemployment was caused by new technology. From influential trade union circles, not least SID, came the demand that workers and local unions should have co-determination and a voice in the introduction of new technology at plant level, and that dismissals should be forbidden. It was also proposed that government and the unions should formulate a technology policy aimed at central management for the introduction of new technology, and geared to the development of employment. The attitude in these circles was thus rather negative, but after profound studies of the effects of new technology versus effects on employment and real wages of *not* keeping pace with other industrialised countries, the official LO attitude changed in a positive direction. The LO and the DA were therefore able, without major difficulties, to come to terms on a new general agreement governing the introduction of new technology. It was the unanimous attitude that this was a matter of co-operation, and the agreement was accordingly given the form of an appendix to the Agreement on Co-operation and Co-operation Committees. The LO has formulated a policy stating its willingness to co-operate and to contribute to the successful use of new technology in such fields as industrial investment promotion, vocational training follow-up, and job environment and occupational safety. The agreement does not concede co-determination,but it is the policy of the LO to monitor the effects of new technology on the functioning of society, the decision-making processes, the information flow, etc.

A few years ago the LO took the remarkable step of enlarging its secretariat with a micro-economic research unit. It is staffed with business economists, accountants and similar professionals. The original purpose was to assist employee representatives on the boards of directors, worker members on co-operation committees and shop stewards, where they have to understand and analyse accounts, budgets, etc. To fulfil this purpose, the research unit must collect detailed information about most Danish firms. It is already engaged in a study of owners of Danish shares with the intention of examining the concentration of power in the private sector. This unit may in future prove to be of essential importance as it can supply detailed facts on individual firms and industries, on which the unions can base their wage policy. If the research is continued in a systematic way, the LO and the unions can successively acquire a unique knowledge of private business in Denmark. This will form a solid basis for wage demands and for insight into and assessment of the reliability of an employer's case when negotiating at the enterprise, industry and national levels. It is not yet a stated policy to develop the unit in this direction, but the LO is fully aware of the value of a databank with detailed information on most Danish firms.

The most recent trade union initiative, by many considered sensational, is the establishment of the Danish Business Investment Fund. It is founded on the same basis as most other business investment funds, but with the special purpose of supplying risk-taking capital to private enterprises and thus contributing to the creation of new jobs that otherwise would not have existed. The fund is an integral part of the unions' new employment-promotion policy. At first there was a great deal of scepticism in private business—and above all in its organisations —about the real motives behind the fund. Many feared that the intention represented a back-door move towards economic democracy and wage-earner influence and power over private enterprises at a stage when the wage-earner fund scheme was unlikely to be carried out in the foreseeable future. This impression was apparently confirmed by statements from leading left-wing Social Democrats. The originators behind the scheme were, however, right-wing, responsible trade union leaders and Social Democrats, and it was they who formed the temporary board. They strongly argued that the new fund was part of the LO employment-promotion policy, the only aim being to create new jobs. This being so, the finance and insurance sectors—including commercial banks—and the pension funds were invited to participate with two-thirds of the capital. The trade unions' share would be one-third. These sectors were convinced that the scheme was genuine and worthy of support. The new fund started its business in 1984 with a capital of 300 million Danish Krone, of which the unions have supplied 100 million and banks, insurance companies, pension funds, etc., 200 million. Well-known leaders from big private firms, banks and insurance companies now sit side by side with presidents of big unions on the board of the fund. The fund has already been so successful and has had so many applications for capital that it is now considering doubling the capital to 600 million Danish Krone.

The Danish Trade Union Movement in the 1980s and the 1990s

The above long review and analysis is a necessary background for estimating the future short- and long-term trends in the development of the Danish trade union movement. The change of priority in favour of employment promotion, the reaction and frustrations caused by the collapse of the LO-inspired and supported economic and social policy, and strong internal tensions are just some of the reasons why the LO and the unions are at present in a state of self-examination and reconsideration of their goals and policies, maybe even philosophy and ideology. The internal and external reactions to the past policy, internal rivalry and jealousy, some unions' recent intolerant behaviour and treatment of individuals, as well as bold initiatives to start new unpolitical unions and a growing outspoken unwillingness to be forced to give financial support to a political party through the union subscription, mean that the trade union movement is facing more vital problems and challenges of renewal than ever before in its 100-year history. All these problems have been aggravated and necessitate a quicker solution following the metropolitan bus strike in 1984, when SID and a few hundred activists evinced total disrespect for other members of society, laws and ethical rules.

What kind of society is to be preferred by the individual union member? What should be the role and function of the trade unions in this society? How, if at all, can they co-operate with a non-socialist government? How shall relations with employers be developed? Will and should future wage-differentials, wage systems, wage elements and wage formation be different from those of the past? How will future trade union, and thus the LO, organisational structure be constituted? Should power and decision-making be more centralised or more decentralised? Should wage negotiations be centralised or decentralised? What will, on the whole, be the size of the membership of the affiliated unions, and thus the balance of power and influence within the LO? What should their relation to the Social Democratic Party be? Will the political affiliation to other parties, not least non-socialist parties, of an increasing number of union members influence the traditional LO role as one of the wings of the Social Democratic labour movement? How will changes in the structure of the labour force influence the number of members in the LO-affiliated unions? Will the politically neutral organisations of salaried employees and public employees attract members from the LO-covered areas and thus increase their membership and influence at the cost of the LO?

The importance of, as well as the anwers to, these and similar questions can only be assessed in the context of previous development, priorities and preferences, successes and failures.

Although it is difficult to predict trade union preferences, policies and goals, there are, however, many indications of the most probable medium-term course—a huge body such as the Danish trade union movement cannot and will not make hasty and abrupt shifts overnight. Revolutions do not occur in Denmark. One of the most important indications of the future course was the election of the new LO president on the retirement of the old, powerful president two years ago. The new president, elected without rival candidates, is in many respects a contrast to his predecessor. A firm and strong, but tolerant, quiet and pragmatic personality, he does not want the lime-light: he listens first to find joint interests, and then seeks to co-ordinate, unify and act. He appears to be the kind of leader who will give optimal independence and autonomy to the affiliated unions without losing sight of unity and solidarity. It can therefore be expected that the LO way of acting over the next decade will be characterised as voluntary co-ordination of decentralised union activities. This implies that centralised, massive trade union drives, aimed at structural changes to society or the industrial relations system, are unlikely. On the other hand, there will be considerable efforts to re-establish and strengthen internal trade union cohesion and solidarity and to achieve a more efficient and harmonious organisational structure, one more fitted to coping with the rapidly changing needs of occupational qualifications and thus the need of a higher occupational mobility.

The LO Congress in November 1983 did not adopt resolutions about far-reaching changes of society, more co-determination, corporatism, etc.—not even about the organisational structure of the LO. The new president's report, which was adopted unanimously, on the contrary pointed to the need to strengthen existing private enterprises, to establish new ones, to encourage more private initiative through more public support, and to improve competitive performance through, *inter alia*, relatively lower wage costs. Also stressed were reduced growth of the public sector and thus a lower tax burden, as well as a better infrastructure to act as the basis for an efficient private sector using high technology. There were, of course, formally vehement protests against the new government's cuts of certain social benefits. It would have been remarkable had the report not repeated the wish to see the introduction of wage-earner funds, by and by; but now it is to be achieved by means of profit-sharing and in a moderated form. The report stressed the argument that this would contribute to more investments in the private sector and more employment, as well as more worker participation and productivity.

This report confirmed an impression gleaned from other LO documents and statements from high-ranking trade union leaders; the great majority of the trade union movement does not foresee nor desire any decisive changes of the existing mixed market economy, pluralistic system of society—apart from the proposed moderated economic democracy system. A more equal distribution of ownership, influence and incomes would contribute to a fairer and more democratic society with better sharing of risk and responsibility, and with more efficient and competitive enterprises.

The kind of society that the LO envisages for the years to come, and the economic and social policy to be pursued by the trade unions and the Social Democratic Party, was debated at the Congress. The programme for the period 1984–9 can be summarised under these headings:

improvement of competitive strength of private enterprises;
fairer distribution of the tax-burden;
a changed, improved and more efficient public sector, that could contribute more to welfare;
shorter hours of work;
better and safer conditions of work;
co-ownership;
more and better education and vocational training;
more efficient and economic use of energy resources;
more stable monetary and currency policies;
curbing inflation through a balanced and co-ordinated development of all categories of incomes;
a good social balance, i.e. no group in society shall benefit from sacrifices of other groups, and weak groups shall be safeguarded through wage-earner solidarity.

The LO and most of the unions have realistically acknowledged the turn of the electorate to the right. This they regret and efforts must be made to help the Social Democratic Party regain its strength and rebuild its image. With the exception of the big SID, it is not intended to fight the new non-socialist government (e.g. by directly combating it, or by being unwilling, and even refusing, to co-operate): The LO and most of the unions adopted a balanced course *vis-à-vis* the new government, and at an early stage the LO aired the idea of tripartite contacts for exchange of information with a view to mutual co-ordination, in relevant fields, of the policies of government and of the independent labour market organisations. The issues for such contacts would be mainly incomes policy, industrial policy, new technology policy, job creation, vocational training and a widened interplay and flexibility in the contacts and co-operation between the private and the public sectors. This also indicates that there is not much will in the trade union movement to fight for a different economic and political system in the forseeable future. The prime minister's invitation to tripartite contacts before the next bargaining-round —about the consequences of shorter hours of work—was accepted by the LO, albeit with the inevitable formal reservations and scepticism.

There are no indications from the trade union movement that relations with employers at any level, from the shopfloor to the central organisations, should be subject to change as regards principles. No fundamental change to the main agreements is proposed or demanded. The only exception being that the LO president finds it worth while to consider if certain amendments of the new Technology Agreement are needed, when sufficient experience makes an evaluation possible and it can be judged whether it lives up to its intended purposes.

In the years to come there may, of course, be shifts in the priorities unions attach to employer–worker contacts and mutual relations at all levels. Apart from employer attitudes and behaviour, such shifts will to a large extent depend on internal LO problems and preferences as regards centralised versus decentralised wage negotiations, and on how the LO will be able to formulate and implement a system of voluntarily co-ordinated, decentralised negotiations on the renewal of the wage agreements. The unions are at present far from unanimous on this important subject. On the contrary, skilled workers' unions prefer a far-reaching decentralisation, whereas other unions—above all SID —strongly urge a strengthened solidarity and thus centralisation. It is likely that there will continue to be internal quarrels and compromises, so that some of the traditional subjects are left to decentralised negotiations, whereas other traditionally general demands (e.g. hours of work) will still be subject to central bargaining and uniform solutions. Much depends on whether it will be possible for the LO to have its Executive Committee established as a co-ordinating and monitoring body as is the case in the DA. Over a period of the next 10–15 years, or for the next five to seven bargaining-rounds, it can be envisaged that the trade unions will change the preferences given to centralised versus decentralised negotiations, depending on the internal balance of strength, the need for solidarity action to help groups lagging behind, as well as on economic conditions of different industries and thus differences in employers' capability to pay higher wages.

As long as the unions give high priority to the creation of more jobs, it would be logical for them to focus on decentralised negotiations, while at the same time observing the necessary solidarity. However, in this context it is not always logic that counts. The term 'solidarity' is not well defined, but subject to broad and often emotional interpretation. It should be recalled that there are now, and in the foreseeable future will continue to exist, strong tensions and differing opinions within the unions —above all, SID is claiming central negotiations and low-wage protection. Indeed, astonishing compromises and concessions to SID may prove necessary to avoid a split in the trade union movement.

Many employers' federations, and to some extent also the DA, strongly favour decentralised negotiations, and that wage determination, to the greatest extent possible, should take place at the shopfloor level; DA adds the reservation that a given upper limit for wage development should be generally observed. Thus it should be possible to find common ground for the many union and employer ideas about a co-ordinated, decentralised wage policy.

Whether the LO in future will be the only strong and real representative of wage-earners' interests is a very delicate problem. Indeed, the bus drivers' strike, and in particular SID's role in this context, has made it an acute one. Over the last 10–15 years the number of salaried employees and civil servants has exceeded the number of manual workers. This development will continue, so that in another 10–15 years' time the traditional LO members —manual workers—will constitute less than 40 per cent of Danish employees. Many of the salaried will have a position and a professional training, which excludes them from membership of an LO-affiliated union under the present rules. Although these categories are by no means as well unionised and as interested in union membership as manual workers, and although many of the lower-level salaried—not least commercial and clerical employees —are LO members, the long-term trend indicates that the LO will be less and less representative.

Some organisations of civil servants and other public employees have contemplated affiliation with the LO. This has, however, caused so much unrest and so many protests that application has been shelved. In other cases, it has been decided not to apply for affiliation. This has in recent months strengthened the Central Organisation of Organisations of Public Servants and of Salaried

Employees (FTF); at the same time, the FTF interest in closer contacts and collaboration with the LO, and thereby with the Social Democrats, has diminished. FTF is, according to its constitution, politically neutral.

There are many reasons for this weakened interest in LO membership. Of crucial importance is the fact that many members of these organisations do not feel that they have enough mutual interests with the bulk of LO unions and their members because of differences in social and cultural background, education and attitudes to work and management. Another reason is that they may fear domination by the big and strong old unions within the LO family. A third reason is that they don't accept membership of a union that is closely linked to the Social Democratic Party and the labour movement, and that they will not hand over union subscriptions to give financial support to a party that doesn't get their vote. Recent research proves that less than 60 per cent of LO members vote Social Democratic. It is therefore interesting to observe, as mentioned above, that FTF, following a period of inclination to the LO and the Social Democrats, has been at pains to stress its political neutrality. And as described below, some the LO unions have themselves voiced strong protests against being forced to give support to the Social Democratic Party.

Another really big challenge for the LO in the second half of the 1980s will be to solve the many internal problems and tensions caused by an ever more heterogeneous membership, and in particular by the deep-rooted rivalry, jealousy and widely differing opinions between some of the big unions.

Of the already mentioned 45 per cent increase of the LO membership from 1972 to 1982, 80 per cent are employees for whom it is not a tradition or a matter of course to join a union. Many have joined purely in order to become insured against unemployment. Most of the new members are commercial and clerical employees, or female employees in the public sector. A rough analysis of the present LO membership leads to the conclusion that only 50 per cent belong to the original workers' unions.

The vital question of a new trade union organisational structure is the area causing the strongest and most serious controversies and tensions. The structure has not been changed since the unions were founded more than 100 years ago; it is still based mainly on skills and training. The skilled workers have their unions and the semi-skilled have their huge SID for male and the big KAD for female workers. Only in a few industries has it been possible to merge the unions into industrial unions. In 1971 the LO Congress adopted a resolution on the future organisational structure, namely that eight industrial unions should be established to cover both skilled and specialised general workers. In spite of many efforts, no progress has been made since then; if anything, friction has become more overt—especially between the Metalworkers' Union and SID. The latter is rather undisciplined and left-orientated, and is opposing a good deal of the existing main agreements regulating the industrial relations system. It is there-fore often hesitant to take committed action against members violating industrial peace. This came to a flagrant culmination during the bus strike in 1984. The strike was called to enforce a closed shop against a number of members who refused to pay a levy to the Social Democratic Party. The stoppage was extended by secondary action designed to bring the whole of the metropolitan transport system of Denmark to a halt. The employing authority eventually gave in to the demands of the union, though unlawful, and dismissed the workers who had res-igned from the union. Both the closed shop and the secondary action—which included picketing the railways, oil, transport, newspapers, and mail service—were illegal and the union had to face a massive fine. The strike has raised issues of major importance since it has revealed the vulnerability of society when confronted with a situation of this kind unless the courts, with the support of public opinion, are prepared to enforce compliance with the law by threatening the union with massive financial penalties that would jeopardise its existence.

SID is also fighting for its survival and for its members, whom it fears will be dominated by skilled workers at the shopfloor level (and at any other level, in the case of industrial unions) so that differences in wages and other conditions will become even bigger. Therefore SID has submitted an alternative plan for the future structure that is unacceptable to most other unions.

It is at present impossible to see how to find a compromise and how to unite the contrasting opinions. The 1983 LO Congress simply did not discuss this delicate matter, apparently for fear of a clash of such proportions that it could split the trade union movement. The positive will to find a solution is difficult to trace. SID has even been hesitant to approve experiments at enterprise level to see how a grouping organised on industrial union lines would work.

The 1983–4 winter and spring saw a kind of an open war between the presidents of SID and the Metalworkers' Union, mainly on the subject of structure. Following a meeting in May 1984 of the LO Committee on Organisational Structure, it looks as if the SID president has agreed to give up his own proposal and to consider compromises based on the industrial union idea. The reason for this surprising promise may be that he was in a weak position within the LO after his role in the bus drivers' dispute. So the final solution is still far ahead.

The situation was not made easier by the president of one of the bigger LO-affiliated unions of public employees and civil servants. He proposed that all public employees under the LO should form a new big union. In May 1984 a compromise was reached, so that LO-affiliated unions with many public employees could form a kind of cartel with the mandate to negotiate for these public employees.

Another problem causing tensions between SID and other unions is the vocational training question. The skilled workers' unions demand that the existing training system for skill is maintained and improved, partly because of industry's urgent need for a highly qualified workforce. SID, on its side, demands that the systems for training skilled and non-skilled workers be merged. Here again it is difficult to see how the gap between the conflicting interests can be bridged.

Public employees, who have become an increasing part of the labour force and the LO membership, have also caused problems within the LO framework as regards wage policy. It has long been generally agreed and accepted by all that the public sector just follows the private sector's wage levels and development. However, powerful circles within unions whose members are mainly employed in the private sector have recently intensified their arguments that this course is no longer justifiable, because of the much higher productivity increases in the private sector. They argue that only their personal contributions to the productivity increases lead to higher wages for them. So it is not fair that employees in the public sector, where productivity increases are minimal, have their pay automatically adjusted to the wages in the private sector without making the same efforts to increase productivity. This also leads to a heavier tax burden.

The first reaction from the public employees was negative, but the new government announced at the same time its intention to decentralise and restructure the wage policy and wage-fixing in the public sector by linking wages more closely to individual performance, productivity improvements, etc. This idea has not been rejected totally by the unions and organisations of public employees, so it cannot be ruled out that there will—and within the LO frame—be a positive collaboration aimed at a reform of the wage systems and wage-fixing in the public sector on lines similar to the private sector. It will, however, take a long time. Strong unions' demands for solidarity wage policy may ensure a parallel development of the wage levels for the lower ranges in the two sectors.

Both individual workers and many employers have looked for a renewal of the basis for wage determination, for new wage systems that will link wages more closely with work performance, workers' participation, and improvements to the work climate and to the economic conditions and results of the enterprise. An increasing number of small and medium-sized firms are introducing profit-sharing schemes and employee shares. This is normally welcomed by the employees, although because many trade unions are in favour of both a more decentralised wage policy and of securing workers a bigger share of the net result, they are hesitant to accept and approve such solutions. They can strengthen the ties between the worker and the employer too much and thus weaken trade union solidarity as well as the unions' power to obtain higher wages and better conditions for their members through collective bargaining. It will also be an extra obstacle to the wage-earner fund idea. On the other hand, it is likely that it will prove necessary for the unions to revise their traditional solidarity line within the next decade. They will be under heavy pressure from necessity and from many individual employers and workers, but a thoroughgoing decentralisation of wage determination and very close links between individual pay and profits will probably never be accepted, as this will attack the very *raison d'être* of the unions, whatever their organisational structure.

As long as the LO encourages entrepreneurship through the establishment of more new small enterprises, it must envisage that still more of its members will be offered and will accept such schemes. Most probably, the LO and the majority of the unions will not approve such schemes because of the risk of endangering worker solidarity. Such an attitude will, on the other hand, mean that the unions will miss the chance to get provisions regulating such methods of payment included in the agreements. It may also in this context prove necessary for the unions to acknowledge the change of political attitude and of attitudes to the enterprise within the rank and file, if a split and a strong growth of the new, very active, unions is to be avoided.

The attitude of the DA to an extreme decentralisation of wage determination and to new, untraditional pay elements (e.g. profit-sharing) is not quite clear. Although the DA has been an advocate for decentralisation, it appears that it has aimed more at negotiations between the direct parties (i.e. the unions and the employers' federation). Decentralisation right down to the shopfloor and very untraditional pay elements have as yet not been given high priority in the DA. It should here be recalled that one of the DA's chief responsibilities is to ensure that employer solidarity is maintained (i.e. that members do not attract labour from other enterprises through higher wage bids, or that local wage increases do not spread and are kept within the agreed frame). A very decentralised wage determination based on profit-sharing will imply a very heterogeneous wage development, which may be difficult to monitor and govern.

The economic democracy proposal is still part of the formal and official LO programme. There are, however, a good many indications that the LO no longer attaches major importance to it. The new president has never identified himself with it, as his predecessor did, and during the campaign up to the 1984 parliamentary election both the LO and the Social Democrats 'forgot' to mention the wage-earner fund theme. In an interview in April 1984, a leading trade union representative said that the time is not right for reintroducing the proposal.

Legislation introducing wage-earner funds cannot be expected in Denmark in the 1980s, and maybe never. Instead, one can expect that the LO and most of the unions will give the new Business Investment Fund very high priority and increase its capital and its active job-creating activity. Considering the share of the capital provided by private financial sources and the investment policy which has already been instituted, it does not appear possible to use the fund as a loophole for the introduction of economic democracy.

The very close LO–Social Democratic relations will inevitably be reconsidered within the not-too-distant future, when it is likely that they will become less close. They are already somewhat looser than a few years ago. If the links are not made less formal, it may prove to have an adverse effect on the trade unions and on the LO.

The unrest and rebellions within the big Union of Commercial and Clerical Employees in Denmark (Handels-og Kontorfunktionaerforbundet i Danmark: HK) and among the bus drivers have resulted in resignations and expulsions; indeed, the bus drivers' strike started as a protest against being obliged to support the Social Democratic Party through union subscriptions. The case has been raised in Parliament where there have been proposals to pass legislation forbidding such compulsory support. Both the LO and some unions are considering proposals to make such support voluntary.

Another cause of looser relations to the party is the necessity of co-operation with the present non-socialist government, which will probably remain in office for several years to come. The LO has already declared its willingness to co-operate with the government, and it is obvious that over-emphatic links with the Social Democrats will hamper its manoeuvrability in this regard as well as causing further protests and unrest within the rank and file.

The Social Democratic Party will probably be weakened for several years to come by internal rivalry and discord between its different wings, as well as by reduced support from the electorate. The party has abandoned its previous policy and its traditionally responsible behaviour in favour of a leftwards move, which makes close relations and collaboration between it and the LO increasingly problematic.

As far as one can see, the bus drivers' case and actions within the HK have caused problems of an immediate and long-term character. These problems have many aspects, as already mentioned. The whole matter started as protests against compulsory support of the Social Democratic Party, but this is only the surface. The discontent is far more deep-rooted. One problem is the close relations to the party. Many new non-Social Democratic union members demand that the unions and the LO shall be non-political, as FTF and the new rival unions are. They and a good many old union members want more democracy within the unions (i.e. more decentralisation of the decision-making procedure). In practice, this is the same as a decentralised wage policy and negotiation procedure. Another cause of discontent is, as already

mentioned, that it is impossible to be insured against unemployment without being a union member. Another, and maybe
the most serious, problem—both in principle and in practice—is
the recent union actions for the closed shop. Some unions, above
all SID, have been so flagrant that they have used any measures,
even violation of the law, to force non-members into the union or,
in the case of failure, they have forced the employer to dismiss
non-unionised staff. In the bus drivers' dispute, SID succeeded in
having workers dismissed, although the public employer thereby
was forced to violate legislation granting public employees the
right not to be members of a union.

An interesting aspect of these actions is that they have only
taken place within the municipal sector and only where there is a
Social Democratic and socialist majority on the municipal council,
so that the employer, to some extent, is identical with the trade
unions. It is difficult to avoid the impression that a few unions and
unofficial activists, above all within SID, try to maintain the
principle that employees exist for the sake of the union, and that
membership is compulsory; employees, on the other hand, do not
see the union as rendering such services and benefits as to make
membership attractive and consequently do not join voluntarily.

It is beyond any doubt that both the unrest and loud protests
and many resignations, as well as the actions of the new unions,
have given rise to serious considerations within the LO unions. So
has SID's actions, which are apparently not acceptable to any of
the responsible union leaders.

The most probable future development is that the new unions
will not acquire much influence or many members, nor that the
LO-affiliated unions will be split or otherwise fall apart. It is
unlikely that there will be a number of alternative rival trade union
movements in Denmark. It is, on the other hand, also beyond the
limits of reasonable probability that the old strong labour
movement should separate into its three wings because the LO
declares itself politically neutral. Instead, one can expect a further
lessening of the LO ties with the Social Democratic Party and a
higher degree of tolerance to those who do not wish to be union
members; it is also likely that it will become easier to get unemployment insurance without being a union member.

The Employers' and DA's Future Role and Functions in Society

It is not possible to evaluate the future of the trade unions and the LO without knowing how the employers and their federations will develop and vice versa.

In the future, the employers and their organisations will have an important and responsible function in Denmark's market economy and within a free pluralistic and democratic system under rapid technological development. The DA has not published any long-term policy and strategy, as much will depend on trade union development and policy. In this context, it should be borne in mind that the employers' federations and the DA—for good reasons—have always been mainly defensive organisations. Only since the mid-1950s have they also added a good deal of member service to their functions. When considering their previous policy and role, as well as the whole organisational machinery, it is doubtful if there will be any major changes within the next years.

The new DA president's oral report to the 1984 General Meeting focused on future development and the DA's and member federations' likely involvement in it. It was stressed that a major task would be to contribute to a harmonious introduction of new technology by preparing vocational training and management skills for future technology. This will imply a much higher level of flexibility in these and many other fields of production and will necessitate better management–employee relations and co-operation, as well as a real change to the organisational structures of both the unions and employers' organisations. The president also pointed to the need for a completely new and very flexible structure of collective agreements. This will involve more decentralised wage determination. It was also stressed that the real base for the tasks and work of the employer organisations is to assist the individual enterprise and to help its further development.

There has recently been a debate within employer circles on decentralised wage policy. As mentioned above, the DA has always been an advocate of decentralisation in the sense that its affiliated bodies have always negotiated their own agreements. The two biggest member federations have proposed a much further decentralisation, namely right down to the enterprise level, and that agreed wage-increase frames should not be a general upper limit, but an average limit. Enterprises where increases of productivity, work performance, skills, involvement, etc., justify higher or lower wage increases should be free to make them. This will complicate the DA's role as the body responsible on the employers' side for the general development of wage costs. The DA's staff is not yet geared or trained to master such functions, as they are not yet qualified to evaluate and assess new pay elements (e.g. profit-sharing), and the consequences of their incorporation in wage determination.

An extremely decentralised wage system also makes it difficult and delicate to implement the important Article 23 of the DA's constitution. This article states that no member federation or individual member firm shall enter into collective agreements of normal and general contents without the prior agreement of the DA General Council, and that conclusion of a collective agreement shall always take place under the express proviso of the confederation's approval.

Under present conditions it will be very difficult for the DA to formulate a general policy on wages and other conditions of work, and to implement, monitor and control how this policy is observed. For instance, there might be 20,000 or more enterprise-based agreements of widely different content and with different dates of expiration, instead of the present 500–700 essentially homogeneous agreements that all expire on the same date.

So the DA is facing as big a challenge as the LO, if it is to take on board its president's and leading member federations' proposals about the future development of private enterprises and their conditions as regards their industrial relations system. The biggest challenge may prove to be to persuade the LO and the trade unions to accept such a system and to make it compatible with solidarity wage policy.

2 FRANCE

J. Nousbaum

Population	54,000,000
Per capita GNP, 1982	US$ 10,000
Exports as per cent of GNP, 1982	17
Number of large companies (among the 500 largest outside the USA)	38 with 1,805,000 employees
Governments	1945–6 De Gaulle
	1946–58 The period was dominated by many short-lived coalitions between centre, moderate and left-wing parties in the Fourth Republic
	1958–74 De Gaulle returned and the Fifth Republic involved presidential rule. Gaullist presidents and government coalitions (the governments were rather centre/right-wing coalitions)
	1974–81 A more centrist government under Giscard d'Estaing
	1981–4 Socialist president (Mitterrand) and a coalition government of Socialists and Communists
	1984– Socialist government
Public sector (share of GNP, 1982, including transfers)	51 per cent
Trade union membership	15–20 per cent
Trade unions	Confédération Générale du Travail (CGT) (Communist) is the largest with 1,200,000 members. Confédération Française Démocratique du Travail (CFDT) (Socialist) with 800,000 members in 26 unions. Among other organisations with a preponderance

45

of salaried employees can be mentioned the Confédération Française des travailleurs Chrétiens (CFTC) with 150,000 members, and Confédération Générales des Cadres (CGC) with 200,000 members.

Employers' organisations

Some 90 per cent of French business enterprises are affiliated to the Conseil National du Patronat Français (CNPF). Small and medium-sized firms are organised within the CGPME. There is a double affiliation to both CNPF and CGPME. A third organisation, SNPMI, is seeking full recognition as an employers' organisation.

The Participants in Industrial Relations

Trade Unions

The characteristics of French trade unionism are as follows.

Pluralism. Trade union pluralism is the result of a long historical development consisting of breaks, reunifications and divisions.

The first trade union confederation to be formed was the CGT (Confédération Générale du Travail: General Confederation of Labour), set up in 1895 and finally united in 1902. It experienced a major split in 1921 between the CGTU (aligned with the Communist Party) and the CGT (aligned with the Socialists). A reunification took place in 1936, and a new split occurred in 1947 but this time CGT-FO (Force Ouvrière, aligned with the Socialists of the day) split off from the CGT (which remained aligned with the Communist Party).

The second trade union confederation was the CFTC (Confédération Française des Travailleurs Chrétiens: French Christian Workers' Confederation), set up in 1919 under the inspiration of social Catholicism. After first organising only salaried staffs, it gradually changed its orientation with the large-scale recruitment of workers from a Young Christian Workers (YCW) background. In 1964 it shed its denominational affiliation and became the CFDT (Confédération Française et Démocratique du Travail: French Democratic Confederation of Labour), though a CFTC continued to exist, with its ranks severely depleted but still faithful to its Christian origins.

In 1946 a new organisation was recognised, the CGC, which recently became the Confédération Française de l'Encadrement (French Confederation of Managerial and Supervisory Staffs: CFE-CGC). It resulted from the joining together of various organisations representing professional groups and takes in not only managerial personnel, but also technical and supervisory staff and commercial travellers and representatives.

In addition to these five organisations—leaving aside the FEN (Fédération de l'Education Nationale: National Federation of Educational Staff) which, being concerned with the teaching profession, does not fall within the scope of our study—are the so-called 'independent' unions. These, after many vicissitudes, joined together in the CSL (Confédération des Syndicats Libres: Confederation of Free Trade Unions). They are established in certain major enterprises, especially in the motor industry, but are not recognised for various reasons as being nationally representative.

Representativity. 'Representativity' is a legal concept which confers a certain number of prerogatives on the trade unions.

The legal status of the trade unions (their right to conclude contracts, to acquire assets and administer them, to take legal proceedings, etc.) is of no direct concern to this study, but the same cannot be said for 'national representativity' which has been conferred by the government, in accordance with certain criteria laid down by law, on the five organisations named above: CGT, CFDT, CGT-FO (generally known as 'FO' for short), CFTC and CGC.

The trade unions benefiting from this recognition have a specific right in regard to the negotiation of collective agreements and their 'extension' (a mechanism enabling such agreements to be compulsorily extended to firms not involved in the negotiations), but they also enjoy the right to be represented on various official consultative bodies (see below) as well as to participate in the administration of the social security institutions and jointly administered bodies (retirement, unemployment). They also enjoy privileges with regard to intervention in enterprises, such as setting up trade union sections, monopoly in the nomination of candidates for the first round of works council and staff representative elections, and they receive subsidies from the government, especially in the field of training. The Institute of Economic and Social Research (Insitut de Recherches Économiques et Sociales:

IRES), set up in June 1982 with government involvement, has been placed at the service of these organisations.

Relative Importance and Weakness. Is the monopoly thus accorded to the 'representative' unions justified? It is doubtful when the importance of the trade unions is measured against the number of unionised workers. Indeed, the rate of unionisation in France—which stood at some 20–5 per cent in the recent past—has shown a substantial drop since the economic crisis. The percentage of union membership is thus in decline.

It has to be recognised, however, that the status of the trade unions is not measured only against the rate of unionisation. Consideration must also be given to their ability to express the aspirations of the workers, to mobilise them, to negotiate compromises and to exert an influence on government and on public opinion. In this respect, the trade unions have up to now been seen in France as exercising real power of a rather institutional kind. Do they still have this power? We shall see later how this question can be answered.

Trade union pluralism, moreover, has prompted questions on the relative importance of the various organisations. A number of assessment criteria can be applied to this aspect—none of which, however, is guaranteed to give an accurate reflection of the real position. The main point to consider here is that the development which has taken place since the change of government in May 1981 has been characterised by a heavy loss of influence for the so-called 'revolutionary' organisations (CGT and CFDT) to the benefit of the 'reformist' organisations (FO, CFTC and CGC), in line with the losses incurred by the political parties of the government majority (Socialists and Communists). The significance and scope of the distinction between these two organisational categories will be looked at later under Trade Union strategies.

Trade Unions and Political Parties. The trade unions are defined by law as having the *exclusive* aim of 'studying and defending the rights and material and moral interests' of the workers. The occupational nature of the trade unions which emerges from this definition in principle rules out any activity of a political nature, but the reality is more complex.

It may indeed be noted that while certain organisations are distinctly more highly politicised than others—the CGT, for example—all the organisations have ideological links with political parties. Some political parties go further and seek to establish themselves directly within the enterprises; this is particularly true of the Communist Party, which has enterprise 'cells' and has set up an 'enterprise' section in its Central Committee to which certain large companies are directly linked. Thus, it could be said that the Communist Party has been seeking to transform itself into a 'Fifth Workers' Centre'.

The Employers' Organisations

The structure of the employers' movement is heterogeneous. Firms in France vary greatly in size and legal structure. Following the extension of nationalisation which began in 1981, this heterogeneity has increased.

The CNPF (Conseil National du Patronat Français: French Employers' National Council) is the main employers' organisation, and it is interesting to note that the enterprises recently nationalised continue to be members of this organisation, which did not fail to elicit vehement protests from the CGT and the Communist Party.

The strategy followed by the CNPF is one of 'enlightened capitalism'. While defending the freedom and responsibility of enterprises and repudiating state control, it recognises the need for a dialogue with the trade unions and with all categories of workers and it endeavours to arrive at a general consensus. The application of this strategy, however—even before the change of government in 1981—ran up against the reactions of certain sections less progressive in their thinking and against the special problems of the small business. In addition, after May 1981, the constraints imposed by government on the operation of free enterprise prompted new anti-union reactions in some employers' circles.

Thus the CGPME (Confédération Générale des Petites et Moyennes Entreprises: General Confederation of Small and Medium-sized Enterprises), which is associated with the CNPF, has distanced itself somewhat from the latter. Indeed, a new organisation, the SNPMI (Syndicat National du Patronat Moderne et Indépendant: National Union of Modern and Independent Employers) is endeavouring in certain sectors of the small and medium-sized business community to provide a focus for discontent and to encourage action in support of their demands. The SNPMI does not rule out violence as a means of pressure.

It is also worth noting that there are among the ranks of the employers currents of thought and opinion which find their expression in various groupings, such as CJD (Centre des Jeunes Dirígeants: Young Managers' Centre) and the Club 'Entreprise et Progrès' (Enterprise and Progress Club), which seek to guide the development of employers' thinking along the most progressive lines. Other tendencies find their expression in bodies set up to reflect the size or form of enterprises, such as AFEP (Association Française des Entreprises Privées: French Association of Private Enterprises), which groups together some 40 of the biggest private companies, and, at the other end of the scale as its name suggests. ETHIC (Entreprises à Taille Humaine de l'Industrie et du Commerce: Enterprises of a Human Dimension in Trade and Industry).

Although these groupings do not seek to compete with the CNPF in its role of providing representation for employers, they may cause it to take into account the results of their deliberations. They cannot, therefore, be overlooked in plotting future trends in employers' thinking.

Trade Union Aims in Respect of Company Management

The change of government which took place in France in 1981 has resulted in the adoption of a number of measures corresponding more or less to the objectives of the trade union organisations closest to the political power centre. But it has also given rise to considerable dislocations in trade union strategies. Of course the ideologies remain unchanged, but the complete turnaround in relations between the trade union movement and the state has modified the attitudes of trade union leaders and, in consequence, the reactions of the rank and file towards their leaders. It is therefore necessary, before examining the means of access to company management currently available, to review the various trade union strategies.

Trade Union Strategies

We made a distinction above between the 'revolutionary' and the 'reformist' trade union movements; this distinction needs to be fairly extensively qualified in any contemporary analysis of trade union strategies.

The 'Revolutionary' Trade Union Organisation. The CGT and
CFDT, which profess the 'class struggle' and seek a fundamental
transformation of society, are known as 'revolutionary'. Their
concepts of power in the enterprise ('democratic control' for the
CGT, 'workers' control' (*'autogestion'*) for the CFDT) are apparently close to one another. If we look behind the words, however,
we note that their general concepts of economic and social
organisation differ to the extent that the unity of action which they
had achieved from 1966 to 1980, and which had for nearly three
years survived the split in the 'Union of the Left' (1977), does not
seem capable—although the left is now in power—of reasserting
itself for anything more than purely *ad hoc* actions.

For the CGT—whose doctrine remains closely linked to that of
the Communist Party—company control has become 'the business
of the workers'. A shift in the doctrine of the Communists is
discernible here, however, since they once considered that 'to be
active in the field of company management was tantamount to
playing the game of the capitalists by substituting realism for
revolution'. Now both the Communist Party and the CGT are in
favour of 'intervention in the fields of industrial, commercial and
financial strategies and policies on purchasing, markets, cost
structure, production, investment, research and the introduction
of new technologies', the ultimate objective being 'to show that it
is possible to find resources where none can be found in the
capitalist shambles, that it is possible to generate profit in other
ways but also to redirect its utilisation'.[1] The dual trade union
objective is thus to present demands and to intervene in management in such a way that they can be satisfied. Hence the CGT
has defined new 'criteria of management' aimed not solely at
financial profitability but at 'social profitability' as well.

It may however be noted that, in its parallel defence of the
interests of the Communist Party which following the election of
Mitterand as President, was one of the government parties, the
CGT sometimes had to curb the excesses of its rank-and-file
militants, which could have jeopardised its interests. Thus, it
occasionally put the brake on certain movements and at the same
time accused organisations such as the CFDT—which does not
follow the same tactic—of 'adventurism'.

The CFDT, however, always claims to be resolutely in favour of
'workers' control', but this term is clearer than the thinking behind
it and the means to be applied in order to achieve it. At the level of

principles, the CFDT advocates a 'redistribution of power' at all levels of the enterprise and aims to secure 'maximum worker participation in the actual management of production'.[2] By declaring that 'the crisis may be due in the first instance to the fact that the operation of the enterprise is monopolized by its owner, whether it be in private or state hands',[3] it makes a direct challenge to the decision-making authority of the entrepreneur.

Even so, this organisation has followed a fairly tortuous course of development. After switching in 1978 from a strategy of 'rupture' to 'recentring'—branded as reformism by the CGT as well as by a small number of its own militants—it is now experiencing certain adjustment difficulties. The support it gave to the government in the institution of a policy of economic stringency was considered to a large extent responsible for its electoral setbacks and it now seems to be moving in the direction of offering fairly stiff opposition to the government. (The dispute at Talbot in December 1983 was an illustration of this new stance, which tends in the opposite direction to that of the CGT.)

'Reformist' Unions. FO, which heads this group, always professes to be a 'free and independent trade union organisation'. While continuing to proclaim the spirit of the Charter of Amiens (1906), according to which the revolutionary tendency prevailed in the CGT of the day over the reformist tendency, it nevertheless gives pride of place to 'contractual policy' as a mode of action and holds that within the enterprise and outside it the trade union should act as a 'counter-weight', and not as a 'counter-power'. It considers that it is not the role of a trade union organisation to participate in the taking of economic decisions, at either enterprise or government level. It thus calls on the workers to guard against illusions of fictitious power and to reject incorporation into bodies which would lead to the workers being placed in some form of tutelage. Even so, it advocates 'workers' scrutiny'.

The CFTC, although far removed from FO by dint of its denominational origins, is, like FO, committed to the contractual policy. However, this does not rule out the militant pursuit of demands; indeed, the new right it has just secured to have its voice heard could even encourage it to go further along this road. While opposed to the class struggle, it favours all procedures for mediation and even supports certain forms of co-determination.

Finally, the CGC, although geared to sectional interests, seeks to take its place as a full partner in the social dialogue. Apart from the demands appropriate to the staff categories it represents, it has put forward—notably in the field of industrial reform—a series of proposals which also tend markedly in the direction of co-determination. Nevertheless, encouraged by its recent electoral successes, the CGC has a fairly changeable attitude. Having been vehemently opposed to the government at first, it now seems to be seeking advantages by moving closer to it.

The broad lines of trade union strategies set out above show that it cannot be concluded that there is a 'polarisation' in trade union life. The split between 'revolutionaries' and 'reformists' seems to be rather a thing of the past to the extent that, on the one hand, the CFDT appears to occupy an isolated position on the trade union chessboard and, on the other hand, when it comes to demands and action movements, *ad hoc* alliances may be formed between the different trade union groupings.

Routes of Access to Company Control

An examination of the main routes of access to company control will show us how the strategies described above work out in practice.

Access to Property

Nationalisation. The most extreme form trade union demands can take in a system of private capitalism is, of course, nationalisation. The nationalised sector, as set up in France in 1945, was considerably extended in 1982 by the nationalisation of 39 major banks, two finance companies and five major industrial groups. Altogether, this sector currently accounts for about 20 per cent of the national economy.

With regard to the principle of nationalisation, FO, even before the statute was voted into law, had stated that it did not really consider nationalisation to be necessary except for industries holding a monopoly. As far as other measures of nationalisation were concerned, it had strong reservations even though it did not declare outright opposition. But it was especially concerned to prevent the application in such enterprises of any system of workers' control or co-determination, and feared politicisation which it regarded as a serious risk to the nationalised undertakings.

The CFDT, which favours the socialisation of the financial means to production and trade, was pleased to see in nationalisation the path to economic recovery. In particular, nationalisation of the banking sector would permit the implementation of a financial and monetary policy which would accompany the fulfilment of industrial development objectives. But the CFDT mainly saw nationalisation as a means of moving towards workers' control, the rights thus acquired by the workers of the nationalised undertakings then serving as a model for those of firms in private enterprise.

The CGT for its part was, and continues to be, the strongest advocate of the principle of nationalisation. On this point it identifies fully with the Communist Party, which regards the expropriation of the bank, chemical and steel 'bosses' as one of its greatest successes in the government in which it participated. It is currently the only trade union organisation to demand the extension of the nationalised sector to include, in particular, the motor industry.

The costs involved in the nationalisations which have been carried through and the meagre results obtained in economic terms are such that those responsible for the country's economy are unlikely to embark on new ventures on these lines, but we shall see later what consequences they may have in areas concerned not with the ownership of enterprises, but with their management.

Co-operative Production Societies. The co-operative production society is another means of taking economic activities away from private capital. In France the concept is of long standing and has been applied in many instances, but few co-operatives—in the production sector at least—have prospered while at the same time retaining their original character. Some examples of co-operatives of this original type are still in existence, but they cannot be extended for general application because they are based on factors relating to their particular context.

What we are witnessing today is a resurgence of the co-operative on different lines, the formula now being used is one of keeping unprofitable enterprises alive artificialy. This trend, initiated by the CFDT, began to show itself in 1973 with the LIP affair. (A watch-and clock-making factory which the workers, having been made redundant when the firm was taken into receivership, tried to keep alive. A long period of agitation followed, in which public opinion was made aware of the problem of mass redundancy.)

Although in principle the CGT considers that workers' co-operatives stem from a concept of class collaboration, it is currently strongly in favour of their development. It has indeed prompted the creation, with the aid of public funds, of a large number of such societies to take over either wholly or in part the activity of enterprises which have gone into liquidation. None of these co-operatives has yet proved that it could survive for long on its own resources. The outside support which they need emphasises their artificial character, but they also enjoy, in addition to the fiscal advantages associated with co-operative status, the new favours which the present government grants to the entire sector termed the 'social economy' sector. The latter is regarded as a 'third sector' between capitalism and full collectivisation—in other words, as an example of 'soft socialisation'.

Although it is not easy to arrive at a precise figure, it is estimated that there are currently about 1,200 co-operatives in France employing 40,000–45,000 persons, particularly in the building and engineering industries, in the graphical trades and in the services sector. Their possible extension, with government support and the interest of the trade union movement, could raise a problem for the future.

Participation in Capital and Shareholdings. A compulsory system was instituted by an order in 1967 for the 'participation of workers in the fruits of company expansion'. It provides that enterprises employing more than 100 wage-earning workers and showing a profit must set aside a 'participation reserve', the overall amount of which is calculated from the portion of fiscal profit exceeding 5 per cent of the company's capital. This reserve can be used for the issue of shares in the company to the workforce, for the purchase of bonds or debentures, for payments to blocked accounts in the firm or for the purchase of shares in investment companies or joint investment funds. The issue of shares in the enterprise is, in fact, the procedure least commonly applied.

Altogether, it is estimated that 3–4 million workers are currently covered by this participation scheme and that the financial benefits they draw from it have so far accounted for less than 3 per cent, on average, of their wages.

Apart from this compulsory participation scheme, various legal measures have recently been adopted to supplement older legislation aimed at extending workers' shareholdings in private companies or in the public sector, but none of the schemes applied has so far met with any enthusiasm on the part of the workers; those who do take advantage of them frequently resell their shares as soon as possible.

The unions have never been interested in these various schemes, since the participation of workers in the financial life of companies is seen by some as the manifestation of a spirit of class collaboration which they are against. Generally speaking, therefore, this approach contains no route of access to the ownership of company capital which the trade unions could exploit. Thus it could come as a surprise that the present government has just announced the preparation of measures designed to permit the association of managerial staffs with the capital and results of enterprises by means of new incentives to the purchase of shares. Perhaps this is an indication of the government's concern to take management and supervisory personnel into account and thereby to meet criticism voiced by the CGC.

Wage Funds. A recent legal provision (included in the Finance Law of 29 December 1983) provides for the setting up of wage funds which would serve to finance productive investments or schemes likely to reduce working hours and create new jobs.

Such wage funds respond to a CFDT proposal seeking to devise mechanisms providing for a certain control of investment by the workers and meet the desire of government to see the mobilisation of new savings derived from an element of deferred purchasing power in wages as part of the fight against inflation.

However, the law makes these wage funds optional and stipulates that they can only be set up under contractual arrangements or collective agreements. They can be set up within enterprises, in industrial sectors or even in 'employment pools', a formula which is particularly favoured by the CFDT. In order to encourage workers to participate, tax advantages are offered both on payments made and on the interest which they attract.

Nevertheless, apart from the CFDT, the unions remain very cool towards these schemes. Indeed, in a period in which it is of paramount importance to them to defend the purchasing power of workers' wages, currently under severe stress, they see no grounds for encouraging them to set aside part of their pay for schemes from which they are not certain of drawing the slightest direct advantage. The CGT, for its part, envisages other means of achieving investment control.

Since the conditions under which the funds will be expected to operate have not yet been laid down, it is too early to give an opinion on their chances of development.

Access to the Role of Management

The main mode of access to the managerial function is worker participation in the decision-making bodies of companies. Up to now, however, this formula has only been applied to a very limited extent in private companies through the medium of the representatives who may be appointed by the works council to attend meetings of the company's board of directors. But, while these representatives must receive the same documents as those distributed to other members of the board, they only have consultative status on the board and do not take part in the decision-making. The unions, accusing heads of companies of taking decisions outside the official meetings of the board, regarded this participation as purely fictitious. Do they want to go further?

We have indicated earlier that only the CGC and the CFTC favour co-determination; consequently, they have included in their proposals for company reform a right of worker participation in and entitlement to vote on company supervisory boards. (French legislation provides that limited companies can take the form either of a company with a board of directors and chairman/managing director or of a company with a board of management and supervisory board.) Along with FO, the CGT and the CFDT do not favour this arrangement, but they have approved the law of 26 July 1983 on the 'democratisation of the public sector' which provides for such representation on boards of directors or supervisory boards, not only for the nationalised undertakings as such, but also for their direct and indirect subsidiaries where they employ over 200 persons. For, in this sector, co-determination is no longer felt by them to be a manifestation of class collaboration.

In companies subject to this arrangement, boards of directors or supervisory boards must have one-third of their members elected by the workforce if the company employs over 1,000 wage-earning workers and, in companies employing between 200 and 1,000 persons, two or three members. The worker representatives have the same rights as the other members of the board, but they are not jointly liable with the board members representing the shareholders. The extension of this system to companies in which a nationalised undertaking only has a shareholding could give rise to its generalisation to companies in wholly private ownership in the same economic sector.

We shall have to wait until the boards of the companies subject to the law are set up during the course of 1984 before we can assess the effects of the new arrangement on the operation of the companies concerned. It is, however, to be expected that the unions will endeavour to pursue effective action in this arena.

Access to the Supervision of Management

Supervision of management is today exercised directly through the medium of the works council. In addition, a new right—the 'workers' right of expression'—though not designed with that in mind, may well be used by some trade union organisations for that purpose.

Works Councils. By widening the powers of the works councils and supplementing the means placed at their disposal, the new legislation (28 October 1982) has opened up to the workers' organisations a broader means of access than was previously available, if not to the management of the companies, at least to the vetting of their accounts.

It may be noted in this connection that the term 'co-operation' which appeared in the previous texts on the powers of works councils no longer features in the present texts. The CGT was especially happy with the removal of this term which it felt was used by the employers in attempts to secure 'class collaboration'.[4] This is an indication of the manner in which this organisation, for its part, intends to use the new provisions. Among the latter, mention should be made of:

(1) The multiplication of information of a legal, economic, financial and accounting nature on the enterprise which must be presented to the works council, and the development of its role of consultation on all questions affecting the organisation, management and operation of the company, on plans for separations, mergers, acquisition or transfer of subsidiaries and purchases of shareholdings, on the fixing and surveillance of prices, company research policy and any major plan to introduce new technology.

(2) The widening of the powers of investigation of the chartered

accountant whom the works council may call upon for assistance, and the possibility open to the council of calling in a technology expert and other experts outside the company, with no restriction as to profession (lawyer, economist, trade unionist, etc.).

(3) The obligation to provide members of the works council with instruction in accountancy and the compulsory creation in enterprises employing more than 1,000 workers of an accounts committee with responsibility for studying all accounting and financial documents submitted to the works council.

(4) The creation of 'group councils' (parent company and direct and indirect subsidiaries whose head office is in France), which constitutes a major innovation in the new legislation, for it extends intervention by the works council to centres of decision outside its own enterprise.

Certainly, the works council with powers extended in these ways is still a 'consultative' body, but the powers of surveillance it can exercise, with the new resources at its disposal, may enable it to take indirect action against the management of the company. Thus the CGT expects to include in the information which must be supplied to the council 'the state of the company's relations with its banks' and investment programmes in order to 'verify their conformity with the initial plans'.[5] Under the slogan 'Let's Open up the Accounts', it demands the setting up of a 'committee for the surveillance of cost and price formation'.[6]

Similarly, the CFDT plans to use the works council to facilitate 'the intervention of the workers in the appropriation of company results, particularly for investment'.[7]

The possibility of calling in 'experts' chosen by them gives the unions very considerable new powers of investigation in this area.

Among the powers of the works council relating to the surveillance of management, special mention must also be made of employment control. Certainly in this respect too, the joint consultative committee only has a role of 'consultation' prior to any redundancy on cyclical or structural economic grounds, and the last word remains with the administration, but the conditions under which the council can exercise its powers—notably by extending the deadlines laid down by law—constitute a serious impediment to the conduct of the company's affairs and exacerbate its difficulties in such a way that the reductions in manpower cannot take effect when the head of the company judges them to be essential to maintain equilibrium in its activity.

In the course of the debates which preceded the vote on the new laws on the rights of workers, the CGT and the CFDT had demanded that the works council be given a genuine 'right of veto' on the matter of redundancies. FO, on the other hand, was strongly opposed to this arrangement which, in its view, would burden the workers—by giving them powers of co-decision—with responsibilities which did not belong to them. Although the law did not finally accord the right of veto to the works council, the conduct of certain trade union organisations tends to lead to the same result. This is particularly the case where the CGT is concerned: the latter does not disguise its view that the fight against manpower reductions must allow intervention 'at the very heart of the company managements'.[8]

Workers' Right of Expression. Workers' expression constitutes a new right accorded to them by law on 4 August 1982. The text adopted, which had given rise to severe reservations, notably on the part of FO and the employers (on very different grounds), is in the end fairly cautious, since it does not itself lay down the procedures under which this right is to be exercised but leaves them open for discussion in the enterprises. Only in 1985 will a legislative text, taking into account the arrangements arrived at by negotiation, be adopted. Also, it limits the right of expression to 'the content and organisation of work' and to 'the definition and pursuit of action designed to improve working conditions in the enterprise'. It does not, therefore, affect the operation of the enterprise, still less its management, and does not involve any new distribution of the powers of decision in the enterprise, even on matters covered by the right of expression.

The trade union reactions to this new right vary greatly. The CFDT came out most strongly in its favour since it views the measure as a decisive advance towards 'the socialism of workers' control' and an excellent means of 'promoting the workers' own autonomous conduct in relation to the power of the employers'. In this connection, it rejects the role of the hierarchy, the objective being to 'undermine the power of the employers over the organisation, the distribution of tasks and the discipline of the enterprise'[9]. The CFDT thus situates itself squarely within a perspective of workers' control extending well beyond the confines of the Law.

The CGT, by contrast, is only interested in the new right to the extent that the unions are able to give direction to their workers through the medium of their elected representatives and officials. Company management must have no place in this area, which indeed must provide a platform for the denunciation of the failures of management and the rejection of all reference to private property.[10]

The concern of the CGT is thus also to make a very broad interpretation of the law, venturing out into 'criticism of entrepreneurial management and the elaboration of industrial solutions'.[11]

FO for its part continues to voice hostility towards the law, because it sees in the right of direct and collective expression of workers a challenge to the primacy of the trade union organisation. It also sees in it the risk of exploitation for political purposes and the danger of the institution of a parallel hierarchy, placing the establishment, particularly the supervisory staff, out on a limb.[12]

The latter view is of course shared by the CGC, which fears that the workers' right of expression encroaches on the role of management. It also fears that it constitutes a risk of destabilisation of the economy through the development of subversive activities such as took place recently in the motor industry.

In the present state of affairs, however, the law seems to have been correctly applied to the extent that the agreements concluded (covering some 2 million workers) are limited to the purpose intended and entrust the direction of meetings, in 75 per cent of cases, to the management. But the example of nationalised undertakings, in which the right of expression is set out in more precise terms and is exercised in 'workshop councils', will certainly be used by the CGT and the CFDT as far as possible to deflect the law from its purpose in the private sector.

Access to Means External to the Enterprise

The external influences acting on an enterprise are many and varied in an economy which, especially at a time of crisis, is increasingly subject to government intervention. When the government, as is the case at present in France, takes pains to obtain the agreement of the trade unions, or at least some of them, the demands of the trade unions fall on more fertile ground. Thus the implementation of the various measures designed to assist industrial adjustment and company restructuring is often inspired by social preoccupations, alongside which concerns for profitability are of secondary importance.

Thus it is particularly in the field of employment that the representations of the trade unions are most insistent. We have seen above that the works councils only had a consultative role in this respect and that the last word rested with the administration, which had sole competence in the matter of rejecting or authorising redundancies, subject to the means of recourse open to the enterprise to challenge the administrative decisions. But in fact the trade unions deploy their action outside the works council, seeking in the first instance—depending on the case in question—to secure alternative jobs or to trigger reactions among the rank-and-file workers, subsequently intervening with the government in order, sometimes, to force it to go back on its own decision. This was the case recently in the Talbot affair, in which restructuring redundancies authorised by the government were challenged by the CGT, although it had been party to the decision authorising the redundancies, and by the CFDT which took an even more aggressive stance. Similarly, the agitation provoked and sustained by the CGT in connection with the restructuring of Papeteries de la Chapelle Darblay was a determining factor in the solution finally adopted, which has been embodied in an agreement negotiated and signed by that organisation with the foreign group which took over the business.

Trade union action meddling in the management of companies on the pretext of defending jobs can take other forms. The 'employment–training–production' contracts which the former Communist Minister for Employment endeavoured to put into effect provided an opportunity for this; the object of these contracts is to establish contact between two enterprises, one of which previously imported the various products needed for its manufacturing processes, products which the other enterprise would be able to produce subject to the recruitment of new workers, which would be facilitated by government aid. The trade unions will inevitably attempt to intervene in the enterprises concerned.

The trade unions are also paying close attention to the possibilities offered them by the institutions with consultative status set up by the government with the precise aim of associating the workers with the preparation of the main lines of economic and social policy or with the application of the legislative and regulatory texts governing it.

Among these institutions at national level are the following: the Conseil Economique et Social (Economic and Social Council), whose function is to deliver opinions on all draft legislation of economic and social importance, particularly the draft plan; the various committees responsible for the preparation of the plan; the Commission Supérieur de la Négotiation Collective (Higher Collective Bargaining Council); and the Comité Supérieur de l'Emploi (Higher Employment Committee).

Representatives of the trade unions nominated by the government—and not elected, such as the workers' representatives entrusted with the administration of the social security system—sit on these various bodies alongside representatives of our socio-occupational groups and of government departments. Their weight is not therefore decisive, but the debates which take place may nevertheless affect the final decision of the government, which will take particular account of the views expressed by the trade unions linked to the political parties forming the present majority.

At local and regional level, moreover, the trade unions are also represented on the economic and social committees and on the various consultative bodies, which must take on increasing importance with the policy of decentralisation currently pursued.

This external action on the part of the trade unions is thus far from negligible. This is shown by the CFDT in particular, when it states: 'The policy of extending workers' rights tends in the right direction if it does not stay within the confines of the enterprise. Local committees on employment, planning and taxation reform are all means to be made use of.'[13]

Finally, among the external means may be cited the effect which the trade unions are endeavouring to produce on public opinion. They seek, of course, in the first instance to influence the media, with the aid of well-trained communications experts, but they also achieve public prominence by organising events of various kinds (sports events, folklore displays, cultural events, etc.). In this respect, the CGT puts a great deal of skill into making use of the possibilities offered by the local authorities favourable to it.

Future Prospects

The outlook for the future—looking ahead to the 1990s—reveals simultaneously factors of continuity and factors of change, and their interaction calls for the utmost caution in drawing conclusions. It is not possible, therefore, to make predictions without placing them within the context of the various hypotheses likely to arise in the political sphere, on the one hand, and in the economic sphere, on the other. The development of trade union action will itself be conditioned by these factors.

The Effects of Political Trends

The political situation in France following the departure of the Communists from the government is still too uncertain for any serious forecast of developments in the medium term. Whatever happens, certain changes of direction may be expected after the parliamentary elections in 1986. (In the following scenarios, the terms 'right' and 'left' are used for the sake of simplicity, but it should be remembered that the reality is more complex and that, in particular, a new 'centre-left' could emerge.)

In the hypothesis of a return of the 'right' to power, which would be subsequently confirmed by the presidential elections in 1988, nationalisation would be the first issue to come up for review. The timescales and procedures for the return of the undertakings recently nationalised to the private sector would, of course, require certain adjustments (in particular, access for the workers to the capital of the undertakings concerned could be favoured). But should we also expect a radical review of the terms of employment resulting from the law on the democratisation of the public sector? The answer to this question is not so obvious, but it can at least be said with certainty that strict limits will be set to the application of the law and that its extension to the sector which previously remained in private hands need no longer be feared.

The participation of the workers in the decision-making bodies of private companies could not be ruled out entirely, however. Of course, only the CFTC and the CGC have advocated a measure on these lines, but it had been the subject of draft legislation prior to May 1981. Because of the opposition of the CGT and the CFDT, but also FO, and reservations on the part of the employers, it was not debated. Nevertheless, it could reappear on the agenda.

On the other hand, the question would also arise whether certain of the measures to extend the powers of the works council would be reviewed: intervention by 'experts', for example, and the trade union monopoly enjoyed by the 'representative' organisations. A sizeable group in the employers' camp would like to see this happen, but it might be questioned how far it would be wise to go in risking a confrontation with the trade unions on this matter.

The 'workers' right of expression', which was already one of the concerns of many company heads and certain parties of the 'right' prior to May 1981, would certainly remain, but the formula of detailed legal regulation would be removed in favour of leaving the question to be resolved through contractual arrangements.

In the event that the 'left' were to remain in power, there could be either a hardening or a relaxation of positions on the problems relating to company management. In the hypothesis of a hardening of positions, it might indeed be expected that, if the government policy of austerity were to be maintained on the grounds of economic constraints, concessions would be made in other areas to the unions close to the power centre. Thus the least that could happen would be a widening of the powers of the works council along the lines sought by the CGT and CFDT (pp.58–60).

But a relaxation of positions is also a possibility. With economic realities continuing to make their effects felt and with a recognition of the vital need to maintain companies in good health, there would be no alternative but to provide them with the means to operate normally. An easing of excessively restrictive measures might then be anticipated which would enable enterprises to defend their competitiveness.

Effects of Economic Trends

Projections in the economic context are also fraught with imponderables because, apart from internal factors, others relating to the international picture also have to be taken into account (cost of raw materials and energy, international tensions, difficulties in European organisation, relations with the Third World).

Whatever happens, however, a high rate or growth cannot be expected in France for the years ahead. It will not therefore be possible to release sufficient resources to cover all requirements (payment for imports, investment, maintenance of advantages secured for all workers, new advantages for the least well-off and guarantees of employment for all). Faced with this situation, the reactions of the trade unions will take one of two forms. Some organisations, notably FO and the CGC, will concern themselves mainly with the defence of the material interests of the groups of workers they represent through the medium of negotiation; the

CGT and the CFDT will in the first instance see in the persistence of difficulties a new proof of the failure of the liberal economy and will increase their pressure for a collectivised economy (CGT) or an economy under workers' control (CFDT) which would be better able, in the view of these organisations, to meet the material demands they would continue to press.

Foremost among these will be demands related to the problem of unemployment resulting not only from cyclical economic difficulties, but also from difficulties of a structural nature.

The modernisation of enterprises, which is of crucial importance in maintaining their competitiveness, indeed involves far-reaching technological changes which, under any system of government, will necessitate industrial redevelopment, and on this point the trade union organisations will continue to quarrel with one another, with the employers and with the government.

Future Trends in Trade Union Development

In order to assess, within the context of the various hypotheses we have outlined, the possible results of trade union action in the years to come, it remains here to determine the influence effectively exerted by the unions on those they claim to represent and possible future developments.

At present in France we are inclined to speak of a crisis of trade unionism stemming from the declarations made by the unions themselves, the causes of which call for analysis.

Among these causes are first and foremost the economic crisis, which is preventing the unions from obtaining satisfaction of their traditional demands and, in particular, from achieving the increases in purchasing power to which the workers had become accustomed in the years of prosperity.

But mention must also be made of the difficulties of the trade unions in adapting to socio-cultural change. Technological change has indeed had an effect not only on the volume of employment, but also on the very structure of the world of work. With the development of computer systems, office automation, etc., the interests of occupational groups take precedence over general interests, the more so as there is no tradition of trade unionism among these groups. There will also be increased 'segmentation' in the pattern of employment, due to irregular work, part-time work, work at home, work under 'flexible hours' arrangements and perhaps also undeclared work—all of them forms of employment which keep workers away from the centres at which the trade unions can carry on their activities.

The trend towards 'corporatism' which will result from this situation may of course be used by both the revolutionary and the reformist unions, since an ideological justification can always be found to defend specific interests; but that will not necessarily strengthen the hand of the trade unions unless they are able to develop new strategies capable of providing solutions to problems raised by economic, technological and social change.

The workers indeed seem at present to feel the weight of the trade union 'apparatus' as that of ponderous institutions which are no longer in direct touch with their preoccupations. This 'institutionalisation' of the trade union organisations—which some of them, such as the CFDT,[14] have themselves recognised—is indeed increasingly criticised as rendering them incapable of solving day-to-day problems and providing the workers with the services they require. Are the French trade unions capable of evolving in order to rectify this situation? The answer to this question requires some qualification.

The CGT will certainly not alter its strategic line but will pursue the tactics best suited to the interests of the Communist Party. It will thus sustain its offensive in the field of company management and, in parallel, will support sectoral demands, which will enable it to increase its clientele on the Socialist left.

The CFDT, aware of its own difficulties, is currently seeking the right means of acquiring a new credibility.[15] It would certainly be a mistake to think that it could develop along lines fundamentally different from those it has followed up to now. Nevertheless, economic constraints are prompting the CFDT to reconsider certain of its positions with regard to the enterprise, recognising that there are 'employers—large, medium-sized and small—whose day-to-day conduct of their affairs represents a positive vision of the industrial challenge'.[16] Thus, what finally emerges with the CFDT is a discrepancy between sometimes constructive 'discourse' and 'conduct in the field'. The result is an impression of inconsistency which it is at present trying to shake off.

FO, the CFTC and the CGC are not and will not be demanding more power in the enterprise. FO in particular affirms and will reaffirm at any opportunity that it has no plans to participate in the framing of economic and industrial policy and that it leaves company management to those whose responsibility it is, which leaves it free to promote its demands in the material area.

Conclusion

We might be tempted in conclusion to consider that the freedom of management in French companies is today already seriously eroded but should not in the years to come experience further encroachment, when we take into account the relative weakening of the 'revolutionary' compared with the 'reformist' organisations and the general recognition of economic realities prompted by the economic crisis. However, we have also seen that it is necessary to guard against any conclusion as final and as clear-cut as this. The data relating to the problem in France are particularly complex, and it has not been possible to develop all the aspects of this complexity. We shall therefore return here, in order to explain them, to those aspects which are of special importance to the analysis of possible future developments.

Characteristics of French Trade Unionism

These characteristics, especially the pluralism and divisions of the trade union movement, may be seen as a factor of weakness in the collective strength of the workers, but may also constitute an incentive for the unions to compete with one another in demands and promises and be used by some for political ends. When we also take into account the low rate of unionisation, we might wonder how the trade unions can really perform their role within the enterprise.

It should be pointed out at the start in this respect that a low rate of unionisation does not necessarily mean that the workers are completely indifferent to the activities of the unions. Thus it may be noted that, in works council elections, the trade unions win over 80 per cent of the votes cast.

Except in those works councils in which the trade unions enjoy the extended facilities already described, the trade unions present their case in the enterprise through the staff representatives elected by the workforce under the same terms as the members of the works council (their field of activity is limited to that of presenting claims), but also through the trade union representatives appointed directly by the unions from the enterprise 'trade union sections'. The latter—the existence of which only won legal recognition after 1968—are on the increase, despite the depletion in trade union membership (their number rose from 11,775 in 1970 to 30,601 in 1979) and this increase in particular reflects a better

'multi-union' establishment. Trade union sections were only compulsory prior to 1981 for enterprises employing at least 50 workers.
Since the law of 28 October 1982, they may be present in all
enterprises which, together with the obligation to conduct annual
negotiations at enterprise level (on real wages, the actual length
and organisation of working hours) also imposed by law,[17] aims to
impart new impetus to trade union action in enterprises of any
size. The scope of this impetus cannot yet be measured, however,
since the economic situation is hardly favourable to the conclusion
of many agreements.

Diversity of French Enterprises and Importance of the Public Sector

The very wide diversity of French enterprises as regards size, legal
structure, the nature of their activities and their regional dis-
persion render it impossible to group them together in a single
appraisal. There is no doubt that, in spite of the new legal provisions aimed at introducing unions into small firms, it is in the big
companies that trade union action is and will remain strongest.

But the current importance of the public sector also prompts the
question whether trade union strategies might not show
differences as between this sector and the private sector. No such
differences emerge from the examination of these strategies, but
there is no doubt that the special facilities available to the unions
in the public sector cannot but give them a taste for further
incursion into management, particularly in the area of company
secrecy, and this inclination will not stop at the nationalised undertakings.

Thus several industrial agreements being negotiated between
French firms, whether nationalised or not, and between French
and foreign companies have recently been brought to the attention
of the public by the trade unions themselves, and it is they who
have sometimes sounded the alarm over difficulties facing certain
companies,[18] perhaps without realising that such indiscretions
could wreck negotiations which would otherwise have had beneficial results or could accelerate the demise of companies in
difficulty.

Also, no difference in strategy is to be seen in the fact that more
strikes are currently taking place in the public sector than in the
private sector. As they involve public service employees, these
strikes are carried on by workers who, since they enjoy security of
employment, run no risk in demanding the maintenance of their

purchasing power. In the case of sectors such as the nationalised steel industry, the object is to defend jobs threatened by the restructuring plan drawn up by the government. Indeed, the workers' disappointment is that much greater because they had thought that 'nationalisation' meant job security. Whatever the case may be—whether the issue is pay or jobs—they think that, if they win through in the public sector, they will get satisfaction more easily subsequently in the private sector.

Trends on the Employers' Side

Trends on the employers' side are a crucial factor in the outlook for the future. Will heads of companies be able to set up a new system of relations with the trade unions? That is the question being asked today.

Here, too, we meet with a variety of positions. An important current of thinking among employers is represented and will continue to be represented by a purely defensive and, consequently, anti-union attitude. But there are other company heads who recognise that the trade union is and will remain a valid discussion partner and that it would even be dangerous for it to be weakened to such an extent that there was no longer any collective expression of the interests of the workers.

The division between the two currents does not necessarily manifest itself at the level of the big employers' confederations. Certainly, in the present configuration, the SNPMI needs to be set apart from the rest, being an organisation for the defence of small and medium-sized business opposing both the state and the workers' trade unions by forms of action which may extend to violence. It may be noted that, after the left came to power, the government, thinking to take advantage of a split in the employers' ranks, planned to recognise this organisation as having representativity. Indeed, a letter from the prime minister of 25 February 1982 proposed to include it 'in those bodies in which there is provision for the representation of socio-industrial organisations'. But since then, although the SNPMI has won 14 per cent of the votes in the elections to the conciliation council in 1982 (compared with 2 per cent in 1979), the government has become concerned over the conduct of this organisation and has not carried out its intentions. The SNPMI thus remains an isolated organisation whose future influence is uncertain.

The CNPF and the CGPME, on the other hand, while they have

no legal or financial links, are in continuous liaison with one another. Moreover, the representativity of these two organisations, which is recognised, overlaps to some extent, since a number of companies are members of both.

Nevertheless, while declaring itself in favour of the contractual policy *vis-à-vis* the workers' trade unions, the CGPME has not signed all the major national agreements signed by the CNPF and increasingly inclines towards an independent strategy. The extension of new workers' rights to small and medium-sized enterprises has rendered it particularly sensitive, because its policy is to defend the style of leadership and authority which is the traditional hallmark of the small employers. But, while sometimes engaging in vigorous public demonstrations to put its views across, it points out in the face of the SNPMI's excesses that it 'will never present that attitude as systematic union policy'.

The CNPF for its part states its mission to represent all categories of enterprises: small, medium and large. Thus its current president, elected in 1981 and himself the founder of ETHIC, can claim to refute the criticism levelled against the CNPF that it is dominated by the technocratic employers of the big corporations and assert that, on the contrary, it represents the 'human scale' enterprise just as well.

Even if this claim of the CNPF to represent enterprises of all sizes may today give rise to a certain amount of friction with the CGPME, it seems that in the present state of affairs the two organisations will avoid a confrontation. They sit side by side on official consultative bodies opposite the workers' organisations, defending their points of view in terms which may indeed differ, but which are presented only after prior consultation to enable any difficulties arising to be sorted out. Thus at the elections for the conciliation council in 1982, a CNPF–CGPME joint list was put forward which won nearly 78 per cent of the votes.

No attempt should be made, however, to hide the fact that the division in employers' attitudes referred to above is to be found in every organisation in which varying tendencies are in evidence and that, while there is agreement on the rights of company heads in the matter of authority and management—rights which derive from their responsibilities—divergences emerge on the question of devising the means to achieve 'social consensus'.

As we are concerned here with drawing a conclusion on future prospects, we should like to direct our attention to the positive directions of the quest.

These positive tendencies are indeed to be found in companies which, in their concern to safeguard their competitiveness, seek in the first instance to show that the trade union movement does not have a monopoly on social progress: thus they seek to respond to the individual aspirations of the workers by introducing more flexibility into working conditions, for example by developing 'self-sufficient teams', 'quality circles', 'flextime', etc. In the same way, they have no hesitation in applying the workers' 'right of expression' under the terms of the new legislation to the extent that it makes it possible to accommodate their real aspirations, the managerial staff having a particularly important role to play in this respect.

In parallel, company heads who are in touch with their workers in this way also admit that this effort to take account of the individual interests of the workers through a hierarchical approach must go hand in hand with the role of the trade unions in providing expression of their collective interests. If the unions present in the enterprise are truly representative of its workforce, it should be possible and it would be worth while, according to the employers, to develop in the union representatives an awareness of the economic problems. This is what the head of a plant servicing the shipbuilding industry, which is currently in difficulty, was referring to when he said that union representatives needed to be given 'an object lesson in the management of a company': 'We cannot expect our workers to give us their best in the future if we do not first give them correct information on the economic realities; what items go to make up the cost of an hour of work, how to estimate a price, how to plan a project. All these things are important and our workers should know about them.'

The 'social consensus' could therefore come into being in this spirit, with the two sides of industry seeking understandings with one another and at the same time keeping a certain distance *vis-à-vis* the state. On this point, there are grounds for criticising many company heads who declare themselves opposed to state control, while at the same time constantly demanding from the state measures to help them out of their difficulties. But there is another, more consistent attitude, that of the company heads who merely demand an easing of restrictions in order that they can maintain their freedom to be competitive.

Similarly, it may be noted that the unions politically close to the present government at first relied on it for the satisfaction of their demands but that changes in government policy have led them to reconsider their position. The fact that it is now in the nationalised undertakings (steel industry) that the most serious difficulties are being experienced, having to do with the industrial changes laid down in a government plan, is consistent with this change of attitude, which is tending to separate the unions from the state.

Conversely, a spirit of reappraisal of the private company is beginning to make itself felt in trade union circles themselves. Whereas, paradoxically, in the years when there was full employment and purchasing power was constantly increasing, private companies met only with indifference and even hostility in these circles and in public opinion, a realisation is now dawning in the wake of the crisis that jobs will be best protected only through the competitive power of companies and that private initiatives should therefore be developed.

With a full awareness of these tendencies, it should be possible to foresee a future pattern in which employers and union—at least, many of them—decide to rely more on each other than on the state in order to reconcile economic necessity with social aspirations.

It is in this eventuality that the freedom of management of enterprises could be safeguarded.

Notes

1. Alain Obadia, member of the Confederal Committee of the CGT, *Spécial-Options*, April 1983.
2. CFDT, *Aujourd'hui*, no. 59, January–February 1983.
3. Edmond Maire, *Cadres—CFDT*, no. 306.
4. Maurice Cohen, *Le Peuple*, no. 1148, January 1983.
5. *Le Peuple*, 15 October 1982.
6. Hispano/RATP affair, *Vie Ouvrière*, no. 1981.
7. CFDT, *Aujourd'hui*, no. 60, March–April 1983.
8. *Le Peuple*, no. 1151, March 1983
9. CFDT, *Aujourd'hui*, no. 58, November–December 1982.
10. *Le Peuple*, no. 1148, March 1983.
11. Ibid.
12. *FO HEBDO*, no. 1739, 19 January 1983.
13. CFDT, *Aujourd'hui*, no. 60, March 1983.
14. CFDT National Bureau, 4–5 January 1984.
15. Ibid.
16. E. Maire, *Projet*, January 1984.
17. Until the law of 13 November 1982, which imposed compulsory annual negotiations at enterprise level, collective bargaining was mostly pursued at the level of industrial or occupational sectors. Now, therefore, there is a double negotiating level.

18. A law of 1 March 1984, due to take effect by 1 March 1985 at the latest, grants new rights to the works councils in these areas: right to call attention to a situation, power to challenge the auditor, right to demand explanations if the situation of the company gives cause for concern, increased information in cases of amicable settlements, etc.

3 FEDERAL REPUBLIC OF GERMANY

H. Müller-Vogg

Population	62,000,000
Per capita GNP, 1982	US$ 10,500
Exports as per cent of GNP, 1982	27
Number of large companies (among the 500 largest outside the USA)	58 with 2,808,000 employees
Governments	1949–66 Coalitions led by Christian-Democratic Party with the support of the Bavarian Christian Socialists and sometimes of the Liberal Free Democrats 1966–9 A large coalition led by the Christian-Democrats and also including the Social Democrats 1969–83 Social Democrats in coalition with Free Democrats 1983– Christian-Democrats/Christian Socialists in coalition with Free Democrats
Public sector (share of GNP, 1982, including transfers)	49 per cent
Trade union membership	1982: 40 per cent
Trade unions	Deutscher Gewerkschaftsbund (DGB) is Europe's second-largest trade union organisation with 7.7 million members, of whom 5.2 million are workers. The largest of its member unions is IG Metall with 2.7 million members; 800,000 public sector salaried employees are organised in DGB unions. In addition there are two purely salaried employees' organisations outside DGB: Deutscher

75

Angestellten Gewerkschaft (DAG) with 500,000 members; and Deutscher Beamtsbund, which has 800,000 members mainly in the public sector.

Employers' organisations

Bundervereinigung der Deutschen Arbeitsgeberverbände (BDA) has a dominating position—more than 90 per cent of all employees in the private sector work for companies that are affiliated to BDA.

Trends and Demands

The German trade unions[1] are in a new and unaccustomed position. The economic trend which had been the norm for so long, characterised by relatively minor fluctuations but constant growth, has been replaced by a distinct ebb and flow, sometimes with a real decline in Gross National Product. Moreover, the general economic trend has lost its paramount importance to the position of the labour force as a whole. Sectors of outright growth now stand side by side with sectors in which, while the speed of the process of decline is not yet certain, there is no doubt about the general direction of the trend. Even in one and the same sector, gaps are widening between successful and less successful companies.

This dilemma for the trade union leaders is exacerbated by the fact that considerable reserves are available in the German economy as a whole for productivity increases or rationalisation —depending on the terms in which the replacement of human labour by machines and systems is expressed. In addition, the need to catch up with innovations, and hence for radical restructuring in large areas of German industry, is immense.

The more complex trends in the economy become, the more difficult is the relationship between the trade unions and the works councils, the legally sanctioned machinery to represent the interests of the workforce at plant level. Although the DGB (Deutscher Gewerkschaftsbund: German Confederation of Labour) unions hold the overwhelming majority of seats on these committees, there is frequently no co-ordinated policy between the trade unions and works councils. In practice, these plant-level bodies representing workers' interests make extensive use of their independence from the trade unions, which is laid down by law.

This leads to a situation in which the works councils in prospering companies regularly secure a supplement to the pay rates laid down in the collective agreement negotiated between the employers and the union, with the consequence that the agreement is invalidated. In the event of closures and similar negative developments, the works councils threaten to thwart the official trade union policy in two ways: either by radicalism or —much more frequently— by pragmatic arrangements with the company management. Generally speaking, the works councils, when in doubt, do what they consider to be right from their own 'plant-centred' point of view.

The unions are in a certain sense powerless in the face of these challenges. On the one hand, this is related to the fact that, basically, they have never been able or willing to understand that the impressive growth rates of the 1960s and early 1970s could not continue for ever. In any event, they have not so far devised any new programmes to prepare for a different development. On the other hand, the German trade unions have had painfully to adjust to the new political situation. The DGB is personally and ideologically associated with the Social Democrats who, in opposition, can take up the demands of the unions without any regard for a Liberal coalition partner. However, it makes a big difference whether, as an interest group, you are, as it were, a 'third coalition partner' —which is basically what the DGB was during the period of the SPD–FDP* coalition from 1969[2] on—or whether you merely have the largest of the two opposition parties in the Bundestag (Federal Parliament) on your side in the political decision-making process.

The DGB and its 17 affiliated unions have up to now made no effort to redefine their tasks in the face of a completely changed economic environment. There are no indications that it will yet do this. For, with all the pragmatism shown by the German workers' organisations in the past, the unions have always been extremely rigid in programmes and ideology and have always carried the traditional Marxist positions along in their baggage. Thus they continue in their programmes to attribute all the deficiencies and failures of modern industrial society to the 'conflict of interest' between capital and labour. Almost without change since the foundation of the DGB in 1949, calls have continued for the transfer of important sectors of the economy to 'common ownership'.

* SPD = Sozialdemokratische Partei Deutschlands (German Social Democratic Party); FDP = Freie Demokratische Partei (Liberal Democratic Party).

Now, it might be said that anyone in the DGB who has not in the past allowed its programmes to prevent him from doing what was necessary will continue to act likewise in the future. This would be a rash conclusion. As long as the size of the cake to be shared went on growing year by year, the achievement of material successes made it relatively easy for the predominantly 'right-wing' union leaders to justify 'renunciation' of the continued pursuit of social change. Thus, since the mid-1950s, they have no longer seriously pressed for the nationalisation or socialisation of certain industries or even threatened to make use of the strike weapon in order to achieve major political objectives, such as the extension of co-determination.

But the outline conditions have changed; a resurgence of the ideologues and programme-makers is therefore a probability. Since the previous economic configurations—high growth with relatively low rates of price increase and a preponderance of demand on the labour market—will not return in the foreseeable future, traditional trade union programmes will become increasingly topical. In any case, according to an unwritten law of trade unionism, no union official can allow himself openly to dismiss as non-binding or unimportant the objectives and demands embodied in the programmes—the 'decision basis'.

Ideology: From Regulative Factor to Counter-power

The tendency to regard the state as the source of all that is good in the economic field actually presupposed profound confidence in the capabilities and sense of justice of government institutions and bodies. The German trade unions never doubt the efficiency of state administation, despite the many examples of 'squandering of public resources'. On the other hand, their confidence that both the executive and the legislative arms of government act 'justly'—i.e. when in doubt, favour the workers—is rapidly dwindling. This process of 'disillusionment' over the true nature of representative and pluralist democracy seems to have just begun. The trade unions are still far removed from considering the state to be the 'agent of capital'. But there are signs that scepticism concerning the 'system', particularly among the younger officials and members, is growing.

Those officials, who see themselves as a 'progressive alliance' within the unions, are playing a major role in this opinion-forming process. They belong mainly to the Metalworkers' Union, the Commercial, Banking and Insurance Workers' Union, the Printing and Paper Workers' Union, the Educational and Scientific Workers' Union and the Wood and Plastic Workers' Union. They are still a minority both on the union executives and in the establishments of officials, but they are systematically extending their positions in preparation for the change of generation which is not yet complete in most DGB unions. These elements, who belong almost exclusively to the left wing of the SPD, are particularly active in trade union youth and training work. For that reason alone, their influence on tomorrow's trade union policy is greater than their numbers would suggest. In addition, this group, on almost all questions of internal union conflict, is able to refer to a distinctly 'left-wing' body of union policy rules. There is no doubt that the 'progressive alliance' is working on a continuous refinement—or, more accurately, radicalisation—of existing programmes.

This group is calling for a new trade union self-perception—and with considerable success. In its interpretation, the trade unions are no longer interest groups alongside many others, competing with one another to exert the influence to which they feel they are entitled on political decisions. According to the 'progressive' interpretation, the trade unions are rather a special kind of interest representation. According to this theory,[3] as organisations representing 'all workers'—hence 80 per cent of the population in almost all sectors and at all political levels—they have special rights.

This claim to power found its doctrinal embodiment in the 'Programme of Basic Principles' adopted in 1981. This states that the trade unions 'look after the interests of all workers and their families, thereby serving the requirements of the common good'. In other words, by their activities alone, whatever form they may take, the trade unions serve the good of society as a whole. One corollary immediately springs to mind: according to this theory, the trade unions cannot conflict with higher-ranking interests. Whatever serves their purposes is good for society too.

This change in trade union self-perception will not be without its consequences in the years to come. An indication of what repercussions may flow from it was already seen in the autumn of 1983. A number of individual unions were then quite openly trying to win support for the idea of using a general strike to prevent the deployment of US medium-range missiles within the framework of NATO rearmament. The fact that this did not happen was not only due to the opposition of moderate union leaders and to the clear legal position, according to which political strikes against decisions legally arrived at by democratically elected institutions of state are against the law. There was a much more practical reason for the rather academic character of the general strike debate: even the most radical officials did not see the slightest chance that such a call would be followed by any significant number of workers.

The discussion was not entirely without its consequences, however. The DGB Federal Executive called on all workers to join in a 'five-minute token stoppage for peace' on 5 October 1983, in protest against the deployment of new missiles on both sides of the Iron Curtain. The success of this action varied considerably. The fact of the call for a stoppage in itself, however, was an ecouraging sign for the 'progressive alliance'. After all, the top DGB leadership, which opposed all general strike plans, had found that the only way to placate its own internal opposition was to call the first political token strike in the history of the Federal Republic of Germany. The precedent has been established for the future.

The trade unions have thus developed their thinking systematically to the point of forming themselves into a kind of 'superparty'. While affirming parliamentary democracy and its decision-making machinery, a growing number of officials seek to reserve for themselves a right of final comment on decisions taken. On questions of 'fundamental' importance, therefore, there may be a threat of 'demonstrative' and 'political' work stoppages. And it would be entirely up to the unions to decide what is of 'fundamental' importance.

The trade unions could, of course, become a 'superparty' in another, less spectacular way—by the fulfilment of all their plans for co-determination in industry as a whole. Although in formal terms it is not the intention of the desired 'economic and social councils' to limit the independence of freely elected parliaments, their creation would amount to the same thing. In the final instance, there would be a need for non-socialist or non-Social Democratic parliamentary majorities to ensure that their decisions went against the trade union half of the councils and hence 'against the workers'. That would always be possible in legal terms, but not in the long run in political terms.

Against the background of the current debate on the political strike, a related development is gaining force. The smaller the chances, in the face of the changed economic and political circumstances, of achieving spectacular successes in the traditional field of trade union action—in confrontations with the employers and in political lobbying—the stronger is the inclination of the unions to address themselves to general political questions. It is therefore to be expected that they will increasingly see as their main 'battlefield' those political questions in terms of which, on the one hand, the 'class nature' of society is easily explained and in relation to which, on the other hand, emotions are quickly kindled. The catalogue of these themes is predictable: peace and ecology, basic democratic rights and professional exclusion (*Berufsverbot*: the exclusion of persons holding extreme political views from certain professions, such as teaching or the civil service), 'liberation movements' and development aid, 'worker-oriented' science, education and training, women's questions and the problems of various social minorities.

Vehement debates had already raged during the 1950s and 1960s inside the DGB on whether the unions should regard themselves as a 'regulative factor' or as a 'counter-power'. 'Regulative factor' in this context means that the unions should in their basic field of activity—mainly collective bargaining—resolve certain matters together with the employers and ensure adherence to the agreements reached. The role of 'counter-power', on the other hand, includes the political function. According to the counter-power theoreticians, the unions should function *within* the existing, in their opinion, capitalist system as well as *in opposition* to the system—as an anti-capitalist combat unit, as it were.

As has been pointed out, the theoretical debate on the subject has a long tradition. In any case, there is not really any clear dividing-line between the two concepts. Indeed, it is quite possible to represent the interests of the workers within the existing pluralistic and parliamentary system, thus performing a regulative function, and at the same time to work with the utmost vigour, but through exclusively legal means, to bring about fundamental changes in this system. To this extent, the unions are always both things: both a regulative factor and a counter-power. The key point is which function they emphasise more strongly. In practice, the German trade unions have operated for almost three decades mainly as a regulative factor. In the meantime, there is a growing tendency in many DGB circles to consider the unions primarily as a counter-power and to proclaim action on appropriate lines.

Regulative Policy: More Direction, Less Market

The call for more direction and planning is a theme which runs unaltered through all the economic policy programmes of the trade unions since 1949. Of course, they carefully avoid pinning themselves down to a particular theoretical concept or a foreign example as a yardstick for the change they seek in the economic system and in government economic policy. Neither does the DGB in its economic policy pronouncements refer directly to the concept of a social market economy, either in positive or negative terms. To a certain extent, the unions shrink from explicitly re-pudiating the 'third German way'—which is quite popular in large sections of the population and the workforce—between a centrally administered economy and a free competitive economy unfettered by social obligation. Neither is there any official trade union demand for the abolition of private ownership of the means of production.

Their regulative policy considerations clearly amount to a move away from the social market economy, however. Thus the 'Pro-gramme of Basic Principles' not only places competition and planning side by side as instruments having equal status; it also comes out in favour of an economic outline plan through which all economic policy measures would be co-ordinated. It would take in all regional and sectoral projections and thus provide companies with the 'orientation' data necessary for them to take their de-cisions.

The same programme demands the 'tuning' of private and public investment to the structural and cyclical 'requirements' of the economy as a whole. This would be achieved by a system of investment control under which the big corporations would be required to declare their plans for investment and their con-sequences for employment to an 'investment declaration centre'.

A third key element in trade union regulative policy is the transfer to public ownership of key industries and firms which dominate market and economic processes. Economic and social councils, on which employers and workers would each occupy half the seats, would participate in the decision-making on all these matters in the regions and at Länder and Federal level. In addition, there would be co-determination in all large companies, on the coal and steel industry model.[4] The decision-making possibilities of companies and employers would also be restricted in favour of the unionised workforce by the further means of a ban on lock-outs during an industrial dispute.

Outline planning, investment control, socialisation and co-determination would all serve the—in the eyes of the trade unions—most important aim of economic policy; full employment. In the last analysis, the 'right to work' is, from their point of view, one of the 'basic human rights'.

There can be no doubt that the realisation of all the programme objectives would so restrict the decision-making capacities of companies and would so erode the power of disposition of the owners of the means of production, that it would no longer be possible to speak of a 'free' economy. In addition to this—as experience throughout the world has shown—the profusion of measures proposed by the DGB would give rise to an ever-increasing amount of state intervention. What would remain in the end is not a system of central economic direction, but an economic order in which those companies subject to trade union co-determination and faced with 'orientation' as to state intentions, would no longer enjoy much scope for forming their own policy.

It seems to be of great importance to future trade union policy that this 'decision basis' is in reality capable of almost any interpretation, so that many individual interventionist or economic planning demands could be drawn from it. This has been happening for several years—with an increasing trend. For with continued high unemployment, the attraction of the social market economy might become less apparent to the mass of workers, which in turn increases the chances for the advocates of a planned economy and their arguments.

It is therefore to be anticipated that the trade unions, particularly their local organisations, will in the future make even more strident calls on the state. This is especially likely at times when mass redundancies are about to be declared, the collapse of a company is threatened or the difficulties of industries or firms —real or assumed—are having consequences for the labour market in a region. The immediate demand is for the nationalisation of a firm threatened by bankruptcy or of undertakings in an industry which has got into difficulties. That is what happened 15 years ago in the mining industry and is now being repeated in the steel and shipbuilding sectors.

It is interesting in this connection that the workers' organisations increasingly talk of 'socialisation' or 'transfer to common ownership' without defining precisely what they mean by it. Once they realise—for example, in the case of a steelworks or a big shipyard—that the state as the majority shareholder is also unable to provide protection against the consequences of changes in the division of work in the world economy or against distortions in international competition due to varying levels of national subsidies, the trade unions will clearly not be content with a change of shareholders.

By references to socialisation or transfer to common ownership, therefore, they seek to point out that the same decision-making rules cannot apply in an undertaking belonging to the people as apply in a private or state-capitalist enterprise. In other words, the trade unions want to secure more rights of co-determination for themselves in socialised undertakings. It is not at all clear how they see this working out in practice. It is not currently under discussion. That is, however, not an indication that the subject has been consigned to the archives. More likely, the unions at present fear that public discussion of 'common ownership' might reopen the affair of the trade-union-owned building concern, Neue Heimat,[5] which has by no means been forgotten. The matter is therefore not on the agenda for the immediate future.

There is also uncertainty and indecision among the trade unions over the nationalisation debate for another reason. The 'traditional' candidates for nationalisation have, in their eyes, always been the key industries, particularly the basic raw materials industries. Today the coal and steel industries are economically of secondary importance,[6] and it is not clear what other industries are to take the place of the old key industries. Moreover, realistic trade union officials are well aware that more state or 'social' influence in crisis industries will not favour the idea of nationalisation or socialisation; finally, the state can at best only provide a certain social cushioning of the inevitable contraction in those industries.

For this reason, ideas are gaining ground that the trade unions should give precedence in the application of their public ownership concepts to outright growth industries and, in particular, to the highly profitable banks. The Commercial, Banking and Insurance Workers' Union (HBV), in particular, is pressing this idea. The

'Programme of Basic Principles' also calls for a reorganisation of the banking system in order to exclude the control of companies by banks. But these are merely tentative forays. Actual attacks by the trade unions on the private capitalist structure of the banking system are not yet planned. The next nationalisation offensive could very well involve the electrical and electronic sector (micro-electronics). Indeed, to this very day the DGB supports technical progress only in so far as it can be used for safeguarding employment and for the humanisation of work.

For the German trade unions, it is inevitable that future increases in productivity will depend more on the introduction of new production technology than on growth in the economy. On this assumption, unemployment is bound to rise. Since even the nationalised undertakings can do no more than slow down the rate of manpower reduction and ease the process for those affected by means of financial aids, an increasing number of trade union officials are advocating a 'predictive' structural and industrial policy. The model here is the activity of the Japanese Ministry of International Trade and Industry (MITI), which promotes research and development with financial incentives and, through informal channels, aids the formation of internationally competitive enterprises and protects the home market, where necessary, by visible and invisible tariff barriers.

An issue of significance to the relationship between the two sides of industry is co-determination in the undertaking. 'Social consensus' has rightly been seen in the past as an important 'production factor' in the German economy; not without reason, the predominantly peaceful mode of settling disputes has been attributed to the institution of co-determination in the undertaking. Even so, the course of co-determination legislation in the postwar period shows that the trade unions will never be content with what has been achieved in this area but will always seek new and more far-reaching co-determination facilities. This is shown by the attitude to co-determination in the coal and steel industries. Although the unions have, since the early 1950s, unstintingly demanded the extension of the arrangements covering those industries to all large undertakings, the scope for influence in the coal and steel industries is no longer really enough for them. Under existing law the Annual General Meeting, even in the coal and steel industries, can itself take decisions which are normally the prerogative of the supervisory board; the shareholders have thus, by roundabout means, retained the right of final authority in decision-making. Precisely for that reason, the DGB wants to remove this option.

The extension of the coal and steel co-determination model, modified on these lines, will thus continue to be one of the aims of the German trade unions for years to come.

In view of the current political majority position, however, the unions seem to be giving priority to a review of the Law on the Constitution of Enterprises (Betriebsverfassungsgesetz: BVG), which regulates possibilities for the participation of staff representation bodies at industrial establishments (works councils) in decisions on staff and social matters. In particular, the unions might be expected to press for increased involvement of works councils in the introduction of new technology. A consequence of greater influence for the works council in this area would be that the consent of the workers' representatives would be tied to certain conditions. These would probably include, in the first instance, a stipulation that any employees made redundant should not be dismissed and, in the event of possible employment in less highly skilled jobs, should not suffer any financial loss. That could lead to a situation in which it becomes so expensive to use micro-electronics as to preclude their introduction—with all the disadvantages that this would entail for the competitiveness of the company and the jobs it can offer.

The ideas of the trade unions on the public sector are also of significance to regulative policy. Both the individual unions which organise Federal, Länder and local government employees[7] and the entire DGB call for the removal of all differences in status between established civil servants and local government officers, on the one hand, and workers and salaried staffs, on the other. The declared aim of this levelling-out is to place established officials and other employees on the same footing in regard to the right to strike. According to existing legislation, civil servants cannot take strike action because of the special loyalty they owe to the state. This 'handicap' should, in the view of the unions, be eliminated in future. They would then be free to disrupt public life by strike action on the railways, in the postal service or among administrative officials, customs officers and teachers—and thereby increase pressure on the state as an employer.

Independently of efforts to secure the removal of the ban on strikes by civil servants, the Teachers' Union (GEW) has already initiated 'softening-up' action by a campaign of limited in-fringements of existing laws. Here the GEW is following the policy of IG Metall (Metalworkers' Union) and IG Druck (Printing Workers' Union) to reinterpret current legislation. There is a high probability that other trade unionists in the public service will also take this upon themselves.

All things considered, it is unlikely that the unions in the years ahead will conduct a major ideological debate on a fundamental reorientation of regulative and economic policy. Theoretical dis-cussions inside the unions may be expected to address these questions, however. But in the fight for public opinion a different approach is discernible. Here the unions are concerned not to present questions of regulative policy in abstract terms but to link them in a concrete manner with individual economic problems. This removes the need to declare themselves in principle opposed to the market economy system and in favour of a planned and directed system, which in the Federal Republic of Germany has always been tainted by its negative association with the East German pattern. Instead, they may limit themselves to recom-mending state intervention, state-imposed obligations and the transfer of private companies to public ownership in all situations in which the individual worker would—at least in the short term—derive advantage from such action. In this way, the discussion in the country would be less and less about the principles of reg-ulative policy and more and more about state 'aid' in individual cases. To this extent, the adjustment difficulties attendant upon structural change in German industry are providing the unions with an opportunity for launching a regulative policy offensive.

Trade Union Practice: More Radicalism and Less Compromise

A change from a line based on partnership to one of confrontation will take root in collective bargaining policy. The autonomy of each individual trade union in the formulation of pay demands, in the conduct of industrial disputes and in the conclusion of col-lective agreements enables individual unions to pursue a strategy which may be in outright opposition to the official pro-nouncements of the DGB or of other individual unions. Changes in the political majority configuration within an organisation may therefore be reflected most quickly in collective bargaining policy.

Wherever the majority has 'swung to the left' or is about to do so, a radicalisation of collective bargaining policy takes place —radicalisation in the sense that the negotiating of wages, working hours and working conditions is increasingly seen as a 'social power issue' and is processed accordingly. Strident confrontation with 'capital'—to the point of industrial action—then becomes a value in itself, since it serves to promote the 'formation of consciousness' and the 'mobilisation' of the membership and the public in general. Anyone who argues for less compromise and more struggle inevitably imposes demands which make any agreement with the other party extremely difficult from the outset. This was precisely the aim when IG Metall and others in 1983–4 decided to demand the introduction of the 35-hour week with no loss of pay.

The forms of conflict threaten to be more radical in the future. IG Metall has in recent years been trying out a form of action which may replace or be a precursor to an all-out strike. 'Neue Beweglichkeit' (new mobility). What this means is a series of warning strikes—i.e. short stoppages at plant level according to a timetable worked out and co-ordinated at central union level —even before either side declares the negotiations to have failed. In this way, the pressure on the employers is increased. Since it is allegedly a case of spontaneous stoppages of a few hours only, the union is not obliged to compensate its members for loss of wages; the strike fund thus remains untouched. Because of the short duration of these work stoppages, the employers are also unable to respond with lock-outs, since in this case the principle of 'commensurate response' would not apply. As in many other cases, it may be that IG Metall has carried out pioneer work for other DGB unions here; the 'warning strike' weapon will also be used in the years ahead by other DGB unions.

The Printing and Paper Workers' Union (Industriegewerkschaft Druck und Papier) may also have played a trail-blazing role. Since its annual conference in 1983, this union's executive is no longer obliged to ballot the members prior to declaring a strike. The hurdle of a ballot in which a 75 per cent majority is required for a strike has restrained many a union in the past from pressing ahead with preparations for industrial action. On the one hand, a vote of the membership in favour of action is for the union leadership a means for escalation and threat. On the other hand, an executive which wants a strike but gets a rejection from the rank and file would be forced to back down. The print union has now eliminated this risk. There is a second factor: IG Druck, according to the latest policy decisions, no longer has to give strike pay in every instance. This has also increased the executive's room for manoeuvre, since the possible intensity and duration of a dispute need no longer depend on the size of the reserves set aside for strikes.

While individual unions are sharpening the strike weapon, the DGB as a whole is concerned that each individual union should support the others in the event of an industrial dispute. Although sympathy strikes are not permitted under existing legislation, the unions have already shown through the 'new mobility' that in cases of doubt they will go to the limits of law and jurisprudence in their action and will not from the outset refrain from methods of dubious legality. It is conceivable, moreover, that a union may by means of a short stoppage declare 'sympathy' for another union and its aims, while formally organising a 'warning strike' for its own purposes. An extension of the right to strike to public service officials would, of course, considerably widen the scope for the warning strike expedient.

The aim of the 'co-ordination' in pay disputes sought by the DGB is to provide staff, organisational and financial support. If this is successful, it could mean that small unions will in future conduct industrial disputes of their own with the aid of the big unions. And this would in turn open up possibilities for the large organisations to get other unions to take action in their own disputes at relatively low cost. Since strikes as a rule lead to a mobilisation of the workforce and increase readiness to join a union, the individual unions supported could emerge strengthened from such a compaign.

In the context of the closer collective bargaining co-operation desired by the left-wing DGB unions, it is conceivable, finally, that the DGB staff and the DGB organisations at Länder level will take on at least a large part of the public relations work of the union involved in the conflict. This could lead to stronger solidarity action on the part of union members not involved in the dispute. This all looks more likely, the more fundamental and political the industrial disputes carried on by both unions and employers in the years ahead become.

Because of its repercussions, collective bargaining policy is of considerable significance to the economic situation; because of the manner in which results are obtained, it has a lasting effect on the social climate. Co-determination in the company and its establishments is of at least equal importance to relations between employers and unions. Although co-determination is much less spectacular in its connotations than pay disputes, decisions are taken in this context which are often of more direct and therefore greater relevance to the company and its workforce.

The German trade unions have now exhausted all the possibilities of co-determination offered them by statute in the Law on the Constitution of Enterprises and the various co-determination laws. They have also succeeded in securing additional 'extra-statutory' co-determination rights in companies through formal or informal agreements. The range of these possibilities, which are conceded predominantly in large companies associated with the coal and steel sector or influenced by government, is wide and varied. They include agreements on the release of all joint consultative committee members, although the law prescribes only a certain number—or the 'reservation' of the post of board member for personnel and social affairs (worker director)—for a member of the works council or a trade union official.

In the past the unions have always recognised their joint responsibility, even in the event of unpopular decisions. Of course, the economic situation for a long time made it easy for them to do this. The decision which undeniably comes hardest to the employee representatives on company boards is always consent to plant closures and the associated dismissals. As long as demand exceeded supply on the labour market, dismissal for the employee concerned was not synonymous with unemployment. In addition, companies showed considerable generosity in the final pay settlements for departing employees, so that the conduct of the works council or of the worker representative on the supervisory board gave rise to little criticism on the part of the workforce.

With the continued high level of unemployment, it has become increasingly difficult to maintain this policy. There is, therefore, the danger of a hardening of attitudes on the part of the employee representatives on co-determination bodies. The price to be paid by companies for the consent of the workforce may be expected to rise accordingly. The battle lines may thus be drawn up more frequently between the shareholders and the employees—a situation that was once the exception rather than the rule.

As long as supervisory board decisions were in the final instance taken with the consent of the employee representatives, the trade unions could not avoid taking their share of responsibility for them *vis-à-vis* the workforce and the public. If the workers' representatives have been outvoted, however, they will also refuse to accept decisions taken against their will. Their participation in the decision-making processes in this way threatens to become co-determination without co-responsibility.

The extraordinarily high degree of stability which has always characterised the German economic system has much to do, amongst other things, with the fact that many compromises were reached between company managements, on the one hand, and the works councils and unions, on the other—without the employees affected knowing about them. If, however, the probability of conflict increases —for objective or ideological reasons —the unions will be concerned from the outset to discuss the matter at issue in public. This in turn exacerbates the difficulty of reaching compromises.

It should be noted in all of this that the fixation of many trade union officials with 'struggle' takes away the basis for co-determination. This is perhaps where the greatest danger to industrial peace in the Federal Republic of Germany is to be found. For the unions have such an abundance of facilities for co-determination and participation in company business—in pay policy, in public institutions and even in jurisdiction—that it is of vital significance whether co-determination is seen as an instrument for the balancing of interests or as an instrument of the class struggle. Indeed, the voices are increasingly heard on the trade union left of those who see co-determination at best as a field for the pursuit of conflict, while others even see in co-determination a factor which limits the combat-readiness and fighting strength of the union side. It is not likely that the German unions will abandon co-determination; the power of practical reality is too great for that. On the other hand, it would not be surprising if the co-determination possibilities were increasingly used to draw attention in demonstrative ways to the 'basic contradiction between capital and labour'. Thus, already in the steel industry meetings of supervisory board committees are increasingly accompanied by walk-outs, demonstrations and the appearance of employee representatives in the meeting room, as soon as closures and redundancies come on to the agenda. The employee representatives on board committees and the works councils hold back from these demonstrations—if only for legal reasons. It goes without saying, however, that they appear to approve of such tactics.

These activities might be expected to encourage emulation, as has been the case with a recently 'discovered' means of stepping up conflict: plant occupations by workers fearing for their jobs. The trade unions have not yet sanctioned this procedure as an official means of struggle since, quite apart from anything else, legal considerations would advise caution. Nevertheless, the annual conference of IG Metall at the end of 1983 'instructed' the leadership to prepare as soon as possible a plan for future action against companies, going beyond the 'legally permitted forms of resistance to job destruction' which have hitherto been the norm. It is unlikely that the executive will come out in favour of plant occupations without reservation along the lines advocated by those who presented the proposal. It is much more likely that employees will in the future 'occupy' their plants on their own initiative, but with tacit union support. Finally, such actions will be readily emulated, which promises a great deal of public attention.

In other unions, further new forms of 'struggle' are being discussed. These include the 'rolling strike', which will involve the largest possible number of workforces in the dispute, while at the same time limiting the possibility of the employers declaring a lock-out. Also, temporary occupations of departments or machines will contribute to the mobilisation of the workforce.

Organisational Policy: More Self-seeking and Less Predictable

Two tendencies have often opposed one another in the history of the German trade union movement: to function as a union whose sole concern is to represent the interests of its own members and of the organisation, or to function by subordinating the action of the union to more general interests. During the period following the Second World War, however, one theory has had a very distinct influence on practice: the theory of the trade unions as a 'social movement' acting on behalf of all workers and their families, regardless of whether they are members and pay contributions or not. This concept has strengthened the political weight of the unions, since they have not only claimed to speak on behalf of 'all workers', but have also acted accordingly. Thus, although there have been repeated moves inside the unions to secure 'favoured treatment clauses' in collective agreements to the advantage of union-organised workers, this aim has never been seriously pursued.

The fact that the size of the cake to be shared out has objectively become smaller, however, and, in particular, the surplus of demand on the jobs market are developments that have tended to give the unions the character of institutions representing the interests of workers in employment. Thus, during the time of the SPD–FDP coalition, the unions secured the adoption of a number of laws to the advantage of the labour force under which the legal and financial hurdles making it difficult to dismiss workers were set considerably higher. For this reason, it is now practically impossible for a company to dismiss a worker solely in order to take on another with better qualifications. The same efffect may be expected from laws for the protection of particular groups of workers such as the disabled or pregnant women; the restriction of employers' staffing policy freedom has inevitably reduced their readiness to react to changes at other levels by building up the workforce. This has resulted in a distinct reluctance to recruit new staff and in increased rationalisation.

There is particular danger in the fact that dismissals on grounds of closures or restructuring operations (mass redundancies) are possible only when the company has reached agreement with the works council on financial settlements (Social Plan), and it is a matter of complete indifference whether the workers concerned have new jobs in prospect or not. The effect of this provision of the Law on the Constitution of Enterprises is frequently such that a company, because of the high costs of the Social Plan, cannot undertake the staff reductions it needs in order to save itself and therefore goes into liquidation—an especially grotesque outcome of a rigid policy for the 'preservation' of jobs.

The policy in favour of the 'holders' of jobs is further manifested in the fact that the workers' representatives at company and plant level practically agree to closures, restructuring and rationalisation only if those affected are either retrained for other work or are able to go into early retirement; for the company and the state (pensions insurance), this is a costly option. This has dangerous consequences. To begin with, restructuring is rendered more expensive and is thus to some extent prevented—to the detriment of the firm's competitive position. Second, the workers affected are relieved of the need to look around for alternative employment—to the detriment of flexibility on the labour market. And third, the profitability of the company is eroded and public funds are burdened—to the detriment of investment capacity.

In their endeavours to preserve jobs regardless of their economic viability, the unions also act in their own interests; mass re- dundancies, after all, deprive them of members and membership dues. Since at the same time relatively few new jobs are being created, the absolute number of union members has been falling since 1982. There is another reason for this, of course. As the new jobs arise mainly in the service sector, where readiness to join a union has traditionally been below average, even a sustained re- covery will not automatically give the unions a large number of new members.

Already the membership structure no longer corresponds to the composition of the workforce: 68 per cent of all DGB union members are manual workers and only 22 per cent are salaried employees, while the proportions of these groups in the workforce as a whole are 47 per cent and 43 per cent respectively. The structure of the membership is not representative in one other respect: the organisational focus is in the 'old' industries and in the large corporations. These anomalies threaten to become more acute as new jobs are expected mainly in small and medium-sized businesses. It is not that the members are deserting their unions; just that there is no inflow of new members.

There is thus no shortage of efforts on the part of the unions to strengthen their position in the salaried employment sector, par- ticularly among women. But here they are falling back on a dangerous strategy. Since salaried employees are traditionally not very receptive to the old trade union slogan of 'Solidarity Among All Workers', they are the preferred target groups for trade union warnings of 'job killers' in the form of microchips and data-processing systems. If solidarity is not to be achieved among those in paid employment, then at least there should be solidarity among those who fear for their jobs. Success in this strategy would certainly lead to a higher rate of unionisation among salaried employees. In the end, there would also be a considerable degree of scepticism, even hostility, towards new technology.

A sustained decline in absolute membership figures or stagnation will provide ammunition for the advocates of moves to open up the unions to the unemployed. The activists of a more political trade union movement have already chalked up their first successes here. Individual unions are willing to recruit as members young people who can prove that they have undergone training in a relevant occupation. On the other hand, as things stand at present, anyone who was not organised while in employment remains excluded in the event of unemployment. Whether the 'progressive alliance' will acquiesce in that position is open to doubt. In the final analysis, the pool of unemployed could provide a source of recruitment for precisely those members who would advocate a more radical stance in their own interests. Of course, in this case the unions would load themselves with serious internal difficulties, because a large number of unemployed members would hardly be likely to reconcile themselves to a policy of preserving existing jobs, which are already occupied. It will therefore be preferable for the foreseeable future—even for out-and-out radicals among the officials—not to be dependent for re-election on the votes of a large number of unemployed union members.

Another development is of importance in terms of organisational policy. As was the case for other democratically organised associations and parties, the 'wave of democratisation' triggered by the 'extra-parliamentary opposition' at the end of the 1960s did not pass the trade unions by. The consequence of this for the union bureaucracies is that their room for manoeuvre in decision-making has been reduced by more vigilant and more critical surveillance systems. This does not in fact mean that the ordinary member today has a greater and more direct opportunity for contributing his voice. 'Democratisation' has tended instead to be integrated into the existing decision-making structure. This means that the annual union conferences—the supreme authorities of any union, which are attended mainly by full-time union officials and by works council officers—make greater use of their scope for influence than in the past. The same applies to the collective agreement committees, which accompany collective agreement negotiations and whose vote finally decides the question whether the union negotiating team should put its signature to a particular result or not.

A similar pattern is discernible in the relationship between the works councils and the unions, the size of plants and the rate of unionisation of the workforce being important factors here. In small and medium-sized enterprises with a rate of unionisation of less than 50 per cent, the members of the works council are usually dependent on the advice and support of the local trade union bureaucracies. This dependence often results in even works council members who have been elected as 'independents' joining a union after taking up their duties. No change in this situation looks likely.

The workers' representations in large establishments, on the other hand, have acquired a considerable degree of independence *vis-à-vis* the trade union machine. They are generally so well endowed with staff and finance that they have no need of union support in the performance of their actual tasks. With the increasing importance of the 'constellation of firms' unaffected by the general economic trend, therefore, the tendency of these works councils to take decisions and act independently of trade union policy is increasing. This does not necessarily mean greater pragmatism at plant level. Indeed, plant occupations have provided evidence of a new 'plant-level radicalism'.

For a long time now, the trade union head offices have no longer been able to counter this increasing 'plant disaffection' by references to decisions and rule books; the development has gone too far for that. Instead, there are moves in the trade union machine to make the general 'political struggle' the unifying bond of the organisation. Here the thinking of the ideologues could quite possibly coincide with that of the pragmatists concerned for the maintenance of organisational strength.

All these developments mean less power for the top officials. Since the latter—unlike the big union leaders of the 1950s and 1960s—have to operate with a smaller fund of confidence and without 'blind loyalty' from their followers, they are hardly in a position to reach agreement with the employers, and only then to go back to their members for approval. In the final analysis, this weakening of their negotiating partner's position consitutes a major disadvantage for employers' associations and company managements; after all, it makes them less dependable.

Altogether: Dangerous But Not Inevitable

The development trends in the German trade union movement outlined here may have a sustained, i.e. negative, influence on industrial peace and the economic situation in the Federal Republic of Germany in the years ahead. But it is not inevitable that it will all come to pass. The extent to which the ideological resurgence is reflected in trade union radicalism will, on the strength of all past experience, depend on three factors.

(1) The German worker was and still is politically inclined to the centre; many socialisation demands of trade union officials back in the 1950s and 1960s fizzled out in the face of this basic attitude. To this extent, the future general political 'climate' will also have its effect on the trade unions.

(2) The actual economic situation has had little influence on the programmes of the German trade unions, but has determined their practical policy. A positive change in key economic data, such as levels of unemployment, the level of real wages and growth, would therefore have a dampening effect on the radicalism to be observed in many quarters.

(3) The unions are not alone in the arena of political confrontation. It will also depend on the conduct of the employers to what extent the unions are able to realise their industrial policy ambitions.

Potentially disastrous plans in the regulative policy field have been made difficult, delayed and even prevented in the past because German employers and trade associations were not willing to compromise on fundamental issues and took on board the possibility of conflict. That will continue to be the case in the future. In contrast to the situation in past confrontations over questions such as the legal regulation of co-determination or capital formation, however, future disputes will not be limited to influencing the centres of political decision-making and public opinion. On the contrary, there is the threat of a resumption of the debate on principles which arose at the beginning of the 1970s on the reconciliation of private property and free competition with a democratic form of government, now supplemented by the emotionally charged environment issue.

The degree of preparedness for this confrontation varies from one employer to another, but the associations are better prepared than the individual companies themselves. Salaried managers and owner-directors alike are indeed inclined to leave social policy conflicts to the officials of both sides. This sometimes leads at plant level to compromises with works councils which run counter to organisation policies. Another attitude among the employers gives grounds for concern: the hope that a firm 'no' to all trade union demands will settle the matter once and for all. There is a lack of viable proposals for the further development of the social market economy, as well as for adjustment to changed economic, social and political conditions.

Of course, the employers must clearly recognise their limitations. They cannot themselves effect the 're-ideologisation' of the trade unions. There only remains the indirect way: to demonstrate the advantages of a free market economy through convincing company models for consultation, profit-sharing or flexibility in working hours.

Notes

1. The term 'German trade unions' refers here to the German Confederation of Trade Unions (Deutscher Gewerkschaftsbund: DGB), with its 17 individual unions. At the end of 1982, they organised 7.85 million workers, including 2.58 million in the Industriegewerkschaft Metall (Metalworkers' Union) alone.

The main unions outside the DGB are the Deutscher Beamtenbund (German Civil Servants' Association, 812 515 members), the Deutsche Angestellten-Gewerkschaft(German Salaried Staffs' Association, 501 037) and the Christlicher Gewerkschaftsbund (Christian Trade Union Confederation, 297 234). These organisations play a much less important role in public life than their membership figures suggest, however. This has to do mainly with the fact that these organisations only conclude independent pay agreements in a small number of partial sectors.

The DGB is a unitary trade union organisation in two senses of the term. First, it organises on the principle that all the employees of an establishment or a branch of industry should be represented by the same union, regardless of their occupation or status (manual worker, salaried employee, official). Second, the DGB claims to be a unitary organisation in the political sense, in which workers of all democratic parties co-operate. This second claim is not entirely valid, however. There is considerably more agreement on questions of principle between the DGB and the German Social Democratic Party (SDP) than between the DGB and the Christian Democratic Parties (CDU-CSU). Also, nine out of ten full-time trade union officials are members of the SPD.

2. The DGB also had considerable political influence during the period of the 'Grand Coalition' between the SPD and CDU-CSU from 1966 to 1969.

3. The Marxist trade union theoreticians in Germany speak of 'autonomous' unions in this context.

4. The coal and steel sector model provides that the supervisory board should consist half of workers' representatives and half of employers' representatives. In addition, there is a 'neutral man', who must be appointed by agreement between the two sides. The board of management must include a member who has responsibility for staff and social matters and is otherwise a full member of the board (worker director); this member may not be appointed against the wishes of a majority of the employee side.

This arrangement is currently applicable to about 30 companies in the mining and steel industries. The DGB would like to see it extended to all companies which meet two of the following three criteria: 1,000 employees, a balance sheet total of DM 75 million, a turnover of DM 150 million.

5. In 1982 it came to the notice of the public that board members of the trade-union-owned building enterprise Neue Heimat had transacted a considerable amount of private business 'on the side' through the company. Also, leading trade union officials had participated in Neue Heimat depreciation projects in order to minimise their own tax liability.

6. The mining and iron and steel industries in 1982 accounted for 2.6 per cent and 3.5 per cent respectively, of the total turnover of the goods-producing industry. (For comparison purposes: chemical industry 11.1 per cent and automotive industry 11.4 per cent.)

7. Seven of the 17 DGB unions organise public service workers. They include the Gewerkschaft Offentliche Dienste, Transport und Verkehr (OTV: Public Service and Transport Workers' Union) with a total membership of 1.18 million, Deutsche Postgewerkschaft (DPG: German Postal Workers' Union) with 456,930 members, Gewerkschaft der Eisenbahner Deutschlands (GdED: German Union of Railwaymen) with 392,484 members and Gewerkschaft Erziehung und Wissenschaft (GEW: Union of Educational and Scientific Employees) with 372,994 members. A total of 827, 916 officials are organised by DGB unions, i.e. 10.6 per cent of all members.

4 GREAT BRITAIN

B. C. Roberts

Population	56,000,000
Per capita GNP, 1982	US$ 8,500
Exports as per cent of GNP, 1982	21
Number of large companies (among the 500 largest outside the USA)	87 with 6,728,000 employees (Shell and Unilever are reckoned to be 50 per cent British and 50 per cent Dutch)
Governments	1945–51 Labour 1951–64 Various Conservative 1964–70 Labour 1970–4 Conservative 1974–9 Labour 1979– Conservative
Public sector (share of GNP, 1982, including transfers)	47 per cent
Trade union membership	1985: 46–7 per cent (1979: 54 per cent)
Trade unions	Trades Union Congress (TUC)—which has 9,600,000 members (1984–5)—is Europe's largest employees' organisation and organises both workers and salaried employees in both the private and the public sector. The TUC has 96 member unions, the largest of which is the TGWU, Transport and General Workers' Union. Among the public sector trade unions is the General and Municipal Workers' Union (GMWU) with 900,000 members and the National Association of Local Government Employees (NALGO) with almost 800,000 members.
Employers' organisations	Confederation of British Industry (CBI). The number of employees in the 13,000 affiliated enterprises is around 7,000,000 of whom some 1,800,000 work for state-owned industries and the public sector. The largest of the CBI employers' associations is the Engineering Employers' Federation.

100

Introduction

Trade unions in Britain are the oldest in the world. They have deep roots in British history and they have played a significant role in the country's social and economic evolution over the past 200 years. Over this time their membership, power and influence, with many fluctuations, reached its pinnacle in the 1970s. At the end of the First World War they achieved a total membership of 8.2 million—some 48 per cent of potential union membership. Union membership then declined to 4.3 million in 1933—which at a density of 23 per cent was less than half the figure for 1920. From 1933 the unions grew without any major setbacks to reach, in 1973, with a membership of 11 million, in a much larger labour force, the density of 48 per cent which they had previously attained 53 years earlier. Over the next few years they made further gains to reach, in 1979, the highest membership in their history with almost 13 million and a density of 54 per cent. Since 1979 they have lost, in the first downturn since the 1930s, more than 2 million members and their density is now almost certainly below the old peak of 48 per cent they first achieved in 1920. However, there has been a relatively much smaller fall in the percentage of union members in employment. With these changes in trade union membership there have been parallel changes in the bargaining power of the unions at the workplace and the enterprise and in the influence they have been able to wield over the economic and political decisions of Labour and Conservative governments. The main purpose of this chapter is to analyse these changes and to suggest possible developments in the future.

1969–79: A Decade of Significant Growth

In the decade 1969–79, in which the unions achieved an increase in membership of more than 3 million, they were also largely responsible for toppling from office both a Conservative and a Labour government and for pushing the British economy into a record level of inflation and a dangerous decline in economic growth.

Bain and Elshaikh (1976), Richardson and Catlin (1979), Booth (1983) and others have shown that the growth and decline of union membership in Britain have been influenced by a variety of factors

which include: the structure of employment, levels of unemployment, rates of change in wages and prices, changes in
establishment size, social tradition, skill, age and sex, the attitude of
employers, the extent of compulsory unionism, the efficiency of
union organisation at the workplace, degree of public support and
legal regulations of the right to organise and be recognised, and the
changes in the perception of costs and benefits of union
membership made by potential union members.

The evidence suggests that the variations in union membership
over time have been the result of changes in some combination of
these factors, but change in any particular factor may not affect an
individual or occupational group in the same way and might produce a different response. Nor is it possible to say with complete
certainty what the effect of a specific change might have been over
time since it might have induced other changes which may have had
a contrary effect, but it is evident that periods of full employment
have been associated with an increase in union membership and
periods of unemployment with a decrease.

Since the Second World War there have been in Britain, as in
most other advanced industrial countries, substantial changes in the
structure of employment. Between 1969 and 1979 the number of
manual workers declined by more than a million, but in spite of this
fall the actual union membership of manual workers rose by half a
million to bring the density of manual worker union members to a
record level of 63 per cent. The number of white-collar workers who
were potential union members went up by 2 million during this
decade and white-collar union membership also reached a record
density of 44 per cent.

White-collar workers were most highly organised by the unions in
central and local government, health, educational and a variety of
other public services, and to a more limited extent in the financial
and other service occupations in the private sector. In 1979 there
were 41 white-collar unions and 20 partially white-collar organisations, with a total membership of 4.3 million —about 36 per cent
of total union membership (Price and Bain, 1983).

In the decade 1969–79 there was also a considerable increase in
the number of female union members. In this period, female union
membership increased by 1.5 million, to a total of 3.8 million; the
density rising from 27.5 to 39.5. A very large proportion of these
female workers were employed in the white-collar occupations.

In the period from 1948 to 1979 employment in the public sector grew from 4.5 to 6.5 million. The overall density of union organisation in the public sector rose from 66 per cent in 1969 to 82 per cent in 1979. The percentage of all white-collar workers unionised rising from a density of 15.4 to 43.7 (Price and Bain, 1983). Probably one of the most important reasons for this increase was the relative decline in the advantages that were associated with employment in the public sector; namely, employment security, relatively high wages, shorter hours, longer holidays and pension provision. As public employees perceived the improvements in employment standards in the large corporations in the private sector, such as banks, oil companies and other large corporations, they increasingly turned to union membership as a means of preserving their relative position.

The increased willingness of white-collar workers in the public sector to join unions in recent decades was encouraged by a number of other factors. Since the First World War it has been public policy in Britain for governments to encourage their employees to join unions and to accept collective bargaining as the established method of determining pay and other conditions of employment. Union membership has also been stimulated in the public sector by the fact that those in the highest levels of administrative authority are also unionised. Although there is a division of interest and responsibility between those who determine policy and those who carry it out, this is not as clearly drawn as in private enterprise. Moreover, since public service organisations are generally large-scale units of employment—and thus follow highly routinised bureaucratic procedures—employees feel a strong need to belong to organisations which are capable of protecting their interests where these are threatened by what may appear to be arbitrary decisions taken at a level remote from where the effect will be felt.

The Royal Commission on Trade Unions and Employers' Organisations

Although it has been public policy to provide a legal framework which would facilitate the growth of unions and the process of collective bargaining since 1871, there has also always been an element of concern at the possible economic and social consequences of the use of trade union power. As the unions grew stronger in the period after the Second World War this concern began increasingly to trouble governments. When the Labour Party was elected in 1964, determined to bring about a radical reform in the British economy through the adoption of a national plan for economic growth, it was well aware that its intentions might be entirely frustrated by the determination of the unions to push up wages above the real rates of economic growth, to resist the introduction of new technology and change in the methods of working and to refuse to co-operate in reducing the massive levels of over-manning which existed. It therefore decided to establish a royal commission to find a solution to the problem. In spite of the fact that the unions shared a common ideology and common allegiance with the Labour Party they were reluctant to co-operate and did so only when they secured acceptable terms of reference and the appointment of the General Secretary of the TUC as a member of the commission.

When the commission reported three years later it pointed to the need to bring about a more orderly system of industrial relations at the plant level, especially the elimination of unofficial strikes called by shop stewards. A majority of the commission rejected the suggestion that this might be achieved by imposing legal restrictions on the role of unions. It was argued that the commission's goal could be most effectively attained by strengthening the power of the union at the workplace; this could be achieved by imposing obligations on the employer to recognise the key role of the union; formalising the bargaining process; giving the shop stewards a more formal responsibility by an extension of their functions; recognising the need for their training and for the provision of facilities that would enable them to carry out their tasks more effectively.

The Labour government accepted the commission's analysis of the problem of reforming British industrial relations, but it showed no faith in its reliance on the unions voluntarily accepting an obligation to reform their role. It therefore proposed legal changes to strengthen the unions, balanced by penalties on strikers who failed to heed the government when it called upon them to return to work. This proposal created a major breach with the unions which threatened to disrupt their links with the Labour Party. The government gave in to the unions, withdrawing its proposal, but soon afterwards lost the general election at the end of its term of office.

The Heath Government's Attempt to Reform Industrial Relations

When the Conservatives took office they were prepared and committed to introduce a comprehensive reform of the industrial relations system. The 1971 Industrial Relations Act which was passed sought to promote more orderly collective bargaining and to improve employee rights by establishing a new legal framework to be administered through an Industrial Relations Court, an extension of the role of industrial tribunals and the continuance of the Commission for Industrial Relations, which had been established on the recommendation of the royal commission by the Labour Party, to promote voluntary change.

The trade unions would have nothing to do with the Act which, after a period of hesitation, they decided to oppose in every respect. Many personnel managers in the larger corporations had been greatly influenced by the analysis and conclusions of the royal commission—that more orderly industrial relations and responsible union leadership could be best achieved if the unions were strengthened at the workplace by voluntary action— sympathised with the union opposition to the 1971 Act and made no attempt to use the opportunities it provided to make collective agreements legally binding and to constrain the closed shop.

In a second bitter conflict with the miners' union, in which the union refused to respect the government's pay policy, picketing of the power stations forced the government to limit factories to the use of power supplies only on three days a week, and the miners, supported by other unions, again brought a government to its knees and to defeat at the next election.

Legal Support for the Unions

When the Labour Party returned to power in 1974 it honoured its promises to the unions, sweeping the 1971 Act away, removing all restrictions on the unions and extending individual employment rights and abolishing the Industrial Relations Court.

Although the unions were strongly opposed to the 1971 Industrial Relations Act because it imposed some limitations on their freedom to act without legal restraint, they enthusiastically welcomed the 1974 Trade Union and Labour Relations Act and the 1975 Employment Protection Act passed by the Labour government, which imposed legal obligations on employers. The 1975 Act gave the unions the right to use the aid of the newly established Advisory Conciliation and Arbitration Service to secure recognition through a statutory procedure; it made discrimination against union members and shop stewards unlawful and gave them legal rights to take part in union activities, to have time off for this purpose and to undergo training in those aspects of industrial relations relevant to these duties.

This restoration of traditional union freedoms from legal regulation was welcomed by many managers, especially those responsible for personnel and industrial relations, who had neither liking for, nor confidence in, a resort to the law to achieve good industrial relations. They were ready to believe the pleas of the unions that more orderly industrial relations and responsible trade union leadership could be achieved if the unions were strengthened at the workplace. Under a sympathetic government, the unions were on the ascendancy and managers felt they had little choice but to accept the legal obligations imposed on them.

Under the umbrella of the Trade Union and Labour Relations Act which restored all the immunities which the unions had enjoyed before the 1971 Industrial Relations Act, and the Employment Protection Act which extended legal support, the unions embarked on a vigorous campaign to increase union membership and to extend the role of shop stewards and consolidate collective bargaining at the plant level, which they achieved with the help of the employers. By the end of 1978 more than 5 million employees were covered by compulsory union membership voluntarily agreed by employers.

Employers were also ready to help the unions maintain their membership by deducting union dues from employees' pay cheques. This practice, which had begun to develop in the public sector many years earlier, has now become widespread in all sectors of employment. The check-off guarantees the unions a regular flow of contributions, overcomes weaknesses in union organisation and transfers the cost of collecting contributions to the employers.

During the 1970s the number of shop stewards increased considerably and in the companies employing more than 1,000 employees a full-time convenor or chief shop steward became normal. The wages of full-time shop stewards and the costs of their facilities—probably including an office, telephone and clerical assistance—were usually entirely paid for by the companies in which they work. It has been estimated that by 1978 the number of full-time shop stewards had reached 5,000 and was approaching twice the number of full-time union paid officials operating from union offices. (W. Brown, 1981) This remarkable growth in the number of full-time shop stewards again underlines the extent to which management was willing to support the strengthening of workplace union organisation.

Failure of the Royal Commission Thesis

Unfortunately, the results of strengthening the unions were not as predicted by the royal commission and its supporters on both sides of industry. In the 1970s, in spite of the fact that union membership grew rapidly, that the number of shop stewards greatly increased and that the bargaining power of the unions was greatly enhanced, there was no improvement in industrial relations. Conflict grew worse and inflation soared as unions raised their wage demands. Union resistance to the introduction of new technology and new methods of work protected the massive over-manning that had become almost endemic in every branch of British industry and the public services. High labour costs and low productivity undermined competitiveness and brought down profit levels in real terms almost to zero, destroying the ability of private and public enterprise to fund new investment without resort to subsidies and increases in indebtedness which fuelled the inflation.

The union leaders at the national level paid lip-service to the need to improve the efficiency of British industry, but they continued to urge policies that were massively inflationary and unlikely to bring about the improvement in industrial relations and more efficient performance which they claimed to have at heart.

In the absence of positive leadership from the top from employers and unions, industrial relations in the private sector became more and more centred on the enterprise where reforms were slowly and painfully beginning to occur, but they were constantly frustrated by the national climate of giving in to profligate and intemperate union demands. After the unions, aided and abetted by the Labour Party, had brought down Edward Heath's Conservative government in 1974 they continued to press for excessive wage increases; the TUC and the Labour government tried to contain these by a 'social contract' which lasted three years, but in the end they also destroyed the Labour government following the 'winter of discontent' against the efforts of the Chancellor, Mr Healey, to bring down and hold inflation at 5 per cent.

During the 1970s the Confederation of British Industry made a number of attempts to develop a national approach to the fundamental problems of inefficiency and inflation which were paralysing the British economy. In notable reports on *The Future of Pay Bargaining* (1977) and *Pay: The Choice Ahead* (1979), the CBI set out a programme of economic and social reforms and changes in the collective bargaining system aimed at bringing about a rationalisation of bargaining units between plants, enterprises and industries; to compress the annual pay round by synchronising it within a period of three months before the budget, and to revise pay structures so that differentials had a rational basis related to skill and responsibility.

These proposals to have a meaningful effect required the support of the Trades Union Congress, but this was spurned. It is doubtful if many of the national union leaders understood what was happening to the efficiency of the British economy. They were more concerned with redistributing income by social welfare schemes, subsidising the nationalised industries and maintaining jobs by opposing redundancies and any slimming down of the enormously padded pay rolls of public and private enterprise than with achieving the fundamental changes that were required to bring about the rejuvenation of the British economy.

Industrial Democracy Committee Proposals

Although strongly opposed to Britain's entry into the European Economic Community in 1973, the unions became aware of the possibility that a British government might at some stage be called upon to legislate to introduce the principles of industrial democracy embodied in the draft Fifth Directive. During Mr Callaghan's government it was decided with the support of the Trades Union Congress to establish a Committee of Inquiry on Industrial Democracy under the chairmanship of Lord Bullock. The TUC, which up to this time had opposed the concept of worker directors on the boards of directors of private enterprises, gave evidence in favour of this development subject to three principles. One was that there should be parity of representation between management and workers' representatives. The second was that there should be a single channel of representation, through the union, which would be responsible for nominating and electing workers' representatives. Third, the implementation of policy should be through the collective bargaining process.

When the Bullock Committee reported it was clear that it had been strongly influenced by the TUC and its supporters. The majority of the committee proposed that any union which represented more than 20 per cent of the labour force should have the right to request a secret ballot of all employees (in the great majority of large companies with union membership agreements these would be union members). If a one-third majority was in favour, then the unions with negotiating rights in the company would be entitled to establish a joint representation committee. This committee would then agree on a list of union representatives drawn from employees of the company. There would be a single unitary board on which employee and shareholder representatives (2X) would have parity, plus a third group (Y) of independent directors jointly agreed by the union and shareholders' representatives. The third group Y would always be an odd number and smaller than X. This formula was designed to give the unions effectively a veto and to preserve the principle of single-channel representation.

The minority report, signed by the three employer representatives on the committee, objected to the terms of reference of the committee which gave the inquiry no option to reject employee directors in principle. It was opposed to the parity principle and favoured one-third from employees, one-third from shareholders and one-third independents. It was also against the single-channel principle and supported the concept of an employee council not limited to trade union members. The minority report was also against employee directors on a single management board. Employee representation ought, it claimed, to be on a supervisory board on the German model.

The Labour government responded to these proposals with caution. In a White Paper the government opted in favour of a flexible approach and suggested that joint representation committees should be established from the recognised unions, but representatives of non-union employees might be admitted by

agreement. Employees would have a statutory right to be represented on the boards of companies—which at the option of the
company might be of the two-tier type. The White Paper left the
issue of limiting employee representatives to union members only
open to agreement on how employee representatives should be
selected.

Although the response of the Labour government had not been
entirely enthusiastic, this did not allay the virtually unanimous
opposition of the employers to its proposals. The Bullock Report
was perceived by employers as an attempt by the trade unions to
extend collective bargaining into the boardroom and to give the
unions the power to veto any decision which they might believe
was not in their interest. Employers were becoming increasingly
aware of the need to make radical changes to enable industry to
become more efficient and they were certain that if the Bullock
proposals were translated into law, it would probably be the
death-knell of many firms, since the unions would be in an even
more powerful position to block change.

A New Era: Recession and Legal Reform

The election of the Conservatives in May 1979 and the onset of the
deepest recession since the 1930s created an opportunity to bring
about radical changes in the legal framework of industrial relations, and had a dramatic effect on the power of the trade unions
to resist the restructuring of employment and to maintain inflationary levels of pay settlements.

Since 1979 there has been a dramatic fall in union membership.
By the end of 1982 trade union membership had declined by
almost 2 million, with some large unions losing as much as 25 per
cent of their membership. This trend has continued through 1983
and is likely to continue through 1984 and beyond.

The decline has been brought about by the rise in unemployment, the fall in inflation, new legislation, a change in the
attitude of employers, and a hostile public opinion towards unions.

The increase in unemployment to well over 3 million has been
most severe in the manufacturing, processing and construction
industries where the unions have been most highly organised.
With the fall in the level of price inflation and the equally
significant reduction in the level of pay demands and willingness to

strike, there has been a change in the climate of wage bargaining. This has almost certainly weakened the impulse of many workers to join a union which seems to be considerably influenced by the frenetic scramble to keep up with other workers when the rate of wage and price inflation is soaring upwards.

Further growth in the closed shop which had been a major contribution to the rapid increase in union membership in the 1970s was brought to halt with the passing of the Employment Act of 1980. This Act makes it extremely difficult for unions to achieve new closed shops, since they need to obtain an 80 per cent majority of the employees concerned to persuade employers to sign a compulsory union membership agreement. The 1982 Employment Act, which came into effect in 1984, will compel employers and unions who were covered by closed-shop agreements made before 1980 to hold ballots to test whether employees want the compulsory union membership agreement to continue. As with new closed shops, an 80 per cent majority of membership covered or 85 per cent of those voting is required to give them legal protection. Unemployment and the effect of the 1980 Act had led to a reduction of almost 1 million employees covered by closed-shop agreements by the end of 1983. It is almost certain, so long as the provisions of the 1980 and 1982 Acts remain in force, that the closed shop will continue to decline—thus making it more difficult in the future for the unions to recoup their lost membership.

Lawful picketing, since the new legislation, is limited to picketing only the employer of the pickets at their own place of work. Secondary picketing was thus made unlawful. Similarly, a lawful strike by workers is limited to a strike against their own employer, and limited to disputes wholly or mainly concerned —not simply connected with—the following: (1) terms and conditions of employment; (2) engagement, suspension and termination of employment; (3) allocation of work; (4) matters of discipline; (5) membership or non-membership of a union; (6) facilities for union officials; and (7) recognition of union rights to represent workers and procedures for negotiation and consultation. The effect of this legislation has been to make sympathy strikes in many cases likely to be unlawful, and since immunities have been withdrawn from unions authorising industrial action they are liable to injunctions and damages. Inter-union strikes are no longer immune from action in tort; nor are strikes called in relation to matters occurring outside of the UK, unless those taking action in Britain can establish that they will be affected in respect of one or more of the seven matters with which a strike must be 'wholly or mainly concerned' listed above.

The effect of these changes in the law has already been felt in relation to the use of unlawful picketing and industrial action. An attempt by the National Graphical Association to force an employer to grant the union a closed shop and to reinstate six members lawfully dismissed following a strike, resulted in the union being fined a total of £675,000 for contempt of court when it refused to obey an injunction granted to the employer to restrain the union from unlawful picketing. When the union appealed to the TUC for support of its unlawful action, the General Council decided, after a protracted and bitter debate that it would only support union actions that were within the law.

It is too early to be certain that the new legislation will always be effective, but the decision of the TUC not to ask affiliated unions to violate the law was in marked contrast with its attitude in 1971 when it led the trade union movement in a vigorous campaign against the Industrial Relations Act.

The new legislation in the 1980s has not been received with the same degree of hostility as greeted the 1971 Industrial Relations Act. Although the Labour Party has given a pledge to the TUC that it will repeal the 1980 and 1982 Acts and the 1984 Act, there is no evidence that public opinion would be in support of that step. Opinion polls have shown that rank-and-file union members were deeply concerned at the trend of union policies during the 1970s, which they blamed for the damaging level of strike activity and the upward rush of inflation.

Polls have shown that there is widespread support, even among trade union members for the 1984 Trade Union Act, which requires: (1) union executives to be elected by a secret ballot of all members; (2) secret ballots before industrial action; and (3) ballots every ten years on whether the members wish the union to have a political fund. The unions are deeply split on whether they should accept subsidies which are available from the government to cover the cost of administering postal ballots.

The principal objective of the Conservative government's legislation has been to attack the corporatist role of the unions, which has evolved over the past 100 years, as an important element in a broader strategy to make the British economy more dynamic, and private enterprise, nationalised industries and the public services more efficient. In addition to seeking to curb the bargaining power of the unions by giving employees and employers encouragement to get rid of the closed shop, the government has sought to define the limits of lawful strike action by abolishing secondary picketing and removing the total immunities enjoyed by the unions; it has also endeavoured to reduce the influence of militant, ideologically motivated activists by making the unions more responsive, through the use of the secret ballot, to the wishes of the great majority of their members. In altering the law governing the right of the unions to establish and maintain a political fund and the way in which contributions to the fund are collected from members, and in denying the Trades Union Congress frequent opportunity to engage in a lengthy dialogue through private access to the prime minister and in making it quite clear that while ministers are prepared to have consultations with trade unions this implies no obligation to do more than listen to their views, the government has implicitly questioned the value and economic role of the trade unions and their influence on the government as this has developed in Britain.

Trade Unions and the Labour Party

Trade unions in Britain came into existence as a spontaneous response by working men to the vicissitudes of a market economy. They were born out of the Industrial Revolution and the principles of liberal capitalism that made the modern industrial society possible. British unions were not the creatures of a political party, but at various times and with varying degrees of attachment they formed alliances in the nineteenth century with Tories and Liberals. After the end of the century, though still deeply influenced by liberal idealism and the ideology of pluralism, they turned towards a more corporatist pattern of society in which the state had a larger role. In 1900 they formed an alliance with the co-operative societies and socialist organisations to form a Labour Party. At the end of the First World War the Labour Party, with the support of a majority of unions, adopted as its goal the achievement of a socialist system of society in which the means of production would be owned and administered by state bureaucracies; individual interests and aspirations would be subordinated to collective requirements determined by the doctrine of equality.

For the whole of this century the unions in Britain have been dominated by a dualism in their philosophy and a dualism in their organisational structures and policies, brought about by their adherence to the principles of free trade unionism, the right to organise freely, the right to bargain freely, and the right to strike freely, while at the same time they supported policies of state control of the economy, state-provided welfare and winning of power for the Labour Party and its commitment to socialism.

The Trades Union Congress had been in existence 32 years before it took steps to create a Labour Party, and it was careful to ensure that it would retain its organisational independence. Each has its own functions and each follows its own policies. Trade unions may affiliate to either or, as the majority of the larger unions do, affiliate to both. The TUC has no individual members, unlike the Labour Party which also permits the affiliation of socialist societies and the Co-operative Party. The aim of the Labour Party is to achieve a Labour government through the election of Labour Members of Parliament; the aim of the TUC is to co-ordinate the activities of all its affiliated unions and to urge on the government, whichever party is in power, the wishes of the unions as established by the annual Trades Union Congress.

Since they share a common heritage and broadly similar philosophies, there is a relatively close relationship between the TUC and the Labour Party. However, when the latter is in office as a Labour government this may sometimes lead to bitter re-crimination and disillusion, as it did in 1931, 1969 and 1979.

The status achieved by the TUC as the representative of the unions was once described by Winston Churchill as an 'estate of the realm'. The meaning of Churchill's phrase was that the TUC had been recognised by all governments as the legitimate voice of all workers in relation to their vocational and related economic and social interests, and it enjoyed the right to be consulted on all issues of governmental decision-making within these legitimate spheres of interest.

It is clear that the readiness of Mr Churchill, when he was President of the Board of Trade and responsible for introducing Trade Boards and Employment Exchanges before the First World War, to work closely with the TUC has not been seen as either necessary or desirable by Mrs Thatcher's government. Since it was obvious to the latter that the TUC was in total opposition to its economic and social policies and its determination to bring about a reform of the law relating to the trade unions and industrial relations, agreement was impossible and compromise was not acceptable to either side. In this situation the government wanted to make its position quite plain and for it to be understood that it would not be by the weak stomach of some of its supporters, nor by threats that this would lead to the breakdown of consensus politics with the TUC. The view of Mrs Thatcher and her senior ministers that firmness of purpose would isolate the TUC and weaken its ability to lead an effective opposition to the government's legal reforms, has clearly been amply confirmed.

The issues that were calculated to elicit the most intransigent opposition from the unions, since they touched on the most sensitive areas of trade union autonomy—their constitutional practices and their affiliation to the Labour Party—were postponed by the government until it had secured a fresh mandate bolstered by a greatly increased majority in 1983.

On all these issues—the election by secret ballot of union executives, pre-strike ballots and the political levy—the case for reform was extremely strong and had wide public support, including trade union members. It was the political levy that promised to raise the most controversial and politically dangerous problems.

Under the 1913 Trade Union Act unions are entitled to establish a political fund which may be used to support the campaign of candidates in national and local government elections and other political activities if they obtain, in a ballot vote, a simple majority of those voting. The fund is raised by a levy on all members except those who have signed a contracting-out form. In practice, the unions make this right difficult to exercise by not drawing the attention of new members to it and by lumping the contribution to the political fund in with the general contribution paid by the member. Thus, a very large proportion of members pay the political levy in ignorance; to make matters worse, however, although less than 40 per cent of union members voted Labour at the last election, the unions affiliate only to the Labour Party and give support only to Labour candidates.

The money contributed to the Labour Party and Labour candidates by the unions is of crucial importance, since it amounts to 80 per cent of the total income of the party and it gives the unions a dominating voice in the making of party policy. Any change such as the substitution of 'contracting-in' for the 'contracting-out' procedure would, it is believed, reduce the number of union members paying the political levy by up to 50 per cent. This would not only seriously damage the Labour Party, it would also weaken the links between the party and the unions, with significant implications for all the major political parties and for the unions.

Although the Conservatives would like to see the unions less closely linked to the Labour Party, they have no wish to compel the unions to contribute to the political parties according to the voting pattern of their members, since this would benefit the Liberals and Social Democrats, who they believe constitute a major threat to the Conservatives in the long run. They are also worried that any sharp fall in its funds from the unions might cripple the Labour Party and lead to demands for the end of contributions from employers to the Conservative Party, and for the public funding of political parties, which would greatly benefit the Liberal–Social Democratic Alliance. The government has therefore accepted a pledge from the TUC that it will ensure that unions make their members aware of their right to contract-out. In exchange, the new law has been limited to calling for a ballot vote endorsing the existence of a political fund every ten years. What the Conservatives are apparently aiming to do is weaken the links between the unions and the Labour Party without benefiting the centre parties to the extent of encouraging the possibility of a coalition between the Liberal–SDP Alliance and the Labour Party. Such an eventuality could lead to the defeat of the Conservatives at the next election and possibly keep them out of office for decades.

The Conservative government's concern about the political role of the trade unions is not confined to their organic links with the Labour Party. It is also deeply concerned, as were Labour governments, at the extent to which radical Marxist groups are able to infiltrate the unions and, by dint of unremitting activity, to gain positions of power out of all proportion to the number of union members who support their ideological beliefs and political objectives. In February 1983 the government issued a certificate under the provisions of the Labour government's 1975 Employment Protection Act, with the intention of withdrawing the right of union membership to civil servants employed at the highly secret defence communications centre at Cheltenham. This decision was based upon the number of times since 1979 that the unions had deliberately sought to bring pressure on the government by asking their members at the Centre to take part in industrial action. This disruption was not a specifically communist-inspired plot to damage a vital element of the Western nations' military defence system, but there had long been attempts by communist and other left-wing groups to gain control of the civil service unions involved. Since the militancy of civil service unions in the 1970s cannot be dissociated from the growing influence of believers in left-wing ideologies who had been elected to national executives and other posts of leadership, this problem must have exercised some influence on the minds of ministers. Since civil servants have always had the legal right to belong to a union and to strike (though up to the First World War this was not encouraged, and up to that time taking part in industrial action could have led to dismissal), the unions were afraid that this ban would further weaken their influence and bitterly attacked the decision as a violation of the fundamental right of individuals to belong to a union.

These issues relating to the political role of the unions have inevitably sharpened the conflict between the unions and the government. At the same time they have added to the division between those members of the General Council of the TUC who believe that the unions must come to terms with the fact that the majority of union members not only no longer vote for the Labour Party, but also have a low level of confidence in the leaders of the unions, and those members who believe that all that the unions and the Labour Party face is a temporary setback. The left-wing leaders cling to Marxist ideas of socialism and believe that private enterprise should be throttled by a Labour government's imposition of political controls, put under continuous pressure from closed-shop unionism with untrammelled power to obstruct change, and forced by the use of militant tactics to make concessions which inhibit efficiency and promote inflation. Their opponents believe that co-operation between employers and unions to achieve change is essential if the unions are not to continue in decline. This struggle was highlighted by a discussion document on strategy for the future which was sent to all unions in January 1984 by the General Council of the TUC. The document projected a new realism by candidly recognising that the unions must accept their responsibility for their part in the changes that had been forced upon them during the past four years and that they must play a more positive role in the future. The paper called upon the unions to recognise that they had been out of touch with their members. They must come to terms with workplace-centred trade unionism, improve communications and raise the professional standards of their officials.

The objectives of the strategy were primarily 'to make sure that the unions cannot be ignored in terms of their organisational strength and effectiveness'; (1) 'this means a massive effort to prevent a further decline in union membership', (2) 'demonstrating their readiness and competence to tackle the problems generated by the changing environment', and (3) 'maintaining and improving their representative capacity to speak on behalf of working people'.

The need to retain the right to strike is stressed, but the paper urges that this is, and should be, rarely used. It recognises that unions have to accept that collective bargaining in the future must be a means of accommodating to industrial change, and its objectives will have to take account of the needs of employers as well as of the unions.

The importance of this discussion paper was that it sought to analyse the place of the unions in British society in the light of their historical evolution and the challenge which the dramatic decline in their membership and economic and political power has presented. It saw the role of the unions in the past and in the future as complementing parliamentary democracy. The unions would continue to support the Labour Party, but it was argued that much of the activity of the TUC in bringing pressure to bear on governments was not party political.

This analysis of the role of the TUC and its affiliated unions was implicitly rooted in the belief that the prime role of the unions should be to protect the vocational interests of the members; in order to do this, they must reflect the desires of a membership which is more interested in accepting the benefits of a capitalist society than in supporting the establishment of socialism.

Unfortunately, in the immediate aftermath of the publication of the TUC report on strategy two events occurred which blanketed discussion of its implications. These were the decision by the government to ban union membership at the General Communications Headquarters (GCHQ) at Cheltenham, and the second was a national miners' strike.

Both of these issues exposed the underlying weakness of the TUC when confronted by situations brought about by Marxist-inspired, hardline radicals whose aim was to destroy the credibility of moderate union leaders and to inflict political damage on the government.

The miners' strike which began in March 1984 and continued for a year presented both the TUC and the Labour Party with a challenge they were unable to meet. In spite of the fact that the strike was brought about by a highly dubious manipulation of the constitution of the National Union of Mineworkers (to avoid a required national ballot), which was found by the courts to be unlawful, and that one-third of the union's membership refused to go on strike and continued to work, the TUC and the Labour Party both endorsed the strike. They were, however, unable to convince the great majority of trade union members that they should give practical support to the miners by observing their picket lines or ceasing work in sympathy.

The effect of this strike is likely to be far-reaching, since it has significantly weakened what has traditionally been one of the most militant and powerful unions in Britain. It will almost certainly be followed by the decentralisation of the classic nationalised industry, a concept at the very heart of the pragmatic socialism which brought the unions and the Labour Party into the organic alliance cemented in the 1918 constitution of the party. The outcome of the strike has not only placed the privatisation of the coal mines on the agenda, it has also dramatically highlighted all the major issues of ecomonic, social and political change which the TUC paper on strategy tentatively and obliquely raised.

Looking to the Future

In seeking to assess how far the role of the unions in Britain is likely to change in the future, it is necessary to examine three possible scenarios. One is that the present government will remain in office for its full term, and will be elected with a working majority at the end of it. The second is that it will not be re-elected and that the Labour Party will return to power in 1987 or 1988 and will be prepared to give back to the unions the full immunities and legal protections which they enjoyed in 1979. The third possibility is that the government is not re-elected, but that it is replaced by the Liberal–SDP Alliance perhaps in coalition with either the Labour or Conservative Party.

It is safe to assume that during its present period of office the Conservative government will continue to give a high priority to keeping inflation down to levels as close as possible to those of the USA, Germany and Japan by maintaining a strict control over the money supply and over public expenditure, by reducing the size of the public sector, and by encouraging the expansion of private enterprise. The government's policies are not likely to bring a sharp fall in the level of unemployment and many economists believe that, even with a vigorous expansion of the money supply brought about by lower interest rates and a large increase in public expenditure, it is probable that unemployment will continue to remain at a high level. The leader of the Labour Party, Neil Kinnock, has stated that the policies which the party is advocating as necessary to create several million new jobs in five years would probably only succeed in reducing unemployment by a much smaller amount, still leaving possibly 2 million unemployed in the 1990s. Thus, a change of government would probably make little fundamental difference to the level of unemployment and the effect which unemployment has on employee attitudes and union behaviour. Nevertheless, a Labour government would make a difference in other respects since its efforts to reduce unemployment would almost certainly once again stimulate inflation and it would be compelled to try to persuade or force the unions into another compact to hold down pay increases. The Labour Party believes that it could persuade the unions to accept restraint by voluntary means, but previous experience suggests that this would be difficult.

Since the prospect of growth in employment in Britain's traditionally highly unionised manufacturing and process industries is likely to be relatively low, even if Gross National Product continues to grow at the steady, currently achieved 3 per cent a year, the possibility of a recovery in trade union membership will depend upon the unions' ability to organise the growing number of persons employed in the service sector and the high-technology enterprises. There are already more than 6 million non-union employees in the miscellaneous services. Many of these employees are in small firms; a substantial number are part-time employees; many are married women who increasingly return to work when their children reach school-age. All of these categories are notoriously difficult to organise and the unions have not found a way of overcoming their reluctance to become members. Employers in small companies are rarely prepared to help unions to recruit and to maintain their membership in the way that large-scale employers have done over the past 30 years.

During the past decade there has been a considerable growth in high-technology enterprises, but they remain virtually un-organised. Some small towns, which have encouraged this type of enterprise and where they are doing remarkably well, are so far as union organisation is concerned almost like a desert. Most of the workers in high technology have little interest in unions. They have great confidence in their own skills and ability to market their talents if they become dissatisfied with the firm for which they are working or wish to gain rapid promotion. They tend to view unions as outdated, as hostile to modernisation and responsible for Britain's relative economic decline. They prefer the open style of management and good communications which bind management and employees close together in finding solutions to design and production problems. They favour sharing risks and rewards rather than relying on joining the gigantic unions which canvas their membership and which would subject them to bureaucratic rules and require them to engage in industrial warfare, which they believe would destroy, rather than foster, their careers and individual well-being.

If the public sector is also reduced significantly in size through privatisation, though the industries denationalised may remain relatively highly unionised, the breaking-up of the scale of organisation into smaller units with a less bureaucratic style of management will probably lead to a lower level of union membership. If also the legislation on the closed shop has the effect anticipated by the Conservatives, this will reduce the ability of the unions to maintain their membership. Most important of all would be a growing public doubt concerning the virtues of strong unions and an unwillingness on the part of employees to maintain their membership in the absence of coercion. The extent to which disenchantment with the unions becomes deeply implanted in the consciousness of employees will depend not only on the climate established by the government, but also on the way in which employers take advantage of the opportunity they have to en-courage a more positive and co-operative pattern of industrial relations.

There is a conflict of views on the extent to which relations between managers and unions have been soured by the determination of managers during the past four years to get rid of union restrictions and to withdraw from procedures which had seriously inhibited their ability to manage efficiently.

In major industries such as steel, and in many large manufacturing firms, managements, faced by a collapse of demand and large financial losses, have taken drastic steps to remedy this situation. Unions have been forced to accept massive cuts in employment, new methods of working, the end of traditional job demarcation, lower levels of manning, as well as a reduction in the number of shop stewards and the facilities they have enjoyed in the past.

In a substantial number of instances where union leaders at workplace and national levels have called upon their members to come out on strike against the proposals of management for radical change, they have been repudiated. Workers in the private sector have shown a realistic understanding of the need for increased efficiency and the acceptance of changes that before 1980 they would have resisted by every means possible.

There are some personnel managers, industrial correspondents in the media and a great many academics who have criticised management for the firm stand they have taken to improve efficiency and to bring to an end practices which they believed could not be justified by the realities of the corporate situation. This firmness has been described as 'macho management' and warnings have been given that as soon as demand for labour improves, and unemployment begins to fall, the unions will take their revenge. This is certainly a possibility. It is the view of a recent committee of experts of the OECD that nothing has fundamentally changed in industrial relations in the Western countries and that as soon as economic circumstances change for the better, workers will flock into the unions, return to militancy and so make inflation again soar upwards. Since there is a long history of industrial relations being highly correlated with the trade cycle, this expectation cannot be easily dismissed—but it may not be correct.

If there is a return to the levels of inflation which prevailed in the 1960s and 1970s it is extremely likely in Britain, as elsewhere, that industrial relations will tend to revert to a similar pattern to that which existed at that time. If, however, there is no return to very high levels of inflation it is possible that changes in the style of management, union behaviour and attitudes of workers could bring about the emergence of a more co-operative pattern of industrial relations, even in the context of continuing high unemployment.

In the long run, unless they are creatures of a totalitarian state, unions will reflect the interests and attitudes of their members. In the past, union members have been willing to follow shop stewards and national union leaders who called upon them to resist change. They obeyed diktats to engage in conflict for the preservation of archaic work patterns and the securing of levels of pay that could only be financed by massive inflation, because they were convinced that by these means they could overcome the effects of price inflation and keep up with other wage- and salary-earners without endangering their jobs. The flimsiness of the foundation of those beliefs has been exposed and the unions are no longer in a position where they can easily convince their members that excessive pay demands, the obstruction of new technology and changed patterns of work, will bring higher real wages and maintain their employment.

There is a widespread fear among union leaders and the rank and file that new technology will lead to a collapse of employment. In some industries there has been a bitter and prolonged opposition to the introduction of new technology from the unions; in others they have accepted it without overt resistance. The TUC for the past several years has encouraged unions at the establishment to negotiate new-technology agreements which seek to control the introduction of new technology by requiring advance information, consultation and agreement, on its rate of introduction, changes in work organisation, retraining, payment for new responsibilities, and compensation for the resulting displacement and redundancies.

It is difficult to say how many new-technology agreements exist, but the impression is that the number is very small. However, in well-organised enterprises and in the public sector there have been many negotiations with unions on issues raised by the introduction of new technology. In some cases, as for example in the production of newspapers, unions have stubbornly resisted the wish of employers to make use of new technology. They have, however, fought a losing battle, gradually giving way before what has always been in the long run an irresistible advance that may be slowed down, but cannot be stopped.

At the same time as resisting change the unions have demanded job-creating investment and have welcomed, on 'green field' sites, new enterprises using the most advanced technology—even when this has meant accepting manning levels and working methods refused in plants wishing to change from old to new technology.

One of the most interesting developments has been the insistence by Japanese firms, such as Toshiba, that they should recognise only one union which should be responsible for all employees, irrespective of their occupation. The readiness of the Electrical, Electronic, Telecommunication and Plumbing Union to accept such an agreement, together with no-strike provisions, has been severely criticised by the leaders of other unions who also claim the right to recruit and to negotiate for their members. The leaders of the EETPU believe that this type of single-union agreement with a commitment to industrial peace—hitherto largely unknown in Britain—will be the model for organising in the new high-technology enterprises of the future. This model may also become acceptable to the large general unions which have indicated that they would be prepared to negotiate a single-union agreement at the NISSAN motor plant shortly to be established.

Unions and the Next Labour Government

Although impossible to achieve so long as a Conservative government is in power, the role which the unions would like to play in the future is set out most clearly in the report of a TUC–Labour Party Conference, *Economic Planning and Industrial Democracy*.

The aims to which the TUC and the Labour Party are committed are to establish a national planning system linked to a system of industrial democracy. The report calls for the establishment of a new Department of Economic and Industrial Planning which will shift the centre of economic decision-making within the government away from the Treasury, with its concern for financial stability, to the longer-term strategic problems of industrial reconstruction and reducing unemployment by expanding sections of the economy, such as public services, with direct potential for job creation.

Within each department of government there would be planning units staffed with people who understand the Labour government's priorities. These units would be supported by a structure of regional and local bodies and sectional committees on which the unions would be represented. In addition to the machinery of planning, a National Investment Bank would be established which would channel finance towards investment priorities, and a Price Commission which would have a counter-inflationary role, as well as the potential to investigate the efficiency of private industry.

Among the key issues which would feature in an agreed development plan would be the control of industrial purchasing of both the private and public sectors; the control of imports through the negotiation of agreements on both the level and composition of corporate import spending; and the development of a corporate investment plan. 'To ensure that the growth in demand is translated into domestic production rather than price increases,' the Planning Department 'will want to exercise considerable influence over corporate pricing strategy, having regard to the national strategy on inflation.'

The plan would be enforced by the Planning Department which would have 'power to issue directives on a range of industrial matters; powers to invest in individual companies, or to purchase them outright by statutory instrument approved by Parliament; power to ensure that capital assistance to large companies becomes available only through the planning system; powers to exercise discretionary control over corporate purchasing policy; powers to grant exceptions from general policy measures such as price control; powers to provide trade protection through an import control package.'

To make this planning process democratic a strong consultative and participative element would be built into the system at all levels. A major objective of the report is to greatly extend the role of the trade unions as a strategic factor in the development of a planned economy: 'Trade union involvement must be brought to bear at all levels at which planning decisions are made and at all the crucial stages. This will ensure that democratic pressure on decision-making can be systematically applied.' At national level the unions would participate through either a strengthened National Economic Development Council, on which the trade unions have been represented since it was established more than a decade ago by the Conservatives, or on a National Planning Council, which would have more resources at its disposal.

Thus a feature of the report's proposals is to allow trade unionists at all levels to extend their influence through new rights and responsibilities exercised through the unions. 'Trade union machinery must be the basis for building industrial democracy,' the report unambiguously states. 'The principle is important, however, since arrangements which established new structures or channels in competition with existing trade union machinery would be harmful in a number of respects.' The aim, therefore, it is argued, must be to strengthen collective bargaining, since collective bargaining is a central means of extending joint control over decisions in the enterprise at the workplace. It wil be necessary, however, to extend the influence of the unions to corporate decision-making through access to information and effective consultation going far beyond what has hitherto existed.

Unions, it is claimed, should also have the right through the establishment of Joint Union Committees—necessary because of the pattern of multiple unions—to participate through representatives at all levels of decision-making in the enterprise up to, and including, the board level. Management would be under an obligation to respond to the initiative of a Joint Union Committee by entering into an agreement which would give the unions the right to parity representation on the policy boards of enterprises if they wished to take this step. Some unions, notably the Electrical, Electronic, Telecommunication and Plumbing Union, have expressed doubts as to the wisdom of parity representation, but the report would leave them free, if they so chose, to exercise their influence entirely through the collective bargaining process.

The attempts by Labour governments during 1964–70 and 1974–9 to bring about a rapid increase in economic growth by planning and an expansion of demand were frustrated by union and management resistence to the changes required. It would be surprising if similar resistance did not occur again if a future Labour government sought to put into effect the policies outlined in *Economic Planning and Industrial Democracy*. Even with willing management there would be a slowing-down of decision-making; without full co-operation from management and unions, and this is likely to be limited, the result is certain to be a deterioration in union–management relations and decline in efficiency.

During the past few years the efforts of the TUC to encourage the unions and their membership to take a much greater interest in industrial democracy have not met with a great deal of enthusiasm in the current climate. The TUC has, however, had some limited success in its campaign to build support in the unions for a new pension fund investment strategy based on a National Investment Bank and local Enterprise Boards and a new Pension Scheme Act. However, it is far from convincing the government or employers that its aims are desirable. Many Labour-controlled local authorities have been persuaded to invest in local enterprises and to refrain from investing in companies with established interests in South Africa.

Perhaps most significant has been the growth in pressure exerted through collective bargaining at the enterprise level on the policies of company pension fund trustees. This pressure has not been focused on the broader social and economic goals set by the TUC, but on practical questions of administration and benefit.

The interest of the unions at the establishment level in pension fund administration owes something to the courses on this subject run by the TUC for shop stewards and union officials. The TUC also publishes a series of handbooks and bulletins on pension administration.

It is unlikely that the present government would legislate to give unions the sole right to appoint trustees or to make pension trusts observe the code of practice it has advocated relating to the investment of pension funds and the role of trustees. It is almost certain, however, should a Labour government be elected that it would introudce a pension scheme which would follow the proposals of the TUC.

If the Conservatives are defeated at the next election and the Labour Party which comes into power is dominated by a determination to put back the clock to 1979 and to take a giant stride forward to a socialist system, the outcome would be uncertain. It is likely that relations between the unions and a victorious Labour government would soon sour if, in order to carry out its programme of economic expansion, it sought to compel the unions to accept a severe limitation on pay increases. In the past such voluntary incomes policies have had only temporary success and ended in futility. In the light of this experience a radical left-wing Labour Party leadership might feel compelled to impose more vigorous curbs on the freedom of the unions to bargain collectively. If this were to happen, the unions would once again be in bitter conflict with the government and the result would inevitably produce a political crisis which would probably, as in 1969, lead to the fall of another Labour government.

If the Labour Party significantly moves to the right or is only able to form a government as a partner in coalition with the Liberal–SDP Alliance, there is less likely to be a radical reversal of the changes in the law introduced by the Conservatives. A coalition government would seek the co-operation of the trade unions especially in the adoption and administration of an incomes policy. It may also be tempted to experiment with systems of employee representation on corporate boards of directors and to encourage employee financial participation, through co-partnership schemes, or even worker capital funds. The general trend would be towards more corporatist arrangements than the Conservatives are likely to follow, but would give little support to Marxist concepts of radical socialism.

It is a reasonable assumption that in the private sector industrial relations will continue to improve at the plant and company level unless disturbed by the advent of a radical Labour government and high levels of inflation. However, the situation may be rather different in the public sector, which remains highly centralised and where the unions are likely to remain extremely strong. By stoppages of work and other forms of disruptive action, they will be prepared to bring pressure to bear upon any government seeking to hold down public expenditure through the imposition of cash limits which restrict increases in pay and place curbs on manpower.

The Response of Employers to Trade Union Pressures for Economic Planning and Industrial Democracy

Employers' organisations, led by the Confederation of British Industry (CBI) and the Institute of Directors, have vigorously opposed Labour Party and TUC proposals set out in the documents on economic planning and industrial democracy. Though there are differences in the policy positions of these two bodies, they both strongly support the present government. The Institute of Directors has called for effective curbs on union activities and was in the forefront of those who wanted to remove union immunities from legal action to make the closed shop unlawful, to curb secondary picketing and secondary action, and to penalise strikers in industries and services essential to the national interest. The CBI has closer relations with the TUC and, though generally in favour of the government's legal reforms in trade union law, kept a lower profile on this issue.

In terms of response to the TUC's proposals for economic planning and industrial democracy both organisations are very much against. Both have called for policies that would encourage free enterprise and are generally in support of the policies pursued by the present government. The Institute has tended to favour a greater reliance on monetarism, substantial tax cuts and the curtailing of public expenditure similar to the right wing of the Conservative Party. The CBI, on the other hand, has been closer to the so-called 'wets' in the Conservative Party. It has called for reductions of taxes on industry, but has been less vociferous about reductions in income tax. Unlike the Institute of Directors, it has called for a significant increase in public expenditure on the infrastructure—roads, rail, telecommunications and such essential services as water and drainage.

The differences in policy-thrust of the two bodies reflects the differences in the personalities and type of leadership of the organisations as well as their constituencies.

The Institute has a large number of small and medium-type firms, often predominantly family-owned. The CBI, on the other hand, is more broadly based. It is a confederation of over 200 employers' organisations, though it also has 4,500 individual companies as members. It has admitted, since 1969, nationalised industries and public service corporations and the majority of these are now members. There are a number of large firms which, as an act of deliberate policy, remain independent of the CBI, but it is generally in membership of firms in the private service sector and retail distribution that it is weakest. The CBI can fairly claim to be Britain's most representative employers' organisation as it speaks for private and public enterprises employing more than half of the total labour force.

In its structure the Institute of Directors is organised on the basis of district branches. Its headquarters are serviced by a number of policy and advisory committees with a staff very small in comparison with the CBI. Nevertheless, it has a reputation for effective lobbying and public relations.

The CBI is organised differently, since it combines employers and trade organisations and individual member firms organised in 13 regions, each governed by a regional council and serviced by full-time staffs. Its supreme governing body is the CBI Council of

400 members which meets monthly. The council's work is carried out by 29 standing committees of which the most important is the President's Committee. This committee has 26 members which include the chairmen of the most important standing committees. The members of the main policy committees are predominantly chairmen or managing directors of the major private and public enterprises which are affiliated. These would include many who are well known as leading business executives and whose names are frequently in the news as spokesmen for their firms and industries.

The CBI is regarded by the govenment as the most representative organisation of British industry and it provides nominations for the 80 or more national bodies which have been established by the government as advisory or executive bodies (the National Economic Development Council, Manpower Services Commission, Advisory, Conciliation and Arbitration Service, Health and Safety Executive, etc.).

Representation on the trade union side of these bodies was called into question in the TUC following the decision of the government to withdraw the rights of union membership from employees at the General Communications Headquarters at Cheltenham on grounds of national state security. The unions were sharply divided on the wisdom of a policy of withdrawing their representatives from bodies which they had helped to create and which they believed were helpful to their interests. By a majority of 25 to 16 the General Council decided to withdraw from the National Economic Development Council, but to remain on the little Neddies and the other bodies, as the minimum gesture it could make against the government. It returned to the NEDC after nine months' absence. There were some employers and there may have been some members of the government who saw this development as an opportunity to move a step further away from the system of bargained corporatism they heartily dislike by winding up the NEDC, but this was not supported by the CBI and the government gave no hint that it was in favour of such a step.

The Prospect for a New Equilibrium

Under the pressure to respond to the drastic changes which enterprises have been compelled to make, workplace-centred unionism has matured, local union leaders have been forced to change their posture from bitter opposition to reluctant acceptance of the necesssity to accept changes in manning levels and work organisation, the closure of departments and establishments, and changes in pay structures. Though this has been a painful process, both sides have had a common interest in survival and this has often drawn them together in a necessary, but uneasy, alliance. There are those among national union officials and shop stewards who favour, for political reasons, the continuance of union–management conflict rather than co-operation; these will not abandon their commitment to their ideological goals. In some cases their influence may frustrate and delay the development of more integrated industrial relations, but in the long run, if management demonstates its ability to make a success of the policies it has forced the unions to accept and employees tangibly benefit, the foundation will have been laid for the longer-term development of less conflict-dominated industrial relations.

In this context employers and the Conservative government are determined to resist the imposition of European Economic Community-inspired requirements to give employees access to confidential information which they believe would damage their business if revealed, or to elect union representatives on boards of directors, or in any other way to enable union representatives to impose a veto on vital management decisions. Although offically in favour of Britain withdrawing from the EEC, the weakness of the TUC since 1979 has led it to play a growing role in the European TUC. It believes that support for Vredeling and the Fifth Directive is such in the Community that approval by the Council of Ministers is a strong possibility. Therefore the TUC, together with the Labour Party, sought to make support for the Directives an issue in the elections for the European Parliament in 1984. The unions themselves have shown little enthusiasm for worker directors and there has been no evidence of strong support from shop stewards for worker directors and from rank-and-file union members. However, the TUC is convinced that adoption of the Directives would considerably strengthen the ability of the unions to regain some of the control over management decisions they have lost since 1979.

Although strongly opposed to participation systems imposed by legislation, managers have become increasingly aware that in the long run they would be wise to take advantage of the more tractable workplace-centred union organisation which now exists. Their approach involves strengthening the link between managers and their employees by the development of consultative committees, briefing groups, quality circles, the improvement of communications and more open styles of management. In these respects there is a growing body of evidence which suggests that Britain might be entering a new era of employee relations in which unions, having been compelled by weakness and membership pressure to accept changes in the pattern of collective bargaining they have followed over the past 30 years, will be ready at the establishment level to respond to opportunities for constructive co-operation with management.

This is not to suggest that, even if during the rest of this decade union–management relations are more co-operative and collective bargaining is less overtly conflictual, the latent bargaining power of the unions will not continue to be considerable and will probably give rise to economic and social problems.

The problem of pay bargaining may be aggravated by the desire of the government to make the conditions of employment of civil servants and local government employees more responsive to market forces than to criteria determined by internal processes (Committee of Inquiry into Civil Service Pay, 1982) but also to limit the adverse effects of comparability.

Revision of the law so as to protect the community from disruptive trade union action in essential public services has been under consideration since 1981, but the government has so far arrived at no definite conclusions. A possible step might be to make trade union action which disrupts essential services unlawful and to require as an alternative to work stoppages some form of binding arbitration. Another possibility would be to remove the immunity which unions enjoy from civil actions for damages unless they have exhausted agreed procedures, including reference to the Advisory, Conciliation and Arbitration Service. Another alternative would be to establish in the case of all essential services, as in the case of the police and armed services, a standing pay review body with power to make a binding award. A further possibility would be to adopt the US practice of imposing a cooling-off period for 90 days following the declaration that a stoppage of work in an essential service was a threat to national welfare and public interest.

None of these measures are novel and they may not ultimately prevent a work stoppage and a breakdown in a service vital to public welfare. Even so, employers' organisations and the general tenor of public opinion are in favour of the availability of enforceable procedures to prevent a repetition of the ugly manifestations of total disregard for the public interest displayed by the unions in 1979.

There is no denying the moral case for curtailing union bargaining power when its exercise endangers the lives and seriously damages the welfare of citizens who are not in any way responsible for the issue in dispute. However, in a free society there are limits to the extent to which employers and employees ought to be prevented from taking action which they believe is in their interest. In Britain there has been a presumption that unions with members in vital public services would not take advantage of the freedom which they enjoyed from legal coercion not to strike. Unfortunately, this presumption no longer holds good. The government, therefore, may think it necessary to redefine the boundaries of a justifiable withdrawal of labour and to provide alternative procedures to resolve conflicts between management and labour without the disruption of essential public services. Unless the unions are ready to enter voluntarily into no-strike agreements, it is certain that some time in the not-too-distant future legislation will be passed to bring this about.

Though trade union leaders in Britain would prefer to return to the situation which existed before 1980, when the law gave them extensive protection and imposed virtually no limitations on the exercise of their bargaining power, it is now evident that, despite fierce ideological resistance from a militant minority, attitudes are changing: trade unionists, employers and the general public are now ready to accept the advantages of a legal framework which discourages the profligate use of naked power and encourages solutions to conflicts of interest through the development of agreed establishment-centred procedures, the use of the voluntary Advisory, Conciliation and Arbitration Service and, in the last resort, the courts.

Given the maintenance of a balance of power between unions and employers, which is less tilted in favour of the unions than in the recent past, the behaviour of both unions and employers should become less opportunistic, less prone to resort to *force majeure* and more ready to determine goals and policies to achieve them by methods which do not invite the constant intervention of governments and can be accepted as legitimate and beneficial to all sections of the community.

Although the proportion of union membership will be lower than in the 1970s, since it will be concentrated in the large private enterprises and the public sector which will decline in relative size, the unions are likely to be in a position in which they will be able to continue to extract a significant element of economic rent to the advantage of their members. Large-scale enterprises are therefore more likely to be willing to concede high wages and superior conditions of employment to the full-time employees who will compose their hard-core labour force. Temporary and part-time workers, who will probably be employed in larger numbers in the future, will be much less unionised. This will also apply to the increased number of employees in smaller companies and those who join co-operative enterprises.

Even without the closed shop unions will be able to enjoy a relative degree of security, especially while there are long-established collective bargaining arrangements. Although may employers in the private sector have no wish to see the scope of collective bargaining extended, it is unlikely that employers in Britain will become as aggressively anti-union as employers in the USA. A small number of companies—including ICI, Birds Eye Food and Nabisco—are reported to have withdrawn recognition from unions representing management groups, but unless there is a sea-change in the attitude of British employers they are, on past experience, more likely to seek to continue their recognition of unions where this has existed for many years and to foster co-operation through collective bargaining and by other means, rather than to engage in a compaign to rid themselves of unions altogether. It would therefore be surprising if, over the next decade, union membership in Britain fell to the low level of 20 per cent of the employed population which it has now reached in the USA; but it is not possible to be certain this will not happen in the longer run.

Trade union leaders are aware that public confidence in the unions depends not only on how effectively unions perform their tasks at the level of the enterprise and workplace, but also on the influence they are able to exert on governments in shaping national economic and social policies. During the last five years the TUC has been kept at a distance by Mrs Thatcher; although this may continue, there are reasons for thinking that the situation may be changing. Probably neither Mrs Thatcher nor the TUC would be ready at the present time to concede that it might be possible, in spite of their antagonisms, to reach an accommo-dation—but there are signs on both sides that a shift in their previous entrenched positions is taking place.

In spite of its large majority, but probably to some extent because of it, there is some evidence of a drift in the policy of the Conservative government towards its historic centre. The critical attitude of many Tory Members of Parliament towards the gov-ernment's decision to ban trade unions at GCHQ and the evident concern of the government to enter into discussions with the civil service unions, as well as the concessions made by ministers in numerous instances under pressure from the government's own backbenchers, all point in this direction. The agreement reached between the government and the TUC on the political levy shows further evidence of a softening of the government's previous re-luctance to discusss issues of great concern to both sides of in-dustry with the unions.

One swallow and a few gnats to not make a summer, but a change in climate may be encouraged if out of the internal struggles taking place in the TUC, centred on its paper on strategy and the future role of the unions, the TUC General Council is able to loosen its commitment to the more extreme policies endorsed by its Congress and to adopt a more pragmatic position. Though both government and unions are likely to continue to view each other with considerable distrust, there could emerge over the next few years in a warmer atmosphere of steady economic recovery a willingness to seek a more constructive relationship.

This would not take the form of a formal concordat, since that would raise an unwelcome echo, for both sides, of the discredited 'social contract' between the Labour Party and the TUC. It would, however, be a tacit recognition by the government that there was something to be gained by a closer contact with the TUC. It is unlikely, however, that the government would be prepared to accept the concept of consensus policies for which the TUC has called. A shift towards more cordial relations would be helped if the TUC were: (1) to come to terms with the new legal framework and accept that it establishes legitimate boundaries to union action; and (2) if it were to move towards a more neutral political position. Such changes would be strongly condemned by many trade union leaders and local activists, who would fiercely oppose the abandonment of deeply held commitments to bureaucratic socialism and radical, Marxist-inspired bargaining tactics. They would, on the other hand, reflect the interests and desires of the great majority on union members as they are expressed in declining membership, their frequent refusal to support militant strike policies, in opinion polls and in their voting behaviour at general elections.

For many trade union leaders these would be bitter pills to be asked to swallow, but they are implicit in an effective trade union strategy for the future. If the government stands firm on the policies which have brought it success and if these are confirmed, as is a reasonable possibility, by continuing economic recovery and falling, albeit slowly, unemployment, the outlines of a new pattern of industrial relations, which have been laid down during the past few years, will become firmly established. It will not be possible, however, to be certain that a new equilibrium between unions, employers and the government has been effectively consolidated on a lasting basis until after another general election has taken place.

References

Bain, G.S. and Elshaikh, F. (1976), *Union Growth and the Business Cycle*, Oxford, Blackwell.
Booth, A. (1983), 'A Reconsideration of Trade Union Growth in the United Kingdom', *British Journal of Industrial Relations*, vol. XXI, no. 3, November.
Brown, W. (ed.) (1981), *The Changing Contours of Industrial Relations*, Oxford, Blackwell.
Committee of Inquiry into Civil Service Pay (Megaw Committee) (1982), London, HMSO.
Daniel, W.W. and Milward, N. (1983), *Workplace Industrial Relations in Britain*, London, Heinemann.
Price, R. and Bain, G.S. (1983), 'Union Growth in Britain: Retrospect and Prospect', *British Journal of Industrial Relations*, vol. XXI, no. 1, March 1983.
Richardson, G.R. and Catlin, S. (1979), 'Trade Union Density and Collective Agreement Patterns in Britain,' *British Journal of Industrial Relations*, vol. XVII, no. 3, November.

5 ITALY

Federico Butera

Population	57,000,000
Per capita GNP, 1982	US$ 6,000
Exports as per cent of GNP, 1982	21
Number of large companies (among the 500 largest outside the USA)	13 with 1,105,000 employees

Governments	1945–7	Christian-Democrats in coalition with Socialists and Communists
	1947–62	Christian-Democrats in a right/centre coalition
	1962–70	Christian-Democrats in a centre/left coalition
	1970–80	Christian-Democrats, sometimes with support of the Communists (who did not belong to the government)
	1980–3	Christian-Democrats in seven different coalitions with the Social Democrats (a relatively non-Socialist party), Republicans, Socialists (also relatively non-Socialist) and Liberals
	1983–	For the first time since the war the Prime Minister of Italy was not a Christian-Democrat, the Socialist Bettino Craxi. All the Italian governments since 1945 have been dominated by the Christian-Democratic Party, even though it has almost never been able to form a government alone. However, the Christian-Democrats are still the largest party in the five-party coalition

137

Public sector (share of GNP, 1982, including transfers)	54 per cent
Trade union membership	1984: 45 per cent
Trade unions	Confederazione Generale Italiana del Lavoro (CGIL), Communist-dominated with around 4,000,000 members, Confederazione Italiana Sindicati Laboratori (CISL), Catholic-dominated with around 2,000,000 members, Unione Italiana del Lavoro (UIL), Social Democratic-dominated with around 800,000 members. All of them include both workers and salaried employees among their members.
Employers' organisations	Confederazione dell'Industria Italiana ('Confindustria') has around 100,000 affiliated enterprises with more than 3,000,000 employees. There are also separate employers' organisations for state-owned companies (Intersind) and for agriculture, banking and several other sectors of industry.

The Italian system of industrial relations is in the midst of profound transformation. Organisational models of labour and management and patterns of employer–employee relations developed during the early 1970s, grew more and more obsolete at the end of the decade and finally entered a period of change after 1980.

The industrialisation process in Italy during the 1950s was accompanied by limited union power; the unions were divided by ideology into three sections and excluded from direct influence in government. The influence of labour on management and on the national economy and the degree of worker participation was traditionally very low. Labour legislation was weak. Centralised bargaining was not strong, and there were no institutional forms of co-determination or participation and the tripartite regulation of interests was traditionally uncommon. This situation was influenced in the 1960s by the growing industrialisation of Italy, which brought a substantial growth in the membership and militancy of the trade unions. In the 1970s, a pattern of industry and company-centred industrial relations grew—at the national level upon protective legislation and national collective agreements, while at the enterprise it was based largely upon informality, militancy and strong union aspirations to affect management policies. As a result, union trends have been characterised by a mixture of ideological attitudes on influencing the economy, industrial policy and the limitation of management decision on the utilisation of the workforce and *de facto* participation in dealing with company problems.

At the beginning of the 1980s the scene changed radically. With the onset of recession unions were weakened as membership declined and the unitary pact was ended. The basic features of the industrial relations system developed in previous decades—national collective bargaining between the federations of workers' organisations and employers' federations, which in important cases are made effective by the involvement of the government on a tripartite basis—have continued, but in an environment unfavourable to the unions and in which they have been compelled to make significant concessions.

It is hard to forecast the long-term direction of these changes. Difficulties are created by alternative economic and social scenarios, but also by the nature of Italy's industrial relations system which is characterised by ideologically divided central union organisations and a significant element of government-inspired corporatism, together with extreme fragmentation and informality, and the fact that what is codified only vaguely corresponds to what actually happens. Forecasts must cover the evolution of both the formal rules and the practices of industrial relations.

The aim of this chapter is to analyse the two possible evolutions on the assumption that it is unlikely that there will be a trend towards either the classic 'neo-corporatist' or 'neo-liberal' solution.

Before exploring possible new paradigms of industrial relations for the coming years, it is essential to point out that the most significant event in Italy during the 1970s was the great change in the organisation of the big industrial enterprises that took place over the last 50 years.

Industrial relations were part of this event; they were the initial impulse and the constraint, but also the component part of the process of development of the new industrial era.

Four main forces have been active in this process and have characterised four distinct periods in the recent history of industrial organisation. They are: (a) new organisational philosophies, principles and methodologies (1967–70); (b) workers' reactions to the traditional work organisation and union action toward new models of work organisation and participation (1968–74); (c) processes of organisational adaptation to the breakdown of internal rigidities and external constraints and to uncertainties (1973–9); and (d) technological change associated with computerised systems and changes in the economic environment.

As a result of new organisational philosophies, the effect of labour ideologies and goals and adaptation to new technology, the traditional model of bureaucratic Tayloristic organisation in big industries frequently seems to have been replaced by models based upon flexibility, goal-orientation and interaction. Discretion, increase of knowledge, co-operation and operational participation are often required of workers. Opportunities are offered for building up roles and organisational units which optimise both the quality of working life and productivity. Occupational systems based upon new skills and continuous advancement are also possible.

These organisational developments inevitably interact with collective bargaining and institutional procedures (co-determination) and they are likely to challenge the traditional role of the industrial union.

The fundamental thesis of this chapter is that the future of industrial relations depends upon *choices* that will be made in complex systems, companies, cities, labour markets, etc., by a multiplicity of actors. These choices will be based upon a sequence of discrete activities of diagnosis, goal definition, analysis, architectural design and detailed design of institutions and processes at the micro and macro levels.

This development will be different from the corporatist combination of different interests in institutional participation and from the zero-sum defence of interests in bargaining. Organisational change in the big enterprises and shopfloor organisational participation in the 1970s are the origins for what could develop in Italian industrial relations in the 1980s and 1990s.

The Historical Context of Industrial Relations in Italy

Italy is a highly industrialised country but some characteristics make its industrial system quite different from others. Its development has had three main phases.

The Industrialisation Phase (1945–60)

The rapid process of intensive industrialisation is relatively recent; apart from the heavy mechanical industries, most of the industries were born or grew on a large scale only after the Second World War.

In the period 1945–60 industrialisation meant mainly the creation of big companies and large plants, almost exclusively located in northern Italy, the so-called 'industrial triangle' of Turin, Milan and Genoa. At the same time, in the other northern and central regions the traditional small-scale industries (foods, glass, clothing, leather and shoes, etc.) were slowly growing, while southern and insular Italy continued to remain basically rural (with the exception of a few isolated, huge processing plants, or 'cathedrals in the desert', as they were called). In the industrial triangle heavy- and light-mechanical industries—including automobiles, textiles, chemicals, printing, engineering, etc.—were established or developed with advanced technologies and rational organisation patterns basically derived from the US tradition.

The ownership structure of industrial companies is another Italian peculiarity. In addition to the large and small private companies, a substantial number of basic industries were state-owned through two main agencies—IRI, which controlled manufacturing industries such as steel, autos, shipbuilding, heavy motors, aircraft, etc.; and ENI, which controlled the oil industry. Another agency (EFIM) lately joined the former two.

The rapid growth of industrialisation had significant impact on society and on the life of the Italians as it did in most European countries. There followed growth of the big cities, impressive development of transportation facilities such as motorways, availability of durable consumer goods, and changes in the educational system. Some important institutional changes took place as well: private and public industrial management acquired great influence in political affairs with the substantial agreement of the traditional rural and commercial ruling classes of the south. The growth of large-scale enterprises had a powerful influence on economic and social affairs during those years. Industrial growth reinforced the tendency towards political stability. The Christian-Democratic Party, the party of church and capital, ruled the country with the smaller moderate parties until 1962, when the Socialist Party also became associated with the government. The Italian Communist Party, the largest in the Western countries, derives its constituency from industrial workers and has remained continuously in opposition since 1947.

Alongside the political structure existing in 1948 were the unions. They were divided into three main confederations: CGIL, the largest, was composed of communist- and socialist-oriented workers; CISL, at the time basically Christian-Democratic and, later on, attracting socialist as well as Catholic members; UIL, comprising mainly republican, Social Democratic and socialist workers.

In the 1950s, and still in 1984, each main confederation was divided into 'trade federations' (metalworkers, those employed in chemical, textiles, transportation, etc). For instance, the union-affiliated workers of the mechanical industries belonged to FIOM (Metalworkers' Union of CGIL) or to FIM (the same part of CISL), or to UILM (the same part of UIL).

The Rationalisation Phase (1960–8)

The 1960s saw the most explosive period of industrialisation. Some of the distinguishing features of those years were as follows. (1) The reinforcement of organisational rationalisation in the large companies based upon job fragmentation, formalisation of control procedures, increase of bureaucratic rules, strengthening of hierarchical structures, as opposed to traditional organisation based upon craft structure. (2) The expansion of mechanisation, and, in process industries, the first phase of automation. Unlike the previous period, the technical solutions to industrial production were implemented by technicians proud of their technical ingenuity and universal rationality, with technical progress tending·to become a value *per se*. (3) The immense migration of millions of southern farmers, fishermen, craftsmen and unskilled workers to the fragmented, well-paid industrial jobs in the big cities of the north. (4) The increased availability of consumer goods for the burgeoning industrial working class, reinforcing an instrumental attitude towards work and the acceptance of the importance of rationalisation; with unemployment at a high level as the growth of the labour force exceeded the growth of the economy, the bargaining position of industrial workers on the labour market was relatively weak and the salary level was lower than in other industrial countries in Europe. (5) The high levels of profit and competitive position of Italian companies. (6) The start of the industrialisation of central Italy. And finally, (7) the persisting political stability, but continued division of the labour movement.

The Crisis Phase (1969–)

At the end of the 1960s, some of these elements changed. (1) The labour market in northern Italy became more bouyant and brought with it the improved strength of its industrial workers, and a rise of salaries closer to the European level. (2) With the permanent settlement of the immigrant workers there was a rise of expectations related to workers' conditions. (3) As Italian society became more complex the economic and political influence of the big companies decreased. And finally, (4) turbulent international competition, both economically and politically, began to threaten the expectations of the new industrial working class and to undermine the stability of the governing elites.

The Organisational Mutation of the Large Industrial Enterprise as an Explanatory Variable of the Trends in Italian Industrial Relations

The industrial 'model of development', which had emerged in the twentieth century with its requirement of work rationalisation and authoritarian relationships within the firm, and which had been accepted as inevitable by labour, began increasingly to be challenged. The impact of large-scale corporatism upon society, economy, environment, social welfare and democracy, both within the state and the enterprise, raised questions at macro and micro levels which had major implications for the industrial relations system.

Italian workers were infected by and sought to emulate the example of French workers who had broken free from established institutions and processes to secure substantial improvements in conditions of employment by turbulent strikes. In the autumn of 1968 an unprecedented series of struggles was initiated by industrial workers in the big northern factories. The unions soon recognised the significance of this uprising. They introduced directly elected Factory Workers' Councils (Consigli di Fabbrica) and, responding to calls for working-class unity, promoted the process among the three confederations. Work regulation became a social issue as well as improvements in pay. There were demands for change in the prevailing pattern of work organisation which were furthered by means of more or less traditional union claims (improved grade structures, rules for internal mobility, the elimination and regulation of painful or dangerous working conditions, elimination of incentive systems, change of administrative systems of work regulation).

Improvements were achieved, but the unions were more concerned with securing economic and political objectives through national collective agreements than the reform of work in the enterprise. No agreement was reached on the principles of a new pattern of work organisation and no procedure was generally agreed upon for implementing changes.

Nevertheless, a surprising number of innovative changes of work organisation were achieved in the 1970s, in spite of less stringent union action at the plant level. This was due to pressures on management to adapt to constraints and uncertainties.

Workforce rigidity, price increase of raw materials, inflation, export reduction, reduction in investments, etc., were all pushing companies towards more innovative, more flexible, less bureaucratic organisations and a better utilisation of human resources.

There were two types of adaptive response to pressure; planned changes and unplanned changes. On the one hand, the management of a select number of important companies, mainly in state-owned process industries, promoted an integrated series of organisation development programmes including innovative job design and worker participation, training programmes, research, organisation studies, action research, experimentation, etc. The enterprises urged unions to participate in those programmes, but met with cold official responses.

A large but unknown number of small, unlabelled changes in job design in big companies also took place, apparently encompassing new principles of increased autonomy and responsibility in work (longer cycles, job flexibility between production, maintenance and quality control, job rotation, group-based organisation, continuous career, etc.). They were introduced in an unplanned way for reasons concerning production efficiency and effectiveness.

Profound changes occurred also outside the large enterprises. The unprecedented development of small and medium-size companies was not only based upon the decentralisation of production from the bigger ones; in most cases these were autonomous, sound, small enterprises, which displayed a relatively high technological level and an 'organic' organisational structure.

Technological Change

The acceleration of technological development in both large and small enterprises was another driving force of organisational change starting from the mid-1970s.

The rapid technological development did not have any deterministic impact upon job design, occupational structures, conditions of employment, working conditions and participation. Choices of design according to strategies of the social actors were more important.

Employers' strategies in Italy have headed towards the full acceptance of organisational flexibility required by technology and the market, but not towards constraining work organisation to any social model. Job enrichment or autonomous work groups have, in most cases, been rejected as mandatory 'formulas' or abstract models. The pressure to include social parameters together with technical/economic ones has often been refused by employers. The Federation of Metalwork Employers has stated that work organisation is not subject to social agreement.

For their part, unions have sought to insist upon their concept of favourable working conditions (*professionalita*) and training, and have also expressed preferences for models which would maximise benefits for their members.

The Change of the Organisational Paradigm

As a result of these processes that occurred during the course of the decade, the organisation of the large enterprise finally moved away from prevailing mechanistic models to organic ones.

In most cases, a new organisation paradigm emerged in industry which rejected the Tayloristic models of the 1950s and 1960s. In the big enterprises the process of 'making large small' became clearly visible. For example, decentralisation, divisionalisation, etc. Self- contained units became goal-oriented. Control systems have become more sophisticated where both central and local control have increased through advanced information systems. Middle management has become used to controlling results, not people. Today, temporary and matrix organisations abound in dynamic enterprises, breaking the 'dogma' of the unity of command. Partially self-regulated work groups are diffuse. Jobs may be 'rich' or 'narrow', but work roles are identified by results, relationships, actual control of variances. Workmanship seems to be based on knowledge and process control more than on transformation techniques.

Implications for Unions

Firstly, unions have been one of the four motive forces that created an impulse for such developments. Secondly, they have taken part, mainly unofficially, in the new designs. Thirdly, as far as the future is concerned, unions find themselves in an industrial setting which is totally different from that which gave rise to unionism as we know it. Work is no longer defined in terms of clear-cut tasks and jobs measured by time, workers are no longer without responsibility for economic results, and unions are no longer based mainly upon blue- collar workers.

The new rules of industrial relations will be developed around the exercise of continuous design and redesign of flexible sub-systems (shop or firm; city or labour market). In the 1970s the formal responsibility of unions in the process of structural redesign was rejected by employers and refused by top union officers, but an analysis of the experiences of the 1970s, particularly in the restructuring at plant level, can give us some indications for the future.

Most characteristic of the 1970s is the redesign of organisational patterns. Unions and workers have been actively involved for the most part in aspects such as the redesign of jobs, formal qualifications, conditions of employment, working environments, training. At the end of this period the unions obtained rights to the disclosure of information (*diritti di informazione*) which gave them some say in the strategic plans for enterprise restructuring. From there the interest of unions moved towards industrial policy. There have been a few cases where unions have participated in designing a new organisational unit or in introducing new technology. The most well-known examples are in the steel industries. At present, when new technologies are introduced (EDP Application, Robots, CNC, Office Automation, CAD/CAM, etc.) there is some consultation with employees, but not with unions unless problems concerning union prerogatives emerge (employment, grades, training programmes, etc.) or they are associated with company crises.

Significant Aspects of Italian Industrial Relations in the 1970s

In 1973 the three union federations entered into a pact of unity to create a single national federation. The pact had an important centralising influence on the unions and it brought about a certain operational unification at the policy and organisational level. Nevertheless, it failed to overcome their fundamental ideological differences.

Union Strength

In 1977 unionisation accounted for 49.02 per cent of the total labour force (employed), a significant figure given the voluntary system of affiliations existing in Italy. In 1984 the percentage of employees organised had fallen by 4 per cent since 1978. This proportion is relatively high compared with France and Germany, but well below Scandinavian countries.

The high level of union representativeness is greater than unionisation rates might suggest. This is due, to a large extent, to the particular form of union representation at the shopfloor level. Representation is provided by the 'delegates' (or, loosely, shop stewards), elected by all the workers, both union and non-union, by ballot vote. The unions do not put up candidates but recognise whoever is elected as their official representative. As such, each delegate is entitled to have the same bargaining rights as the unions. The ratio between delegates and employees in the company is approximately 1:50.

The whole system of representation is a complex mix of formal rules and informal practices. As a result it provides an extreme spread of bargaining power. A highly fragmented pattern of actions by organised labour characterised the 1970s; from antagonistic to collaborative attitudes, from macro to micro concerns, from negotiation to co-determination approaches, from issues included in traditional union prerogatives to management prerogatives. This fragmentation has by no means disappeared and the breakdown of the unity pact suggests that this situation might recur in the future.

In Italy there is some legislation regulating employment relations, mainly labour rights as in the Statuto dei Lavoratori (Workers' Statute) of 1970. However, this provides only a broad legal framework for an industrial relations system which is largely voluntaristic. In particular, there is no institutional framework for participation or co-determination within the enterprises and, until now, unions have always shown a strong opposition to any proposal in this direction.

There is no formal legislation defining the scope or limits of collective bargaining at either the national or plant level. National industrial 'branch agreements', negotiated every three years, fix minimum wage rates, grading systems (there is no job evaluation in Italy), working hours, information-disclosure systems and general conditions of employment. Application of these items to specific situations at the company level is a matter of plant-level bargaining, as are bonuses, piecework rates, workloads and work environment.

Over the last decade, national branch agreements have had a significant role, regulating the following matters:

(a) Reduction of working hours to a 40-hour working week (1969).
(b) Wage policy, with a strong egalitarian emphasis. Its final and most important feature was the adoption of a 'single grading system' encompassing both white- and blue-collar workers (1973).
(c) Adoption of a 'company information-disclosure system' entitling unions—and hence delegates—to receive information, mainly on company strategies. This is not a formal bargaining tool though it has been informally used as such.

Plant-level bargaining has traditionally been the centre of the industrial relations system in Italy. It is not formally regulated. It may encompass wages, bonuses, etc., application of the single grading system (a major issue of late) and any other problem affecting employment and working conditions. In many cases in recent years, problems like redundancy, shortening of working hours and job mobility have been discussed within the framework of plant-level bargaining, although application of the formal system of company information disclosure was limited.

Action by unions and delegates has systematically aimed at influencing such matters as manning, workloads, work, environment, operational ·norms, required skill levels and internal mobility. By means of plant-level bargaining, unions and delegates could obtain considerable power to control the organisation of work. In many cases conflict resulted from this daily exercise of power, and management was faced with real problems. Nevertheless, it served to encourage organisational change and, in some instances, created the foundation for new experiences of participative organisational change.

Of course, this kind of 'union action pattern', based on the control over work organisation, affected the core of the decision-making process within the companies and presented a major challenge to 'managerial prerogatives'. This is probably the most significant feature of the Italian industrial relations system with respect to other systems in which 'work rules' generally affect only very limited and marginal aspects of the organisation.

Underlying this 'pattern of action' was a very diffuse but never implemented concept of industrial democracy. Extremely powerful in building ideological identity, it was based upon:

(a) 'New' forms of work organisation and different organisational patterns of the decision-making process at the company level. In the expectations of union leaders it could give people real control over information and knowledge about the productive process, and real power to use this on the productive process.
(b) Bargaining power spread over the entire delegate network and applied to all the more relevant company decisions, particularly those directly affecting the use of the labour force and working conditions.
(c) Information disclosure for making union delegates participants in national economic planning influenced by union central offices.

The lack of implementation was due more to unsolved ideological questions than to employer resistance. In fact, real participation in organisation design and strategic planning would have implied — among other things—some sharing of responsibilities of company management and results. In actual fact, intervention in the field of work organisation by the union and delegates resulted in a sort of defensive pattern, based on the introduction of various 'rigidities' in work organisation and on the decision-making process.

Unions' Attitudes towards Participation and Board Representation

The main feature of the Italian industrial relations system is, therefore, the importance that all parties, and the unions most of all, attach to plant-level bargaining.

Unions have, up to now, considered that bargaining power based upon the right of delegates to negotiate virtually every aspect of employment related to the use of labour force is the most suitable form of democracy at the workplace.

Unions have always defended this *de facto* right to bargain against any attempt to institutionalise, and therefore limit, it. They have resisted placing it within a more formalised frame, or shifting it into some form of institutionalised co-determination. For this reason, unions' attitudes towards the EEC Fifth Directive, have been, up to now, rather cool. Nevertheless, the discussion raised by the Fifth Directive itself, and the problem confronting the unions at present (described in this chapter), produced some new elements in union attitudes.

Various parts of unions, and especially those close to the Socialist Party (PSI), both inside CGIL (in which they are a minority) and in UIL (where they represent the large majority), are looking at co-determination with growing interest, though no official statement has yet been made on this matter.

UIL is claiming, officially, a 'legal framework' that would formalise the right to the disclosure of information, provided now by National Branch Agreements; such a 'legal framework' would entitle the unions to be officially involved in managerial choices, and would therefore establish a more formalised role for the unions as bargaining agents, and as subjects entitled to participate in company decisions in some form.

CGIL has developed a different point of view, and even made an official statement about what is called the proposal of a 'Company Plan' (Plano di Impresa). This should be, according to CGIL official statements, an official 'rolling programme' for a five-year period, that companies should present to the governmental authority responsible for industrial policy. It should contain a company's strategic, productive and social objectives, and the means by which these would be realised (human, technological and financial resources). This 'plan' should be presented to the unions and discussed with them, though such dialogue should not necessarily imply any agreement.

This CGIL proposal is clearly intended to provide a tool for a governmental industrial policy and to safeguard freedom of bargaining for the unions, avoiding any form of involvement in managerial choices. It is intended that unions would influence industrial policy by other means, through direct contact with governmental agencies.

The other union, CISL, which has a Catholic background and from its origins has strongly felt the influence of American 'business union' traditions, is the least enthusiastic about any form of co-determination. CISL has, nevertheless, raised a proposal for the institution of a union-controlled 'solidarity fund', to which workers should voluntarily contribute 0.3 per cent of their salary. This proposal met limited interest from other unions, and discussion has not made it sufficiently clear to what use such a fund should be put.

A new element has been brought into the discussion by a proposal of IRI (the state-owned industry organisation) of 'associating' the unions with all the major decisions relating to the urgently needed reappraisal programme of state-owned industry. This seemed to be the occasion for a major change in the pattern of industrial relations in state-owned industries, with an expected influence on the whole system of industrial relations, but it very soon became clear that this proposal raised in the unions the fear of being involved, unwillingly, in some form of co-determination. Management itself was not convinced that this involvement of the unions had any virtue other than possibly to reduce a source of conflict in a period in which important choices had to be made.

For these reasons, and for others which are discussed elsewhere in this chapter, it seems very unlikely that the question of union or worker representation on boards of directors will become a relevant area in the Italian agenda of industrial relations. In more general terms, it has to be said that Italian unions do not oppose property rights and managerial prerogatives, but they wish to 'control' them by means of collective bargaining.

During the long period of economic crisis, in which they had to face many factory closures, redundancies and short-time, unions never sought to achieve the growth of the state-owned sector; the intervention of the state was seen only in some specific case as a last resource to save employment in the more unfavourable situations.

Unions have, on the contrary, regarded the role of the state-owned sector as a means of improving the co-ordination, in the context of a planned industrial policy, between the public and private sectors. Whether the means by which they intended to reach this objective are good or not, is another question; but it is highly significant that unions did not oppose the fact that some companies, after having been taken over by the state and restructured by a state-owned agency, were sold back to private investors. The unions were concerned about the intended plans of the possible buyer, not the principle of private or public ownership.

It must be considered that the chronic 'deficit' of public expenditure, and the already difficult situation of the industrial state-owned sector, present the unions with problems of efficiency and rationalisation in this sector. These difficulties are seen as more pressing than the problem of the enlargement of the sector itself.

Union, Employers, Government at Societal Level

In Italy, in contrast to other countries such as the UK, Sweden or West Germany, the unions have never had direct political representation in government through party affiliations. The CISL is strongly linked to the Christian-Democrats, but it includes a considerable participation of Socialist, ultra-leftist, and non-party members. The Christian-Democrats, who have ruled the country since 1945, asssume that they represent all and offer no special privileges to CISL. CGIL, on the other hand, has a majority of Communist members, but Communists have never been in the government. The issue of political influence of unions on government is extremely complex since there is a lack of correspondence between unions and ruling parties and an absence of the concept of 'political exchange'. When the Socialists, who are strongly represented in all three unions, were included in government they tried to influence labour legislation through the Statute dei Lavoratori, a pro-union law which did not, however, discriminate in favour of one union or another. Generally speaking, the role of the state in industrial relations has been and is notably weak compared to most Western countries. Most foreign observers become confused because the verbal ambitions of the Italian unions—in declarations, claims, comments on economic and social policy at societal level—have, over the last 15 years, been notably higher than in other countries. Economic planning, social policy, labour market policy, industrial policy, fiscal policy, regional development in the south, etc., have filled union documents and have sometimes given rise to monumental demonstrations and strikes. Sometimes these political objectives have been supported by the exercise of the collective bargaining strength of the unions, which has put pressure on employers and the wider community. The response of Confindustria has been to play a more defensive political role, to counter union pressures by seeking to influence the government not to capitulate to union pressure and propaganda. Since 1950 the unions have scored many successes in persuading governments to enact protective laws.

Government Intervention

Since the Second World War laws have been enacted which cover protection of miners (1957, 1971); apprenticeships (1955, 1968); national holidays (1953); domestic work (1958, 1973); individual dismissal (1963, 1966); accident insurance, pensions and social security (1965, 1969); lay-offs (1968, 1975). In most cases they incorporate regulations set up by collective agreement.

The Statute dei Lavoratori of 1970 was a 'strong' intervention by the state in labour relations, defining rights and duties of workers in relation to the employers, limiting managerial prerogatives beyond the union–management agreements.

In addition to legal regulation by statute, there are tripartite organisations in which the unions and employers are represented. The most important of these is the National Council of Economy and Labour (CNEL) which is a constitutional body. Designed in order to promote tripartite co-operation, the council has traditionally performed a cultural more than a political role. In the National Social Insurance Agency (INPS) unions are part of the board, which administers pension funds and the 'Cassa Integrazione', which provides income support when workers are temporarily laid-off. INPS has severe budget problems and unions are not entirely happy to be so much involved in its work. The Institute of Workers' Training (ISFOL) also has unions on the board.

Critical tripartite agencies for regulating the labour market in times of high unemployment and mobility, such as a Workers' Agency, are the object of discussion but have not been founded so far. The Ministry of Labour is frequently called on to mediate industrial disputes, even though it has no formal power of arbitration. Usually, the minister is a member of the cabinet who has the confidence of the unions. Employers try to avoid such a mediation, though they usually have some support from other ministries. The tripartite agreement of 13 January 1983 concerning the indexation of the cost of living seemed like a first step into a neo-corporatist model. But the agreement has substantially failed. The Ministry of State-owned Industries has substantial power to guide the industrial policy of the IRI, ENI, EFIM which control important, large, public-owned companies—in particular, most of the steel, oil, ship- and aircraft-building industries, as well as the motor companies, large portions of the chemical industry, some of the largest banks, and the major automobile, retailing, electronics and food industries. The state-owned industries system was designed in order to facilitate a rapid industrialisation of the country and was successful. A market crisis, political inter- ferences, subordination to the development needs of private in- dustries, and commitment to the unions to increase employment and maintain over-manning brought the system into trouble during the 1970s. Some strong action had to be taken in the 1980s by professional management to limit the influence of the unions and other political groups so as to reduce the losses made by these state-owned industries.

The Ministry of Industry is in charge of economic planning and support to industrial activity. There is no formal procedure of tripartite decision and, unlike some other European countries, there is no formal incomes policy, since this is strongly opposed by the unions. In 1968 a law was enacted for periodic consultation between the government, unions and employers about socio-economic questions. Frequently, unions and employers have been invited to discuss government plans about industrial policy. Both employers and unions have been strongly critical of such plans. The amount of public money invested in industry has been high under the Italian system of tripartite corporatism and the constant pressures exerted by unions and employers in favour of public expenditure of one kind or another.

In summary, employers and union relationships have been for- mally antagonistic in Italy, but the bargaining processes brought substantial agreement. Government has never been a truly inde- pendent third party able to regulate collaborative relations; it has been the object of continuing political and social pressure and subject to processes of mediation which have sacrificed economically efficient decisions to consensus. The unions strongly hold the belief that they are entitled to exert maximum pressure on the government as if it were simply a bargaining party. In the 1970s such influence was exerted not only on policy, but also on actual administrative acts. However, the basis of union power lies mainly outside of the political and administrative institutions since the unions do not control the parties to which they have an ideological affinity and, though they exert pressure, they do not control the administrative processes. Indeed, in time of economic recession their weakness in representation at plant level often places them in a difficult bargaining position.

Present Situation and Visible Trends

These basic aspects of the industrial relations system are currently undergoing profound change. It goes without saying that the economic crisis, redundancies and unemployment affect the strike trend and the orientation of union policies among employees. This could be considered a passing phase that will disappear as soon as signs of recovery are evident, but it is more likely that the change in the industrial structure and technology will permanently affect the industrial relations system.

The transformation of the industrial structure, the growth of multinationalism, the change in the organisation of the large enterprise, the shift from large manufacturing plants to complex networks of independent medium-size producers are changing the social patterns, forms of socialisation and structure of interest groups.

The change in the patterns of dependency on skills and therefore the change in those who are essential in the labour markets plus the growth of new skills, jobs and activities, are giving rise to new employee attitudes and behaviours and new individual and collective strategies for the defence of interests. Thus, the traditional basis, function and methods of the union are under question, as is the *raison d'être* of the union itself.

'Solidaristic' forms of unionisation seem to be decreasing; 'instrumental' attitudes seem to be on the rise. There are also some tendencies towards patterns of action and representation that are typical of the 'professionals'. Nevertheless, those tendencies have not yet taken a clear direction and, although it may be admitted that the old pattern is increasingly outdated, it is impossible to distinguish the emerging one.

The crisis might well push the union to look for a new legitimacy within the political system, seeking an institutionalisation of its role in a centralised 'political exchange', as forecast by students of neo-corporatism. Although a part of the labour movement (i.e. CISL) is aiming at this kind of solution it seems rather unlikely that it will be successful.

During the mid-1970s, an attempt at a neo-corporatist union policy was made. During the so-called 'national solidarity' period (when the Communist Party supported the government majority), the trade union movement offered a more controlled and cautious wage policy and a centralised regulation of conflict within the framework of a general policy for economic recovery and social development.

Although few would have admitted it at the time, this was a typical neo-corporatist political exchange, but, in actual fact, it could never have been realised because of the fragmentation of the industrial relations system and inefficiency of state intervention on the economy.

The attempt to regulate the dynamics of labour costs at a central level by modification of the *scala mobile* (the system of automatic adjustment of wages to the cost of living) was unsuccessful, resulting in a major breakdown among unions and a government decree which substituted the impossible tripartite agreement. The government came close to crisis.

The fragmented Italian political system appears to leave very little scope for a neo-corporatist development. By the same token, the heavy presence of the state in the economy—which is one of the more characteristic features of the Italian political system —makes the development of a true 'neo-liberalistic' policy rather improbable. Nevertheless, the evidence suggests that a more liberal climate is spreading, even within left-wing parties and the unions.

It must be noted that there are differences concerning how the basic problems should be dealt with in the 1980s. The question has led to great controversy among the unions and, once again, there is a fundamental split among CGIL, CISL and UIL. It seems rather unlikely that the situation will return to the ideologically based, head-on conflict of the 1950s, but almost certainly unity in the labour movement has never been effectively realised and any semblance of it is likely to be absent for a long time.

Increased social complexity is likely to produce a greater internal articulation of the labour movement and a greater variety of representation patterns, behaviour and strategies. For instance, a greater formalisation in the representation of workers would bring largely under-represented (e.g. white-collar and technical staffs) or totally excluded groups (e.g. managerial staffs) into the network. These groups might even organise themselves outside the central unions, as is already the case with a large part of managerial staffs. Consequently, relations between delegates' councils and the external unions would change, as would the distribution of bargaining power, probably with a tighter formalisation of the rules, scope and limits of each bargaining level.

All this may produce a greater formalisation of the industrial relations system as a consequence of the increased competition within the labour movement and would represent a major change.

A possible scenario would therefore exclude what has been called the 'end' of industrial relations, in which the existing structure would be replaced by the diffusion of individual bargaining and eventually by instrumental, non-permanent interest coalitions or the emergence of non-unionised corporations in which conflicting interests are mediated through internal procedures and principles of professionalism. A more realistic forecast, radical as it might be, would be a transformation of the industrial relations system, and of the unions within it.

This would take into account a greater formalisation combined with a greater variety of representation and of action patterns, which assume many aspects of the features mentioned above, such as more individualised strategies, different groups represented, etc. This would also imply major changes in bargaining strategies.

The forecast of a tendency towards the centralisation of the industrial relations system seems to be contradicted by the weight of contemporary evidence. The tendency towards fragmentation seems to have been strengthened by the first signs of economic recovery and by the diffusion of new technologies and organisational patterns which seem to have centred union and management interest on the revitalisation of plant-level bargaining.

Paradoxically, it is the diffusion of liberal theories and practices, out of which trade unionism originally emerged, that are weakening the tendencies towards any form of central regulation and are helping to revitalise plant-level unionism. What is likely to change are the form and content of plant-level bargaining.

The emergence of new social and professional groupings, new orientations and behaviour, and new interest coalitions could possibly foster the weakening of rigid egalitarian and solidaristic policies, and the development of greater union interest in recognising (in terms of wages, job grades, bonuses, etc.) the individual contribution to overall performance most likely with respect to quality as opposed to quantity.

Within this framework the bargaining patterns based on rigidities, collective defensive guarantees and the right to veto should lose their weight. The challenge to managerial prerogatives on these bases will probably disappear.

It must be assumed that reactive–antagonistic union action and representation of undifferentiated masses of unskilled and semi-skilled workers may be abandoned and that new patterns of action and new forms of organisation of representation may be sought, according to the needs of the Italian economy.

The basic problem for future industrial relations models emerges from the variety and apparent informality of the relations between employers, government and unions and how to satisfy different requirements of different types of relations between the social partners in a phase of profound mutation of the industrial world.

It may be suggested that industrial relations in Italy will not have a unified pattern in the near future. Three different, as opposed to alternative, component paradigms are probably included whose influence varies according to the level and phases of action. One paradigm is based upon institutional participation with unions taking part in the decision-making process in the societal institutions, through political influence and formal procedures as in the neo-corporatist model. The other paradigm is the bargaining model based upon the representation of interests as in neo-liberalism. The third emerging one is the organisational participative pattern. A triple channel of union action is likely to develop in Italy's industrial relations system.

We can now summarise our forecasts. The first channel, institutional participation, is unlikely to assume the status of a sound, formal procedure, but more the traditional feature of lobbying. The second one, bargaining, will most likely revitalise company-level negotiations rather than reinforce centralised negotiations. The third channel, organisational participation, will increase through a very large variety of formal and informal models. It will be of great importance because it may change the attitude of unions from an antagonistic to a collaborative pattern; from a power to an influence model; from a zero-sum approach to one of evolutionary design. We may expect to see major implications in the change of industrial culture for unions and management and for employees in these categories.

6 THE NETHERLANDS

A. F. van Zweeden

Population	14,000,000
Per capita GNP, 1982	US$ 9,500
Exports as per cent of GNP, 1982	48
Number of large companies (among the 500 largest outside the USA)	12 with 810,000 employees (Shell and Unilever are regarded as being 50 per cent British and 50 per cent Dutch)
Governments	1945–58 Coalition: Socialists and Catholics dominating
	1958–65 Catholic and Protestant centre/right coalitions
	1965–6 Catholics and Protestant centre/right coalitions together with Socialists
	1966–71 Catholic and Protestant centre/right coalitions
	1971–3 Centre/right coalitions with left Liberals
	1973–7 Centre/left coalition
	1977–81 Centre/right
	1981–82 Centre/left
	1982– Centre/right
Public sector (share of GNP, 1982, including transfers)	64 per cent
Trade union membership	30 per cent
Trade unions	The Socialist NVV with 740,000 members and the Catholic NKV with 315,000 members set up FNV, the Dutch trade union confederation, in 1976. Protestant CNV with 300,000 members. In 1974, RMHP, a salaried employees' association, was set up and now has more than 120,000 members.
Employers' organisations	Verbond van Nederlandse Ondernemigen (VNO) is the largest, organising around 75 per cent of all

159

Dutch business enterprises. The other
major employers' organisation is the
Cristelijk Werkgeversverband (NCW).
Many companies belong to both VNU
and NCW. State-owned enterprises do
not have a separate organisation, but
some of them belong to VNO.

Introduction

Labour relations in the Netherlands have always been characterised by a high degree of centralisation. Starting from 1870, a
year which may be seen as marking the beginning of Dutch industrial relations, more and more aspects of the position of workers
have been regulated by central organisations of unions and management, frequently through intervention by the national government.

After the Second World War the Dutch trade unions ranked the
public interest above the immediate interest of the class whose
joint representative body they claimed to be. Throughout the
1940s and 1950s Dutch unions accepted and backed the nation's
industry and economic infrastructure. John P. Windmuller states
in his book *Industrial Relations in the Netherlands*, that the Dutch
trade unions became, even more than their German and
Scandinavian sister organisations, the exponents of 'responsible
trade unionism', the protagonists of the view that macro-economic
considerations should prevail over sectional interests in wage
policy and the advocates of centralised, national decision-making
in industrial relations.

It was only when the period of postwar scarcity was over and
prosperity had returned that the unions turned their policies to
more immediate promotion of workers' interests.

Turbulent Years of Disharmony and Conflict

In the early 1960s the system of central wage determination broke
down under the pressure of a super-tight market. This was not the
end of the process of centralisation, though changes in the system
of collective bargaining could be explained as a growing tendency
towards decentralisation. During the late 1960s and early 1970s the
scope of collective bargaining broadened to incorporate so-called

'immaterial' claims of the unions aiming at workers' participation, co-determination, social policy in the companies and improvement of the quality of working-life. This period was marked by more industrial disputes and polarisation between employers and trade unions.

The Dutch industrial relations system, however, was not uprooted. Its main characteristics—a predominant role of the government in the field of incomes policy, a high centralisation within the organisations of employers and workers, institutionalised consultations on national level between these organisations and a preference for co-operation rather than battle—were unshaken.

The economic depression and mass unemployment of the 1980s urged the trade union movement in the Netherlands to look for new forms of co-operation with employers by acknowledging the need for recovery of the market sector and profitability of companies. Therefore, they have accepted a policy of moderate wage development.

Structure of the Dutch Trade Unions and their Long-term Aims

Three national confederations of trade unions constitute the main force of organised labour in the Netherlands:

(1) the Netherlands Trade Union Confederation (FNV), which was formed in 1976 by a merger between the Netherlands Confederation of Trade Unions (NVV) and the Catholic Trade Union Confederation (NKV);
(2) the Christian National Trade Union Confederation (CNV);
(3) the Confederation of Salaried Employees (Vakcentrale voor Middelbaar en Hoger Personeel, MHP), which was established in 1975.

Their combined membership of nearly 1 million (FNV), 300,000 (CNV) and 120,000 (MHP) comprises about 85 per cent of all organised employees, the other 15 per cent belonging to a number of small independent unions.

Organisation according to religion and ideology has always been a hallmark of Dutch trade unionism, as well as of employers' organisations, political parties, media, press and other social organisations.

Before the Second World War the NVV could be identified with the Social Democratic Party (SDAP), but in the aftermath of the war it disengaged itself from socialism and turned into an ideologically neutral organisation.

The FNV of today still has its links with the Dutch Labour Party (Partij van de Arbeid), but these are much looser than those of the LO with the Swedish Social Democratic Party or of the British TUC with the Labour Party. The independence of the FNV from the Socialist Party was stressed by the merger with the former Roman Catholic Confederation of Trade Unions (ṄKV). This merger can be considered as a result of a process of deconfessionalisation of the whole of Dutch society, which is also reflected in the continuous decline of the confessional political parties.

During the 1960s the NKV loosened its ties with the Roman Catholic Church and the former Roman Catholic political party. A remarkable radicalisation of the Roman Catholic trade union movement, which expressed itself in a sharp anti-capitalist attitude during the turbulent years of labour disputes, facilitated its approach to the NVV.

In this period a new ideological wave was engendered by a revival of class struggle, which marked a sharp deviation from the harmonious labour relations of the postwar decades. More income equalisation, shifts in economic power relations, workers' participation in democratised decision-making and in capital formation, were the new issues. Reforms of society and of the socio-economic order were formulated in the long-term programmes of NVV and NKV, which had been adopted by the end of the previous decade.

Even the more law-abiding CNV, which has always rejected class struggle, advocated reforms in economic decision-making by co-determination and more workers' control of management through works councils and labour representation on supervisory boards. Whereas the Christian trade union movement advocated close co-operation between management and labour on the basis of shared responsibility, the FNV unions claimed a more oppositional role for works councils, stating that more responsibility could not be reconciled with too little control ('Not an Ounce of Control for a Kilo of Responsibility' was a famous slogan of the FNV Union of Industrial Workers).

When the merger of NVV and NKV was officially concluded the

new Trade Unions Confederation formulated its long-term aims in the 'programmatic foundation' of the FNV. Economic democracy should be the ultimate goal of social reform. Capital ownership should no longer be a legitimation of economic power and decision-making. Ownership of the means of production should be uncoupled from economic control. Companies and institutions should be ruled by managers elected by the workers. In large corporations a parliamentary body could be established. The works council could be developed into such a controlling institution inside the company.

In the FNV view workers' self-determination cannot be absolute, but has to be bound to limits which society has to put on it, considering that free competition between democratised companies does not guarantee a socially and humanly acceptable way of production. Therefore the government should steer and coordinate economic processes and capital flows.

The CNV, which refused to participate in the formation of the new Trade Union Confederation because it clung to its own Christian identity, renewed its own programme of long-term aims in 1983. This confederation still has links with the Christian-Democratic Party (CDA), a merger of Roman Catholic and Protestant political parties. Former leaders and staff members of the CNV are Members of Parliament for CDA and from its ranks came several cabinet ministers and under-secretaries. The CNV, which was originally based on Protestant principles, developed into a broader Christian organisation when a number of Roman Catholic unions of civil servants, teachers and police officers joined its ranks.

In its newly formulated programme the CNV advocates a 'just distribution of control as an indispensable condition for everyone to live as a responsible human being'. This point of view comprises equivalence, which has to be expressed in restructuring the whole of society and in income distribution. The CNV is of the opinion that the ideal society cannot be realised in a capitalist, nor in a communist system, but only in a mixed socio-economic order which leaves room for private initiative within certain limits.

In the CNV view labour should not be subordinate to capital, and, consequently, in the long run forms of workers' self-determination will have to be created in all companies. Since the CNV recognises that it is not possible to reform all companies into workers' co-operatives, it advocates expansion of co-determination by giving more decision-making power to works councils.

The Big Trade-off

Postwar labour relations in the Netherlands were shaped by a 'big trade-off', which took place during the 1940s and 1950s when certain institutions were established. For instance, the Foundation of Labour (Stichting van de Arbeid) was set up as a permanent body of joint consultation between management and trade unions; the Social-economic Council (Sociaal-econimische raad: SER) was constituted as the principal advisory body to the government on social and economic policy.

When, still during the German occupation, the interest groups of management and labour gave their consent to the formation of the Foundation of Labour, the main concession came from the labour side which publicly renounced, at least for the time being, any claim to active worker participation in management in return for 'ample representation' in official economic advisory bodies to the government.

Trade unions and employers' organisations are represented in a host of consultative and advisory bodies to the government. Apart from the SER and its many committees and subcommittees, both parties are represented in the following bodies (this list is by no means exhaustive):

the Sick Funds Council (Ziekenfondsraad);
the Work Conditions Council (Arboraad);
the Labour Market Council (Raad voor de Arbeidsmarkt) and its regional affiliates;
the Social Insurance Council and its specialised committees and subcommittees;
the board of the Social Insurance Bank;
the boards of the labour councils which are executing a part of the social security laws;
the Committee of Advice and Assistance to the Social Welfare Act (Algemeen Bijstandswet);
the boards of the General Unemployment Fund and the boards of the Disability Funds;
the advisory committees of the Regional Labour Exchanges;

the Chambers of Commerce and Industry;
the boards of pension funds in the private sector;
the board of the General Pension Fund for Civil Servants
(Algemeen Burgerlijk Pensioenfonds);
the Insurance Chamber and Insurance Council which supervise
private insurance companies;
the advisory committee of the Central Bureau of Planning;
the boards of industrial organisations under public law (PBO);
the managing board of the Netherlands Restructuring Company
(Nehem);
countless permanent industrial committees, for instance restructuring committees.

The institutionalised close co-operation between government
and unions lasted throughout the postwar decades. It was not until
the end of the 1960s that the trade union movement tried to get an
entry into the companies and to the work site by building plant-
level organisation, not unlike local unions and shop stewards in
Sweden and Great Britain. In striking contrast to the plant-level
organisation in these countries, plant organisation of the Dutch
unions never developed into a real power inside the companies.

This phenomenon can be explained by the far more important
role of works councils, with their legal status. The influence of the
trade unions at the level of industrial companies still is of a far
lower order than their impact on socio-economic policy at national
level. Most unions still have no shop-level or work-site structure.
Workplace representation belongs to the works council, which is
an independent institution and by no means a part of the union
structure as it is in some other European countries.

After a series of reforms in the legislation on works councils, the
unions are now in a position to exert more influence on
decision-making by their sections in works councils. For a long
time the unions' attitudes towards works councils could be considered as rather ambiguous. They accepted the role of the works
council as an advisory body in the companies, as long as joint
consultation and a regular exchange of information rather than
collective bargaining was the basic task of the councils. At the
same time they considered works councils as their potential competitors.

This attitude changed in the democratisation wave of the 1960s
when the unions began to regard the works council as a useful

vehicle of gaining more influence on decision-making in the companies. They exerted heavy pressure on government and Parliament to modify the Works Councils Act in order to expand the competence of the councils and to reshape them from mere advisory bodies of management into institutions which should primarily promote the interests of workers. Apart from changes in the legislation on works councils, co-determination at shop level acquired a new dimension by the Work Conditions Act which was adopted in 1980 as a framework law which will be implemented gradually. This Act not only provided for new rules on safety and health at the work site, but also for promoting the well-being of workers in their work. Works councils obtained more influence on safety rules and working conditions in the company, which may imply more impact on the organisation of work at the shopfloor level.

At the national level a new body of joint consultation between employers, employees and government has been created, the so-called Arboraad (Work Conditions Council), which advises the government on decision-making in the field of work conditions, and in health and safety matters. The Work Conditions Act, which stems from the concept of humanisation of work as a means to improve the quality of working-life, can be considered as one of the ways of bringing decision-making in the areas of work organisation and work situation as close as is possible to the control of the workers themselves. This same thought was also one of the main motives for building a plant-level organisation of the trade unions because they observed that quality of working life still leaves much to be desired.

Equivalence of Labour and Capital

In 1971 a Bill on the structure of joint-stock companies was passed in the Dutch Parliament. It followed the unanimous advice of the Social-economic Council, which had based its recommendations on the historical compromise between employers and trade unions of 1969. By this so-called Structure Act, the Dutch legislature chose a dualistic model for the management of joint-stock companies, which was split up into two bodies: the managing board and the supervisory board. A number of important powers, formerly held by the stockholders' meeting, were transferred to the board of directors.

The Structure Act is valid for joint-stock companies with more than 100 employees, and obliges them to install a works council and dispose of a capital of more than 10 million Guilders. This dualistic model is similar in some respects to the German model, though there are important differences. It fits well into the guidelines of the European Economic Community for the harmonisation of legislation on joint-stock companies. Apart from supervision and advice on management policy, the supervisory board has to approve all important company decisions, such as mergers, big investments, collective lay-offs and stock emissions.

Moreover, the board performs two special functions—namely, hiring and firing members of the managing board and the determination of the balance sheet and profit and loss account.

In order to prevent the prevalence of group interests, members of the Dutch supervisory boards are not directly elected by the employees or stockholders. In order to guarantee the impartiality and independence of the board, members are elected by co-option. Each proposal for the nomination of a member has, however, to be submitted for approval to the works council and the stockholders' meeting. One of the main objectives of the legislation on joint-stock companies in the Netherlands is to give employees some impact on management. In this respect, the works council as well as the stockholders' meeting has the right to recommend persons for nomination as members of the supervisory board. Both works council and stockholders' meeting have also the right to make objections against the nomination of a board member and to recommend his dismissal in the case of flagrant neglect of his tasks.

The dualistic structure of joint-stock companies was considered as the expression of the equivalence of capital and labour, both getting equal powers in decision-making.

In April 1984 the Social-economic Council decided to maintain the existing nomination procedure of supervisory board members. The majority of the council (employers and independent members), found no reason to change the rights of works councils and capital owners. They rejected proposals from FNV and CNV for a drastic change in the nomination procedures. From the viewpoint of co-determination and co-responsibility of the workers, both confederations of trade unions strongly advocated direct nomination of board members by the employees or by the works council.

Union Leadership

In the postwar years the Dutch trade union movement was accepted as a respectable partner in the societal order. Its leadership adapted itself to its new role in society. The charismatic pioneer-leadership of the early years was replaced by a more bureaucratic leadership of technocrats and experts, who could speak the same language as their societal counterparts, the managers.

Ideological ties of the rank and file with their organisation are merely a marginal phenomenon. Their influence on the objectives and policy-making of the trade unions is only very remote and formal.

The question why workers in the Netherlands are ready to pay contributions to trade unions is partly answered by an inquiry the FNV Union of Industrial Workers conducted into its declining membership. In trying to find out if there were other reasons for resigning, apart from unemployment and disability, this union ascertained that its organisation remained invisible to the members. Rank-and-file workers regarded wage bargaining as an important task, but this activity took place at a great distance from the union member. In the view of the rank-and-file member, the first task of the union was to represent his interests in the company where he is working, or the place where he is living. In other words, the paramount expectation of the union member is individual service. He considers his union membership as a kind of insurance against unfavourable management decisions and is willing to pay a fee for it.

The union leadership in the Netherlands developed from the self-educated, blue-collar worker into the skilled specialist who makes his whole career in the union apparatus. Union leaders are elected by a co-option mechanism which excludes outsiders and opponents. Dutch trade unionism has become a pillar of the established societal order.

The hard core of this order—private enterprise—was unshaken and never attacked. The struggle between management and unions was displaced from the shop level to the conference table. Dutch trade unions developed from battle organisations into consultative bodies and instruments for maintaining social peace.

Holland still has a record of industrial peace which is only matched by countries like Sweden, Switzerland and West Germany.

Employers' Organisations

The two associations or employers' organisations—the Confederation of Netherlands Companies (VNO) and the Netherlands Christian Confederation of Employers (NCW)—also developed a more professional style of leadership. Since 1973 the VNO has had a full-time professional chairman, under whose leadership a more active public relations policy and political involvement have developed. A striking example of co-ordinated political action was the open letter of nine prominent managers, in which they expressed their apprehension concerning the socio-economic policy of the left-wing Den Uyl government in 1976, an initiative which was well in line with the policy of VNO and NCW.

Forced by worsening economic conditions, falling profit rates and challenged by the trade unions in the 1970s, the employers' associations adopted a hard line of defence against trade union demands and suspect government plans such as proposals for a capital-sharing scheme. They successfully co-ordinated their actions in industrial disputes and appeared to be less inclined than formerly to give in to union demands.

From a passive and accommodating group, the employers became a demanding party in consultations with government and trade unions. The government coalition of Christian Democrats and Liberals which took office in 1982 is meeting the employers' demands for reducing the size and growth of the public sector and the burden of taxes and social premiums. According to their wishes, a deregulation scheme has been adopted in order to eliminate legal and other regulations which hamper free enterprise. A new industrial policy is now taking shape on the recommendations of an independent advisory committee, led by the ex-Shell president Gerry Wagner, which stresses the need for reindustrialisation and industrial innovation by granting more support to promising sectors and projects than to weak and threatened companies.

The employers' organisations in the Netherlands do not represent the owners of the companies, but rather company management, since the role of capital ownership in the country is subordinate to professional management. Large multinational companies—Philips, Shell, Akzo and Unilever—of course play an important part in the board of VNO, the largest Dutch confederation of employers' organisations, but their impact on decision-making should not be over-estimated. Their voice is not decisive, since middle and small companies and powerful employers' organisations like the Federation of Employers in the Engineering Industry (FME) are occupying equivalent positions. Policy-making of employers' organisations in the Netherlands is marked by growing integration as a consequence of joint consultation in committees and councils such as the Council of Central Employers' Organisations (RCO), in which both confederations of industrial employers, the organisations of middle-sized and small business and of agriculture are represented.

There is no doubt that this internal co-ordination has contributed to strengthening the front formation and discipline of employers. Developments in the 1970s and 1980s indicate that they have succeeded better in closing their ranks than they did in the 1960s, when employers met a united front of trade unions.

An integrating factor is undoubtedly the socio-economic situation. As long as there is economic growth, increasing profits and a tight labour market, the integration between employers is minimal and their resistance to union demands weak. When profits are declining and the position of private enterprise is weakening, employers join their forces to improve their position. Owing to these circumstances, the employers' organisations are now in a stronger position to exert influence on future socio-economic developments.

They see as a prerequisite of growing success the need to diminish the size and growth of the public sector. They are also stressing decentralised collective elements in wage formation. In meeting the demands of the trade unions for reduction of working time and job sharing, employers are enhancing the flexibility of working time.

New conflicts with trade unions are not excluded if employers are determined to stress flexibility in order to improve profitability and refuse to give in to union demands for redistribution of existing employment.

Present and Future Developments

During a major part of the postwar period a social-political compromise existed in the Netherlands which contributed to a rather smooth economic development and to the shaping of the welfare state. Socio-economic decision-making was characterised by centralism and a high degree of consensus. The 1970s showed a concurrence of socio-cultural changes in the structure of the Dutch population which were accompanied by growing economic disruption. The organisations of employers and employees, which built up their positions during a period of sustained economic growth, full employment and a continuous expansion of social security, had no response to the uncertainties of a period which was marked by diminishing economic growth and soaring unemployment figures.

Decision-making was more and more characterised by stalemate, because the parties could not succeed in finding a way to handle the new problems jointly. They could only adopt a defensive attitude towards the challenge of changed social and economic conditions. By clinging to their contrasting opinions on the aims and means of socio-economic policy, they lamed central decision-making. The tendency to decentralisation of decision-making was frustrated at the same time by frequent interventions of the national government in wage formation.

A ten-year deadlock in consultations between government and social partners at central level was ended when the central organisations of employers and trade unions reached agreement on a trade-off of wage development against improvement of profits and redistribution of work in November 1982.

For the first time the employers gave in to the wishes of the trade unions for reducing work time. The central organisations agreed on recommendations to parties involved in collective bargaining at industrial and company level, which aimed at recovery of economic growth, improving profitability and sharing of existing employment. This agreement in the Foundation of Labour opened the way to free, decentralised bargaining and forestalled new government interventions in wage formation.

The balance of power in Dutch labour relations has been disturbed by high unemployment. The trade unions have been driven into a defensive position. They have come to believe that they have to give absolute priority to employment above income improvement.

By the end of the 1970s the trade unions tried to develop a new strategy based on job agreements, which should comprise job guarantees by management in exchange for wage restraint. When this strategy appeared to be a failure, the issues of trade union policy were changed into claims for reduction of work time, following the resolutions of the European Federation of Trade Unions for a reduction of 10 per cent in four years.

In the present situation of the labour market, which can be characterised as an employers' market, the trade unions not only have very little to offer their members, but also they are losing much of their impact on national socio-economic policy. Since the conservative government of the Christian-Democratic Party (CCDA) and Liberal Party (VVD) took office, the channels which the trade unions could use to exert influence on policy-making have been closed. FNV and SNV could not find much sympathy for the alternatives they developed to government policy.

The government launched a programme of sharp cuts in public expenditure in order to stop the ever-growing budget deficits and to reconstruct public finance. By diminishing the size of the public sector, the aim of the government was to make room for the market sector.

The trade unions are opposing a policy which, in their view, is deflationist in its one-sided stress on reducing budget deficits. The unions offer resistance to cuts in social benefits and are advocating a more equal distribution of income sacrifices. In the autumn of 1983 a major conflict broke out between the government and the organisations of civil servants when wage cuts were announced. The decision of the government to break with the system of wage formation for employees in the public sector which follows the average wage development in the private sector, paralysed joint consultation between the government and the civil servants' unions.

At the same time employment in the public and semi-public sector has to be reduced in order to meet the objectives of diminishing the size of the collective sector and of lowering the level of public provisions. The painful reappraisal of the Dutch welfare state caused major social tensions and disputes.

During the last two decades a striking difference developed between the fast-growing public and subsidised, non-profit sector, on the one hand, and the diminishing market sector, on the other hand. This development exerted great influence on the trade union movement and labour relations in the Netherlands. Growing contrasts could be observed between unions in the public sector and unions in the market sector. Incomes policy for civil servants and workers in the semi-public sector so far followed the trend of collective bargaining in the private sector (the so-called 'trend policy').

This trend mechanism was uprooted when the government decided to cut civil servants' wages by 3 per cent in 1984. The actions and strikes of civil servants, which unsettled public services for a period of ten weeks, was quite a new phenomenon in the Netherlands. By their actions the unions of civil servants not only resisted what they called a one-sided government decision, but they also tried to compel the government to open real negotiations in order to avoid more cuts in their salaries in the next three years when, according to the government programme, more billions of Guilders must be saved on public expenditure.

Whereas wage formation in the market sector should be free and decentralised, the Dutch government wants to control wages of employees in the public and semi-public sector. This so-called 'trendsetting' incomes policy for the public sector aroused vehement protests among all trade unions, which consider it as incompatible with the freedoms of trade unionism and collective bargaining. So far, no solution has been found for better bargaining procedures between government and unions of civil servants, which still have the feeling that their salaries are forming a balancing item in the government budget.

In a spirit of greater resignation, the trade unions acquiesced in the withdrawal of the Bill on capital growth sharing—a Dutch version of Swedish wage-earner funds—originally proposed by the Den Uyl government, a coalition of Social Democrats and Christian Democratic Parties (1973–7) as an instrument of social reform.

In the Netherlands a reformulation of the basic agreement on socio-economic policy seems to be inevitable. The polarisation of the previous decade has not yet been replaced by a new broad consensus. The institutionalised co-operation of employers and trade unions in the Social-economic Council and Foundation of Labour is still following the traditional pattern of joint consultation. It is not to be expected that this system will be abandoned in the near future, since there is no suitable alternative. The system provides the participants with the opportunity to learn each others' priorities, weak and strong positions and it offers them space to manoeuvre. Within the margins of this space, trade-offs can be made between socio-economic objectives such as income development, employment and public expenditure.

Decision-making at this level has been hampered by the comprehensive system of interlinked income of wage-earners in the market sector, civil servants in the public sector, employees in the non-profit sector and social beneficiaries, which took shape during the 1970s. By this system the interests of government and social partners are so closely entangled that their relationships are becoming ossified. Social rigidities as a consequence of the semi-automated decision-making process on income formation and income distribution may be seen as one of the main causes of the difficult readjustment of the Dutch economy. Government, employers and trade unions are each others' prisoners in a system in which wage development in the market sector determines 60 per cent of the total public expenditure. This is also the main cause of the great impact central government exerts on collective bargaining.

Return to postwar central wage determination, however, is not to be expected, because such a policy would lack the support employers and trade unions gave to it in the 1950s and 1960s. In the Social-economic Council both parties unanimously rejected direct government interventions in primary income formation other than in emergency situations. The SER advice on income policy reflected a change in Dutch labour relations. Employers and trade unions are now both opposing centralism and advocating decentralised bargaining.

Nevertheless, they do not agree on the ways and means to achieve the long-term objectives of socio-economic policy. As a consequence, the necessary readjustment processes in Dutch society will not progress without shocks. The key question is if Dutch society can absorb them without serious social tensions. In this nexus of changing economic conditions and labour relations the trade unions have to make some fundamental choices. Should they promote the immediate interests of their members, or will they cling to their position as responsible partners at the national level of decision-making? Solidarity of wage-earners with the unemployed and beneficiaries of social welfare will be put to the test when they have to pay increasing contributions to social security.

Decline in their membership may force the unions to promote the immediate interests of their grassroots constituency. Loss of faith in trade union leadership has already been reflected in 'wild cat' strikes in the ports of Amsterdam and Rotterdam some years ago. The economic crisis of the 1980s is weakening the position of trade unions in their relations with employers and government. Declining economic growth and burgeoning unemployment make the burden of social security unbearable and put the solidarity principle of the trade unions under severe strain. Moreover, Dutch trade unions are hardly prepared to meet these changes in social and economic conditions.

For the time being, Dutch trade unions will have to suspend their long-term aims of social reform. Recent proposals by the CNV for the formation of employment or investment funds from a levy on the wage bill are a far cry from former union claims for workers' control of investment decisions and capital formation. The CNV now suggests profit-sharing in companies and sectors where reducing working time is not an effective policy, such as in the building industries.

This proposal may be considered as a substitute for the capital-sharing schemes of the good old days when soaring profits and capital growth seemed to justify claims for workers' participation in capital formation.

Union Power

Ideas to restore union power in the Netherlands are most clearly articulated by the FNV Union of Industrial Workers. In its programme for the medium term—*Working in the 1980s*—the union claims to increase union power in the company and on regional and central levels. Workers' determination should be enhanced by delegation of bargaining powers to members of the plant-level organisation and to the union section in works councils. Reduction of working time to an average of 32 hours by 1990, and industrial policy in order to create new jobs, are the main objectives of the union for the 1980s. In its view, industrial policy comprises stimulating technological advance, provided that the human factor is put first and foremost.

The interests of employment should be promoted and the quality of working life improved. With the FNV, the Union of Industrial Workers is ready to fight for maintaining the level of social benefits. In its objectives for wage bargaining, however, the union claims that it will try to diminish the big difference between gross and net income, but not at the expense of the social beneficiaries. Lower social costs by work sharing and the creation of new jobs, as well as higher productivity by technological progress will, according to the union, increase the room for net wage improvements without cuts in social benefits.

Just like the other unions, the Union of Industrial Workers wants to operate as a part of a broad trade union movement, which not only promotes the interests of its working members, but also those of the unemployed. The union does not want to choose only for the market sector, but for the public sector as well.

According to the FNV chairman, Wim Kok, the industrial policy targets of the Union of Industrial Workers are not incompatible with the objectives of the confederation to enhance the strength of the market sector and to defend the public sector at the same time. Nevertheless, differences of opinion between this union and the unions of workers in the food industry and the public sector became manifest; the latter was afraid that the FNV would surrender to the employers if it chose to follow the course advocated by the Union of Industrial Workers in its plan for industrial recovery and entered into negotiations with employers.

Claims by the unions regarding the influence of the employees over capital or investment decisions are now purely theoretical. CNV and FNV plans for introducing so-called investment wages as means to enlarge workers' influence on investment decisions by management are suspended as long as profits are still considered too low.

Consensus or Conflict

In the years ahead the major question in Dutch society will be the size and structure of the welfare state. The traditional conflict of interests between capital and labour is overshadowed by the painful readjustment processes which are enforced by stagnating economic growth. Apart from economic and financial constraints, reduction of the public sector can be considered as an ideological objective of the government coalition of Christian Democrats and Liberals which is strongly endorsed by management.

The Social Democratic opposition defends the gains of the post-war welfare state against attacks of the 'new right', as party leader Joop Den Uyl has stated. In a famous speech during the election campaign of 1981 Den Uyl said that in the near future the central problem of the welfare state will be the defence of solidarity thinking on which the social order is founded: 'In the disguise of individual responsibility the New Right is trying to sell as society-image that it is aiming at giving the helm of society into the hands of a small group of strong and powerful persons. The state retreats on itself under the slogan "Peace and Order, or Resignation without Order".' In this slogan, Den Uyl expressed the identity of Social Democracy in the Netherlands, but it is doubtful whether the Social Democrats still identify themselves with the labour movement.

A growing resistance against the increasing burden of solidarity is manifest among the grassroots of the trade union movement. So far, NVV and CNV strongly oppose government plans to reform the system of social security by an appeal to their members to sacrifice more real income in order to secure the level of social benefits. Their defence of the welfare state may be considered as a rearguard fight, for the time will come when they have to choose between wage restraint in order to restore employment or income sacrifices for maintaining the level of social security.

Estimates of the development of the Dutch labour market indicate a disastrous increase of unemployment from 800,000, or 17 per cent of the working population, in 1983 to 1.5 million in 1990 and 1.8 million by the end of the century. These estimates are not only based on the supposition of stagnating economic growth, but especially on increasing labour productivity and demographic factors such as the growth of the working population by an average of 75,000 a year until the end of this century.

Under these circumstances, the trade unions in the Netherlands will have to make up their mind whether the workers are willing to bear the growing burden of securing incomes of the unemployed, disabled and elderly people. In this context, the system of interconnected and indexed incomes in the market sector and public sector will be put under heavy strain. The government actually broke with this system when it decided to lower the minimum wages and social benefits by 3 per cent in 1984. The whole system of labour relations in the Netherlands might be uprooted if no new consensus is found on the long-term aims of socio-economic policy and the size and structure of the social security system.

The economic difficulties of the last ten years have not served to unite the parties. The remnants of the old corporatist structure of Dutch society now hamper necessary readjustments of the Dutch economy, which is delivering a very poor performance compared with that of other industrialised nations.

Joint consultation between the pressure groups of labour, management and the government on socio-economic policy does not mean close co-operation. A new big trade-off of social preferences is needed, since the old social compromise ended by creating a spiral of compensations which inevitably resulted in growing budget deficits. As a result, the Dutch welfare state failed and became uncontrollable. A prerequisite for a new social compromise will be a disentanglement of the responsibilities the social partners accepted for the interdependency of all incomes. The uncoupling of wages and social benefits is only a matter of time.

The consensus-making machinery in Dutch society is hampered by the fact that the institutions of joint consultation such as the Social-economic Council and the Foundation of Labour, still exist, but are no longer functioning well because of the growing contrasts between employers and trade unions. The tendency towards decentralisation has also contributed to the diminishing significance of the central institutions.

The trade union movement is now facing a process of industrial restructuring and rationalisation on which it can exert hardly any impact. The unions of industrial workers recognise the inevitability of these developments. The new leadership of the Union of Industrial Workers has expressed the desirability of a joint reindustrialisation scheme by management and trade unions which might give the unions some grip on developments. I believe that the trade unions under the actual circumstances cannot expect much advantage from a conflict strategy. They will derive more benefit from coalitions with employers at industrial and company level to promote industrial recovery and prevent further demolition of employment. This means that they have to accept further decentralisation of collective bargaining and, consequently, more income differentiation. The unity of the Dutch trade union movement might be jeopardised if the conflicting interests of the unions of industrial workers and those of civil servants and workers in the non-profit sector are not reconciled. Dutch trade unions are facing important shifts in the working population from which they recruit their membership. Employment in industry will diminish in line with further replacement of labour by capital. Industrial developments will need a more flexible functioning of the labour market, which means less legal protection for the workers against dismissal. The trade union movement will have to sacrifice many of the gains and securities it obtained in a century of battle.

What will be its strategy for the next decade, if the trade union movement has to acknowledge that it failed in restructuring the economic order and economic power relations?

The most logical option, which is consistent with its historical role as a 'pillar of the established social order', is a pragmatic rather than an idealogical or utopian future projection. The fact is that the trade unions in the Netherlands have now to fight for their own survival under the gloomy prospects of economic stagnation, unemployment, loss of faith of their members and unbalanced power relationships. Labour relations in the Netherlands are exposed to heavy strains if this balance is not restored. In order to break the deadlock, the trade unions will have to lay more emphasis on the promotion of the immediate material interests of the workers by building a utilitarian organisation, primarily on the shopfloor, as a countervailing power against management.

A pragmatic strategy will moderate their pretensions for social reform and changing the capitalistic order. Incomes policy will be primarily handled as an instrument of economic recovery, which means that a more equal income distribution will be subordinate to this objective.

At company level, the unions will try to come to terms with employers on the issue of reindustrialisation, which may imply co-determination and workers' participation in work organisation, investment planning, personnel policy and profit-sharing. In this context, a new consensus between management and labour might be attained on the basis of joint interests in a new economic era.

7 NORWAY

Einar Thorsrud

Population	4,000,000
Per capita GNP, 1982	US$ 13,500
Exports as per cent of GNP, 1982	31
Number of large companies (among the 500 largest outside the USA)	3 with 32,000 employees
Governments	1945–63 Labour Party 1963 Conservative-dominated non-Socialist government 1963–5 Labour Party 1965–71 Centre-Conservative coalition 1971–2 Labour Party 1972–3 Centre coalition 1973–81 Labour Party 1981–3 Conservative minority government 1983– Conservative-dominated non-Socialist coalition
Public sector (share of GNP, 1982, including transfers)	49 per cent
Trade union membership	65 per cent
Trade unions	Norwegian Trade Union Confederation (LO) has 750,000 members. The largest LO union is the Norwegian Local Government Employees' Union with 130,000 members and the Norwegian Steel, Iron and Metalworkers' Union with 105,000 members. The dominating salaried employees' union in the private sector is AF with around 95,000 members and Yrkes-organisasjonens Sentralförbund (YS) with 120,000 members, mainly in the public sector.

180

Employers' organisations   The Norwegian Employers'
                                 Confederation (NAF) has more than
                                 10,400 member enterprises which
                                 employ around 385,000 people. There
                                 are also separate employers'
                                 organisations for banks, insurance
                                 companies, commerce, agriculture
                                 and forestry. There are also central
                                 and local government negotiating
                                 organisations.

This chapter has three main purposes:

(1) To emphasise the historical background of unions in
    Norway.
(2) To highlight the nature of basic changes in society in the
    1970s, 1980s and 1990s.
(3) To discuss some areas of trade unions' policy, particularly
    their relations to their members, to employers and other
    major organisations and institutions.

The Historical Background of Trade Unions in Norway

In a brief overview such as this, there is no purpose in going into
Norwegian trade union history in any detail. Nevertheless, it is
necessary to remind outside observers that union development in
Norway has been different from that of other countries with which
we otherwise have much in common.

Norwegian trade union involvement in Labour Party politics
during the whole of this century makes any comparison with, for
example, developments in the USA, very difficult. The Norwegian
Labour Party could not have formed a government in 1935 and
carried out its full employment policy without working hand in
hand with the unions. This established a unique basis for joint
government–trade union economic policy during the 1950s and
1960s.

Union leaders in Norway are shocked to see how a US government can take action against organised air controllers or pretend to be deaf to miners' and steelworkers' demands for protection against unemployment. US union leaders are equally

surprised to see how even a conservative government in Norway is sensitive to union opinions in matters of work environment and workplace democratisation, vocational training and social security.

British union leaders were opposed to and rather critical of the way Norwegian trade unions were involved in industrial and economic restructuring in the 1950s and 1960s. Their Norwegian colleagues were equally critical of the UK trade union policy of resisting organisational and industrial restructuring at almost any cost.

In the early 1960s Swedish industrial and trade union leaders were surprised to see that a joint union–employers' research and development programme on industrial democracy was established in Norway. Their colleagues on both sides in Norway were equally surprised to see the strategies adopted by the main organisations in Sweden. Their strategies on industrial democracy were bound to cause increased polarisation in the 1970s and to defeat some of the major purposes of democratisation of work life. We shall return to this issue in some detail.

Trade union leaders from most Latin countries cannot understand how Scandinavian unions have been able to avoid the splitting of unions along religious lines. French and Italian union leaders find it equally hard to see how little the different ideologies of Communists and Social Democrats have split the Scandinavian trade unions.

It may seem unnecessary to mention these rather general political differences as a background for understanding trade union adaptation to societal changes. But these differences have had quite specific consequences for recent developments in union policies in Norway. We shall therefore mention two more issues of a political nature. One is the nationally unifying effect of the German occupation of Norway in the Second World War. The other is the polarising effect of the referendum in 1972, when Norway decided not to join the European Economic Community.

Between 1940 and 1945 the conflicting interests of employers and unions were subordinated to their common interest of surviving as part of a democratic system. One would have thought that the same would have been the case in, for example, France and Britain. This was not so, at least not to the same extent, if we observe the tendency in these two countries soon after 1945 to move back to prewar politics. In Norway the joint programme of all the political parties established at the end of the war had a lasting impact on government and on union and employers' policies for some 15–20 years after the end of hostilities. Simultaneously, we had a rapid reconstruction and further development of industry, a steady growth in national productivity and real income of 3–4 per cent per year, a high level of social security, almost no inflation or unemployment and no major strikes throughout the 1950s and 1960s. We are not claiming that a trend of participation alone created a trend of economic and social development. The point is that the two trends came about together.

When new demands for revised social, educational and labour policies appeared during the 1960s, unions and managements faced these demands together—not as in most other countries in an adversarial position. There were of course conflicts of interest, but this did not rule out that there were also overlapping interests. If these were not solid enough for joint problem-solving, as they were in many areas of social and educational legislation, they were still kept in mind. The main parties in industry were cautious not to provoke the other side by taking an extreme position on any issue of common interest. The lines of communication were always open.

The employers' organisations were generally opposed to central planning, but kept a low profile when extremists (Libertas) tried to create a political movement against governmental control in the early 1950s. The trade union movement was against strong financial control by a few banks and private owners, but kept a low profile in the debate over nationalisation of industry (the British model). In the 1950s this issue disappeared from the Labour Party programme, in accord with union attitudes.

The employers were initially negative about union demands for industrial democracy in the 1950s, but later agreed to modify labour contracts to enhance the sharing of economic information and new forms of employee participation.

Just as the Second World War situation had a stabilising effect on union–employer relations in the 1950s and 1960s, the 1972 EEC referendum had a destablising effect over the years to come.

After considerable debate during the 1960s within the labour movement, the Social Democratic government negotiated the conditions for Norway's entry into the EEC. A referendum was arranged as the final step before entry. There followed a political confrontation and a polarisation over a wide series of

issues —central versus local power in economic planning, primary
industry versus manufacturing, local culture versus cosmopolitan,
bureaucratic versus popular values, youth and women's
movements versus the establishment. Symptoms of a cultural shift
surfaced in national politics for the first time this century. The
EEC issue triggered off a political chain-reaction. Norway decided
not to join the EEC and the Labour Party and the Trade Union
Council moved back into a defensive position on a number of
other issues.

In 1973 the unions, with Labour Party support, enforced legal
action to introduce employee representation on company boards.
In 1977 the new Work Environment Act was passed by
Parliament. Both of these matters would probably have been
settled through negotiation between unions and employers if the
collaborative postwar climate had not been upset by the EEC
confrontation. During the late 1970s and early 1980s the previously dominant actors in industry drew stricter lines of demarcation between themselves on a number of issues—cost reduction and inflation control, subsidies to declining industries, etc.
It is too early to say how they will work out new roles for themselves in an increasingly turbulent scene of labour relations. They
are not as dominant as before in this scene, where the rules of the
game are changing rapidly. Other unions will influence the Trade
Union Council. The public sector will influence the private sector
of employment.

The Nature of Societal Change after the Energy Crisis

It was not only the oil crisis of 1973 which caused a fundamental
change in the industrialised world. Technological development
had shifted from mechanisation to information systems. Service
industries had taken over from manufacturing as the dominant
form of employment. The new industrial countries had taken a
lead in important world markets, but development had not
trickled down to the poor world as expected. The baby boom after
the Second World War flooded the labour markets with educated
people with a partly new lifestyle. The industrialised culture was
shaken by something more fundamental than an economic recession.

Limits to growth and the age of discontinuity, post-industrial community and the turbulent environment were concepts used to explain what was happening. But what was it that so fundamentally changed the very nature of the industrialised world?

In retrospect there seem to be several new characteristics breaking through at the same time, causing multiplier effects. On the one hand, different sectors of industrial society became more interrelated. On the other hand, each of the sectors became more complex and therefore more unpredictable. With these factors in mind, we ought to take a closer look at two basically different types of environment emerging after the Second World War.

The Unstable Environment, 1965–73

The competitive advantages of different enterprises tell us a great deal about changing environments. During the industrial growth of the late 1950s and early 1960s, easy access to raw materials and energy were critical factors which fit together with economy of scale. These three factors fit together as long as mechanisation is the dominant technology.

Around 1970 a new factor became increasingly important, namely to stay close to the market and to adapt quickly to it. At the same time mechanisation faded out as the leading technology. Automation and information handling started to take over. Production efficiency could in many branches be achieved by smaller units, while large enterprises became increasingly bureaucratised and inefficient.

The organisational patterns started to change fundamentally around 1970. Adaptation to new markets and new technology turned out to be increasingly difficult for large, hierarchical organisations. The principles of scientific management had been unchallenged as long as mechanisation, standardisation and specialisation took place in parallel with continued economic growth and easy access to cheap energy.

A postwar generation of workers and professionals trained in traditional skills and motivated according to a Protestant ethic had kept the wheels of industry turning. Suddenly, large parts of the workforce and large consumer groups turned sour. The assembly-lines started to squeak and complaints over poor quality of work hit the headlines of the new media industry. Even in Scandinavia, with peaceful labour relations as a trade mark of political stability, 'wild cat' strikes emerged on the scene.

The Kiruna strike in Sweden's iron mines came as a shock to the Trade Union Council as well as to employers. Lordstown, 'the most scientific auto plant in the world', became a symbol of failure in US industry. The overbearing attitude of Ford and General Motors towards socio-technical experiments at Norsk Hydro and Volvo in the late 1960s was duplicated in the Japanese auto industry in the early 1970s, producing bewilderment.

In spite of its sophisticated long-term planning, industry walked unprepared into what Vickers (1972) calls the 'environmental trap'. The same happened to the US military machine in Vietnam. But the universities of the 1960s have an equally bad record. In spite of a new big science, social research, the academic world had no idea what was happening inside its own walls. The youth revolt was a symptom of an obsolete bureaucratic system of education and of a declining 'knowledge industry'. Kiruna was also a symptom of declining industries but even more of an obsolete way of organising work, from the bottom of the pits to the top of the management centres.

In short, the major elements in the shift of organisational culture in the early 1970s were:

(1) from mechanistic use of technology as 'given' to information-based socio-technical design;
(2) from closed techno-economic systems of bureaucracy to open systems related to environmental conditions;
(3) from extreme splitting of tasks and jobs to integration of tasks in meaningful jobs;
(4) from centralised managerial planning and control to increased co-ordination as part of all jobs;
(5) from splitting learning and work to integrating work and learning in development;
(6) from wasteful growth and consumption-oriented values to conservation and pluralistic value-orientations.

A most important signal of shift in organisational culture can be seen in new forms of adaptation to environmental changes. In the increasingly unstable environment of 1965–73 the leaders of industry and unions, as well as the political system, had reacted in much the same way as before. Needs for change were registered one by one, and interpreted rather mechanically according to previously known trends. Macro-economic models of planning furnished the basis for reactive adaptation. Cost-cutting and trimming of the traditional organisational system were the corrective means universally applied. International consultancy firms often wielded the axe when cost-cutting meant firing of personnel. Only very slowly did the large organisations start to develop preactive strategies of change—including total redefinition of markets, conscious choice of technology and new forms of organisation. And perhaps most important of all, new forms of coalition rather than traditional competition between enterprises and organisations formed the basis for new strategies of change.

The OPEC coalition of oil producers had sent a shock wave through the industrialised world. Other waves of change caused by new technology and new social forces were multiplied by growing competition from new industrial and commercial powers in Asia. Unions and employers' organisations, linked together by adversarial as well as co-operative arrangements, were shocked into defensive positions and in many cases bitter confrontation and continued polarisation.

In Norway, mainly because of the historical background we have mentioned, the confrontation between unions and employers never reached the level that it did in other industrial countries. In this respect, the difference even between Norway and Sweden was quite striking.

Common Reaction to a Turbulent Phase of Transition

Even if the diagnosis summarised above were correct it would obviously take time before stabilising forces could have lasting effect. All the six development alternatives mentioned are only beginning to take shape. We don't know if they are sufficient, although all of them seem necessary. There is certainly insufficient knowledge about how to integrate the new alternatives into workable strategies. We probably have to live with much of the uncertainty involved in a phase of transition for some time to come. The question is whether we face uncertainty in constructive ways. If not, then the turbulence will be further exacerbated and prolonged.

There are several unproductive or regressive ways of reacting to widespread uncertainty. One is to pretend that the basic problems do not exist—to escape psychologically and morally by claiming that the recession or crisis will soon be over. This attitude is reflected in recurrent statements from the establishments that things will soon improve if those who suffer will only be patient for another six to twelve months. A different type of escapism comes from ideological spokesmen of the extreme right or the extreme left, but the cures they advocate will take a bit longer. Neither a revolution nor a return to the stable 1950s and 1960s are likely.

Another regressive reaction to a turbulent environment is apathy, combined with putting the blame on some scapegoat—an imagined evil power. This reaction was fairly common during the 1970s among leaders of industry and unions and also among politicians. The young leaders from the Second World War and the reconstruction period seemed unable to tackle the emerging turbulence of the 1970s. Or was the situation perhaps beyond the capacity of a social system built on economic growth—on hope and trust? The revolutionary generation of 1968 also turned from 'fright/fight' to 'fright/flight'. Sometimes the flight took the form of drug behaviour, sometimes vandalism and crime. In the extreme case, terrorism became the symptom of the turbulent world of the 1970s.

Some of the fathers of the 1968 generation turned aggressively from 'fright/flight' to a 'fright/fight' reaction. This is, in its extreme form, the third maladaptive response—besides escapism and apathy. Did some of the polarisation in politics and in labour relations in the 1970s occur because of 'fright/fight' reactions? The escalation of international conflict probably did.

A new force—electronic media—entered the social scene in the 1960s and 1970s and had the power to trigger off any one of the three maladaptive responses. Mass media bombarded the brains of people for hours every day with sounds and pictures of a turbulent world. Perhaps the maladaptive responses are not so abnormal as they might seem to be? And perhaps the new information technology holds a key both to a mad world and a more sane one? This is what we seem to find when we explore what kind of future people expect and what kind of future they want.

Beyond Turbulence: What Futures Do People See?

Among the more promising ways social scientists have used to look into the future is the so-called 'search conference'. This method has been used in many countries to establish participative forms of planning. Fred Emery (1981, 1983) and his colleagues developed the method based on research in Norway and Australia, conducted in enterprises and unions, communications systems and education (Williams, 1982). This form of planning conference has been used in local communities as well as in new industries in Norway.

The first part of a search conference is a description and analysis of 'the most probable future' as seen by people in policy-making roles. The following are the major trends for the next ten years outlined for Norway; summarised from search conferences from 1977 to 1984.

(1) Continued economic stagnation. Growth may occur in the form of differentiation and restructuring, not as expansion of production. The leading parts of existing industry (e.g. hydro-electric and electro-technical, shipping and chemicals) will form the basis of new industries (e.g. new oil industry and engineering, communication and transportation systems). Unemployment and distribution of income will be major issues.

(2) Mobility from primary to secondary and to tertiary sector culminates will reach fruition. Traditional sectors will be penetrated by new 'domains' (Schön, 1971) covering several traditional branches (e.g. catering, information handling, transportation systems, clothing services, housing systems, maintenance, health and care systems, energy management, resource recirculation, etc.). The decline of traditional trades will be a threat to blue-collar unions.

(3) Information technology will expand into all traditional sectors and into the new domains. This means that control of new technology will become a major political issue and socio-technical design a major challenge—for unions as well as for managements.

(4) 'Orderly marketing agreements' as practised by governments and enterprises will grow. The new oil industry could give Norway an advantage in this respect, but here existing conservative policies are still dominant. Norway's disadvantage as a high-cost country and its slow development towards knowledge-based industries continue to be

problems. Union–management–government coalitions may engender changes in these areas (as seen in shipping and engineering).

(5) Bureaucratisation remains a basic problem in the public and the private sector. Managements, unions and educators in Norway are perhaps better prepared for reforms than in most countries, but the turbulent environment makes leaders hesitant to take the necessary risks. What is referred to as a decision-making crisis in government prevents new coalitions across sectoral and national boundaries. Governmental control is expected to be high, particularly in domains like oil and communication. A legislative approach to labour relations is not expected to grow.

(6) New forms of organisational structures are developing, but traditions among employers and unions may create some kind of 'cramp', paralysing experimentation and learning. New technology and constructive participation agreements during the 1960s and 1970s are continuing to act as major forces of change. Unions may use these forces to maintain power, but they will need to broaden their base of bargaining as well as their competence to enhance their own restructuring and further development. If they fail to do so, traditionally strong unions will continue to lose members and power. New professional and union structures could emerge through new types of coalitions and prevent inter-union rivalry. Such rivalry may threaten the labour relations system, as we have seen to some extent in the oil sector and the academic sector.

(7) Changing values will coincide with alternative family structures and new career patterns and perhaps also with a basic cultural shift. Improved integration of local communities may strengthen equity and participation, while higher geographical mobility will have the opposite effect. In spite of anxiety caused by recession and industrial restructuring, there are few signs that Norway will see a regression to the male-dominated, centrally controlled organisational environment of the early 1960s. Leading domains like oil, shipping and information industries show interesting signs of family and cultural change towards new lifestyles (Melhuus and Borchgrevink, 1983).

(8) Educational restructuring will follow work reforms. Better integration of work and learning will slowly bridge the gap between schools and work life. The split between theory and practice, between over-professionalised and unskilled jobs will be a major issue for some time to come. Restructuring of trade unions and new coalitions with professional associations will be critical for stabilisation of new labour markets.

(9) New concepts of employment and redistribution of paid work and unpaid care may cause basic reforms or widespread confrontations during the late 1980s. Shorter working hours will enhance more flexible careers. Family members will take on different work roles during different phases of life. Some form of guarantee of minimum income may be necessary for solving the unemployment problems and the emerging cost crisis in health and welfare. Altogether, the unions will move from narrow wage bargaining towards broader issues of incomes policy.

(10) Continued international conflicts in East/West and North/South relations are expected to have at least an indirect impact on local economic and cultural conditions. These matters are no longer left entirely to the political establishments to deal with. On the contrary, popular movements are gathering strength and effective networks have emerged across professional, national and other boundaries. These networks may become acceptable means of socio-political change (e.g. in the form of religious, peace and 'green' movements). Or they may, like Solidarity in Poland, become too threatening to the establishment and trigger off major confrontations.

There are obviously different degrees of consensus regarding the ten major trends summarised above. But, if we are to trust the outcome of different search conferences, the years 1977–84 have been characterised by *growing* consensus. These conferences have had representatives from domains as different as the oil industry and tourism, small local communities and central bodies within the labour relations system.

Trade Union Challenges and Strategies for the 1980s and 1990s

If our analysis so far is correct, a number of critical issues are facing the unions:

(1) How can recruitment be maintained and how can different unions avoid destructive rivalry?
(2) How can unions shift their priorities according to the values of old and new members and the ongoing technological and economic changes?
(3) How can unions reorganise themselves to be able to enact new strategies effectively?

How the unions will handle these and related issues not only depends on what they manage to do themselves; what governments and enterprises will do, separately and through different kinds of alliances, will affect the direction in which the unions move.

Recruitment

The traditional recruitment base for the TUC (LO) unions was industry and mining, fisheries and forestry. LO union membership grew with these industries, and transfer from a declining branch to a growing one was a normal procedure until the 1960s. New members in the offices and technical departments of enterprises were recruited by unionised production workers. A union membership of 60–80 per cent of the total number of workers in a company was normal in large branches of industry. In percentage terms, union membership was always lower in the higher echelons of enterprises.

Recruitment patterns started to change in the labour markets of the 1960s. People with higher education started to unite their interests as workers had done before. Governmental and municipal officers and staff, teachers and nurses, etc., became much stronger in terms of membership and their wage claims. Technicians and professionals increased rapidly in number, and their associations acted more and more like workers' unions in negotiations over wages and working conditions.

Two basic issues, apart from the restructuring of industry, impinged on recruitment to the dominant LO unions. One was the increase in the education of employees, the other was the political coalition between the LO and the Labour Party. These two factors started to interact in the 1960s and 1970s. Then, in 1972, the EEC referendum created a watershed in public opinion and political affiliations.

In the late 1970s the main factors mentioned had created a partly new trade union structure. The professional unions outside the LO had continued to grow and had also increased their strength by adapting LO strategies of bargaining. This could hardly have been prevented by the LO. But something else happened simultaneously. Large new groups of young workers entered branches where the LO could have been in a strong position to get new recruitment. This was particularly the case in oil, retail and service industries and in the new welfare professions. To a great extent, the LO missed these opportunities, while other unions strengthened their position.

Perhaps the clearest indication of what happened in the trade union system is the constitution of a new Confederation of Vocational Organisations (YS). Major groups of bank, insurance and some municipal and governmental employees merged their unions in 1977–8. New groups from defence, tele-services, etc., also joined and in six years the new confederation has grown from 80,000 to 120,000 members. During the same period LO membership has declined from 755,000 in 1981 to 747,000 in 1983. It is no coincidence that the president of YS is a woman, 40 years old, from the union of female tele-service-employees.

The recruitment situation for trade unions in Norway will probably continue to change as labour relations move away from the so-called Scandinavian model. Two dominant partners, the LO and NAF (Central Employers' Federation), used to set the standards for wages and working conditions. Every year or second year, they would decide on the sharing of increased productivity. More and more government and municipal employers will now be on the same side of the table as NAF. The LO and several other union groups will be on the other. Or there will be several 'tables' depending on the relations between employers, on the one side, and between unions, on the other. And now there are no productivity gains—or very small ones—to be shared.

If NAF and the government get into a closer coalition to cut costs and speed up industrial restructuring, the unions will probably move closer to each other. Rivalry between union blocks has started to grow—as, for example, when academic groups pressed for higher wage-differentiation around 1980. But the academic groups, on the one side, and the LO and the new YS, on the other, seem to have settled fairly acceptable demarcation lines between them. Rivalry has not been escalated. Private and public employers will have to act with great care in the next few years not to provoke union rivalry, which is bound to cause further turbulence in the organisational environment.

Bargaining

The criticial bargaining issues of spring 1984 indicate the types of dilemmas which will influence future labour relations in Norway.

The iron industry was as usual first in a series of major negotiations. In 1984 as well as in 1982 the LO/NAF could not agree on 'joint and co-ordinated' negotiations, which means centralised national bargaining. During the postwar period this form of centralisation has taken place with an increasing in-volvement of government. Tax and price subsidies have been part of a total package.

In 1982 the metal workers reacted strongly when municipal and governmental workers set the standards for other branches, through the involvement of a Conservative coalition government. In 1984 the metal industry came close to a major strike, but finally on agreement was reached on several basic conditions. First, that a wage increase will give compensation for inflation (at the rate of some 6 per cent). Second, that a minimum wage level for low-income groups will be maintained. Perhaps most important is the fact that the metal workers are willing to limit their wage claims on the local level for the time being only if the government takes more effective action to control prices and to reduce un-employment. Reduced working hours in the near future is one of the union's demands.

Other branches in the private sector have reached agreements along the same lines as the metal industry.

The public sector did not come to an agreement and a short but effective strike took place. The government decided to resort to legally enforced arbitration because 'vital community interests were at stake'.

There were several paradoxes involved in the strike and the arbitration. Unions of the public sector co-ordinated a strike in-volving some income groups with 100,000 Norwegian Krone and some with 200,000 Krone in annual income. Does this mean that wages and salaries are more or less important than before, or that other issues—unemployment, working hours and working conditions—are common priorities of those unions with growing membership? Both explanations seem valid.

Another paradox is that a Conservative government coalition standing for a more market-oriented economy puts legal arbitration into effect. There is little doubt that arbitration has general support among those who voted for the present government as well as most of those voting for the opposition. Does this mean that governmental involvement in wages and salaries is increasing, irrespective of the basic philosophy of the ruling political parties? Or does it mean that other issues—like inflation and unemployment—are of greater political importance? Both explanations seem relevant.

Social Welfare

Social security and welfare issues could have made the spring of 1984 even more of a turning-point. Parliament passed a law to decentralise the health service from national to municipal level. The government made a new compensation agreement with the Medical Association. A large number of municipalities rejected this agreement and major national unions were against it. They claimed that the Conservative government was breaking the principle of equal rights to social services and security. The government, particularly its centre coalition members, rejected this accusation. Its political future depends on the outcome of the public debate in this area.

Amidst this confrontation cities like Oslo have had to cut their social costs significantly. Suddenly, union representatives of health and social workers started to meet with city authorities to work out joint proposals for substantial cost reductions. This will not be forgotten when national contracts are negotiated.

The priorities of the municipal employees are: protection of social services, particularly for children and old people; safety of employment; and incomes policies (including tax) which will protect real income from inflation. Other major demands regarding work environment and participation in management are maintained from agreements made in the 1970s. It is important to note that the major bargaining claims of the Municipal Employees' Union—the biggest national union and affiliated to the LO—are very similar to those of YS which is independent of the LO. Both have about 120,000 members, significantly more than any other union.

New contracts to be bargained in the oil industry may also be significant for the years to come. In oil there is quite a strong rivalry between unions. It is caused partly by the Labour Party affiliation of the LO unions, and partly by the generally anti-union attitude of large international oil companies. They have preferred to deal with non-LO unions—if any unions at all. NAF has tried to bring order to this situation with the full support of government and at least one of the international companies.

The four different unions in the oil industry, in spite of different political orientations, put safety and related working conditions (shifts, etc.) at the top of their list of priorities, together with stable annual income. This means that oil companies have to deal with safety shop stewards and other union representatives in ways they are not used to. The unions, on their side, have members who are moving towards a new work culture, partly because of the nature of their work and learning in high technology, partly because of oil workers' long periods ashore—where family structure and local communities are changing.

Amidst these unstable labour relations national policy on the oil industry is up for revision. A confrontation has been threatening regarding the role of Statoil, the state-owned company. Suddenly, the government and the opposition, with strong backing from the LO, has started to move towards a compromise. This may mean that the major parties involved realise that critical areas of common interest should take priority. The control of national income from oil and an attempt to avoid inflationary effects from oil into other industries are such major interests. And these common concerns cannot be protected if labour relations get out of control.

This illustrates both the increasing interrelatedness and the unpredictability that we have emphasised. A confrontation on national oil policy and related labour relations will obviously increase the turbulence. Compromises and consensus on major issues will decrease it. These issues are not wages and salaries in a limited sense. They are, rather: national policies to control unemployment; broad incomes policies rather than specific wage claims; shorter working hours and flexible pensioning; high standards of social security and work environment.

Union Involvement in Management of Companies

Nationalisation of industry has been pursued only by small minority groups during the 1960s and 1970s. The fear that it might lead to further bureaucratisation of management has been shared by unions as well as politicians. The issue has been part of the continuous debate over industrial democracy. In the early 1960s consensus was reached simultaneously to develop indirect employee involvement in management and concrete reforms in the organisation of work. The latter objective was pursued through widespread experimentation with self-managing groups, new forms of supervisory and specialist roles and changes in planning and information systems. In no other country where similar reforms spread during the 1970s and 1980s did unions and managements act jointly in these matters to the degree they did in Norway.

When diffusion of the new forms of work organisation did not take place as smoothly as expected the issue of employee representation on the boards of companies came to the forefront again. The EEC referendum sharpened the political climate and the unions pushed for reforms, if necessary by legislative measures. In 1973 the new law on enterprise democratisation was passed by Parliament. If the employers had agreed to settle this matter by negotiation the reform would have been less comprehensive. A two-level representative system was introduced, with employees holding one-third of the seats in each body.

In 1977 the new Work Environment Act was passed and included matters of union representation which had previously been handled through negotiations. Parts of the new law supported diffusion of new forms of work organisation, and the introduction of the law was based on local initiatives and local problem-solving.

Before the national election of 1981 the issue of union involvement in management of companies was brought up again by a joint LO and Labour Party committee; 50 per cent representation of employees on boards and concrete changes in work organisation were suggested. The former claim does not seem to have as strong support as the latter one. Both issues were included in the broader mandate of a governmental commission to deliver a report in 1984. The working method of this commission is interesting, since it has included extensive contact with grassroots developments and considerable time has been spent on searching for a common approach by different unions and employers' groups.

The outcome of the new commission will be decisive for developments in this area during the 1980s. Increased activities to promote new forms of work organisation have certainly been initiated, while significant changes in formal representation are less likely to come. The way in which the commission has worked, with strong emphasis on coalitions between different types of unions and on local developments rather than central control, may be significant for labour relations in the 1980s and 1990s.

There have been no echoes in Norway of the Swedish debate on wage-earner funds. Proposals for special arrangements for employees buying shares in companies have been rejected by the LO, while other unions have not taken a strong position on the issue. One possibility may be that employee ownership comes up in a different fashion. In critical situations, local union and management negotiations may lead to short-term agreements where, for example, unions postpone wage claims. If the enterprise survives on this basis and prospers, it would not be unexpected that part of the following year's profit would be claimed by unions perhaps for some kind of local collective fund. Such an arrangement could have saving effects, apart from its major purpose of solving crisis situations. It could also be combined with different forms of employee-owned co-operatives, a system of ownership which is spreading in some countries, particularly in the USA.

The co-operative movement has for a long time been strong in Norway, in agriculture and fishing and in the retail industry. It has never been strong in the production or service industries. A new trend which has emerged in the USA, and which is slowly gaining ground in Norway, is that small companies in the service industry and in high technology are formed on a co-operative basis. This seems to have considerable appeal to young, highly educated people. It also seems that these small companies are innovative. They may stimulate similar trends in the health and care sector. It may also have an impact on national policies to counteract unemployment. This would mean that a combination of co-operative and self-employment activities would be encouraged on a broader scale. There are some indications that sub-contracting and home-work, in manufacturing as well as in office work, are growing. (This is linked to the controversial issue of informal or 'black' labour.)

On the whole, one would not expect major confrontations or

drastic changes in the next few years in the formal system of *indirect* employee or union involvement in ownership or management of companies. If, however, there is a very slow introduction of new forms of work organisation involving employees *directly* in the control of their own work, the situation may become different. A strengthening of small-scale co-operatives and subcontracting systems could become a major challenge to unions, which could change their attitude to ownership control.

The Internal Dynamics of Union Organisation and Capacity for Strategic Change

Increasing in size and getting more and more involved in national politics at the central level, the LO and some of the other large unions lost some of their vitality during the 1970s. When turbulence increased they were forced on to the defensive or relied on traditional approaches and old alliances.

The LO and the Labour Party tried to hold on to old bastions together: economic growth, full employment and solidarity in wage and incomes policy. More conservative unions found allies within a continuously growing public bureaucracy. Rapidly growing unions linked to new technology and the new welfare professions had their own promoters, as did teachers inside higher education, the most rapidly growing institution in the 1960s and 1970s.

Traditional growth factors—industrial expansion, new technology and higher education—pulled the unions along and gradually made them revert to a traditional philosophy and organisational behaviour. With the mid-1970s and the political reaction to the youth and women's movements, most unions followed the conservative trend. The economic recession made those who had much to lose tread carefully. Those who took a more aggressive approach lost public support and were popularly associated with the die-hards of the Mao movement.

The LO initiated and led the drive towards industrial democracy. In the first phase, between 1962 and 1972, the LO and local unions were on the offensive. The national unions seemed to sit back and wait for a national policy to develop. In the meantime, they were fully occupied as before with wage contracts. In many ways this was the way new policies had customarily emerged during the 1950s and 1960s. The LO, with Labour Party support, initiated new policies and expected them to filter down the organisations. They did in fact do so as long as industrial growth continued.

But this was not the way new ideas took hold in the 1970s. It was the way superficial media went from one popular issue to the next. Union as well as political leadership were pulled into the media world and got less and less chance to concentrate on strategic changes. When the grassroots produced new ideas, which they did in the work reform experiments and in some school and local community projects—often led by women—the top of the organisation structures did not catch the wind. They did not help new policies to develop from the bottom up, or through new social networks.

The LO unions did not capture the new mainstream of young potential recruits coming from higher education. Only to a limited extent did the unions organise the great number of women going to work outside the family, often in part-time jobs.

Long service and collective trust within the movement were basic criteria for election to high trade union office. Consequently, young men and women had to wait in line and very few of them got to the top of unions where they could represent new ideas and new values. Most unions missed the chance to let the new recruitment change the profile of the unions and to modify their structure. The older and larger the union is, the more rigid is its structure.

In the case of industrial democracy, unions other than the LO —those for technicians and staff—earned the greatest benefits. They had well-educated and eager members to use the new representative system, initially promoted by the LO (Englestad and Qvale, 1977). The LO unions did hold their positions as strong stake-holders in enterprise affairs. But this was nothing new for them, while it was very much so for staff and technicians' unions.

In Norway, the LO did avoid most of the employer–union confrontations over industrial democracy which took place in Sweden. NAF took a more careful position than SAF when national unions lagged behind in active support of local experimentation. In fact, it looked as if SAF made a special effort to make managements do it alone. NAF avoided this risk of pretending to take over what the LO had initiated. NAF was willing to give support whenever possible, being quite aware that it would take time before local and national forces could merge. This also turned out to be a wise policy when it came to the introduction of the new 1977 Work Environment Act.

The internal dynamics of unions were to some extent affected by the introduction of the 1977 Act. Very concrete issues were to be analysed and tackled by people who did the day-to-day work. Shop stewards' committees were not unaccustomed to dealing with most of the shopfloor and office problems that came up. The LO–NAF technology, equal rights agreements and the joint guidelines for organisational projects supported the work environment reforms. In many cases, this led to more young people and more women taking on the union responsibilities. But again this was mostly at a local, not a national level.

The adult education reforms, also strongly promoted by the LO and other unions in the 1960s and 1970s, had some of the inspiring effects of the Work Environment Act. But the large union educational organisation (AOF) had great problems avoiding the bureaucratisation which usually follows from large-scale activities. To change its educational paradigm may be as difficult for the union movement as it is to change its basic ideas of work organisation and its approach to the control of new technology.

If we return to the six major elements of a potential shift in organisation culture (p. 186), we find that the LO and other large unions have only just started to initiate the new alternatives. The values, the norms and the structure are basically those of the industrial growth period. And the strategies are seldom preactive.

The large unions are to a great extent ruled by their heavy administrative machinery and run as traditional bureaucratic regimes. And one should not overlook the rigid task structure maintained by regular bargaining and contract administration. When the administrative machinery has sapped some of the energy from basic reforms and when all the meetings and media pressure have taken their toll, the strategic capabilities of unions are seriously reduced.

There are signs, however, that the corresponding elements of a cultural shift outside the traditional domains of unions also have an impact upon union strategies. Family structures and local community values are changing and the gulf between work and learning may be bridged by work restructuring and educational changes. New technologies favouring network communication and step-by-step policy-making through experimentation are on their way (Thorsrud, 1981).

The big question is what effects will result from a long-term recession and increased unemployment? As we have stressed several times, strong pressures for change may facilitate new strategies. Too much pressure and escalated confrontation tend to make large organisations stick to their guns.

The ability of trade unions to develop new strategies of change depend on a series of critical factors.

(1) To what extent can they restructure their own organisations and their bargaining machineries? They must cope not only with traditional issues such as wages and working conditions, but also with new common issues like incomes policies under long-term recession, reforms of the education and welfare system and basically new forms of work organisation and employment.

(2) To what extent can the unions avoid rivalry which may reduce their overall impact and destablise further the labour–management scene? Inter-union coalitions on the new common issues will increase their mutual influence and reduce the turbulence in labour relations. Special affiliations with political parties (the LO–Labour Party coalition, for instance) will decrease inter-union collaboration.

(3) Government involvement in labour relations seems to increase irrespective of political orientation. This may not necessarily mean further steps towards the corporate state. It may mean that government, unions and employers' groups in the private and public sector must agree on certain guidelines at a national level. At the same time they may have to agree that experimentation, development and control at local level will have to increase. Such combinations of centralisation and decentralisation may have been impossible or irrelevant during the phase of industrial growth. They may become a necessity for survival and readjustment during the 1980s and 1990s.

References

Emery, F.E. (1981), 'Adaptive Systems for our Future Governance', in F.E. Emery (ed.) *Systems Thinking*, Harmondsworth, Penguin
Emery, F.E. (1983), 'New Perspectives on the World of Work', in *Festskrift til Einar Thorsrud*, Oslo, Tanum-Norli
Engelstad, P.H. and Qvale, T.U. (1977), *Innsyn og innflytelse*, Oslo, Tiden

Melhuus, M. and Borchgrevink, T. (1984), 'Tidsbinding av Kvinner', in Hernes, H. (ed.), *Kvinners livsløp og levevilkår*, Oslo, Universitetsforlaget
Schön, D. (1971), *Beyond the Stable State*, Harmondsworth, Penguin
Thorsrud, E. (1981), 'Policy-making as a Learning Process', in Gardell and Johansson (eds), *Working Life*, London, Wiley
Vickers, G. (1972), *Freedom in a Rocking Boat*, London, Pelican
Williams, T.A. (1982), *Learning to Manage our Future*, New York, Wiley

8   SWEDEN

Anders Leion

Population	8,000,000
Per capita GNP, 1982	US$ 12,000
Exports as per cent of GNP, 1982	27
Number of large companies (among the 500 largest outside the USA)	19 with 570,000 employees
Governments	1945–51 Social Democrat 1951–7 Coalition of Social Democrats/Farmers' Party 1957–76 Social Democrats 1976–8 Non-Socialist three-party coalition 1978–9 Liberal minority 1979–81 Non-Socialist three-party coalition 1981–2 Centre/Liberal minority government 1982– Social Democratic minority government
Public sector (share of GNP, 1982, including transfers)	68 per cent
Trade union membership	1984: 80–85 per cent
Trade unions	Swedish Trade Union Confederation (LO) with a total of around 2,100,000 members (of whom some 850,000 LO members have agreements with SAF employer associations). The Central Organisation of Salaried Employees (TCO) with more than 1,000,000 members. The Swedish Confederation of Professional Associations (SACO/SR), which organises around 225,000 members.

| Employers' organisations | Swedish Employers' Confederation (SAF) dominates with 35 member associations whose 43,000 affiliated enterprises have more than 1,200,000 employees. |

Historical Background

Origin and Dependence of Institutions

The institutions as they exist at present carry within their structures and power patterns and in the actions of their leading personalities memories from the time of their establishment. The LO, the Swedish Trade Unions Confederation, was founded in 1898. The LO's original statutes stated that its functions were to collect and distribute to its member unions statistical information about trade union activities, and to assist the unions in their defensive conflicts and when the right of association was threatened.

From the very start, the relationship between the LO and the already existing Social Democratic Party—founded in 1889—was the subject of discussion. After the inaugural congress, membership of the unions was slow to build up, partly on account of differences of opinion about the relationship with the Social Democratic Party. At the Social Democrats' Congress held at the end of September 1984, the relationship between the LO and the party was once again on the agenda. A decision was made to retain collective affiliation to the party; by the decision of a meeting of its members, or of its Executive Council, a local union branch can affiliate all its members to the party. In such a case, the individual member must personally apply to leave the party, if he or she does not wish to remain a collectively affiliated member.

The relationship between the Social Democratic Party and the LO has always been a problem-filled one. Nevertheless, collective affiliation has been retained and closer collaboration has been built up in many other spheres too. The chairman of the LO is a member of the party's Executive Committee, members of the government are drawn from the LO's senior cadres, the party executive and the LO's national executive engage in regular discussions, etc. Collaboration on political issues has been especially intensive over the past 15 years (see below).

These institutions can adapt themselves to a changing social and political climate. But it is a difficult process that takes time.

The disturbed situation—by Swedish standards—that we have noted in recent years is an expression of the fact that the established institutions are finding it difficult to adapt to changing conditions.

Saltsjöbaden Agreement and Centralisation of Conflict Funds

Over the past few years it has become increasingly common to refer to the Saltsjöbaden Agreement and the Saltsjöbaden spirit (the 1938 basic agreement between the Swedish Employers' Confederation (SAF) and the LO on labour market peace and co-operation was concluded in Saltsjöbaden) as a means of describing a 'Swedish model' that no longer exists. The background and history of the model are as follows.

Ever since its foundation, SAF has been highly centralised, partly because of the wish to control and spread the cost of the insurance protection against conflicts that membership of the organisation offered. Sweden was a country that was plagued by many serious strikes until the 1930s. The member unions of the LO had sovereign rights to decide on conflict action—indeed, even individual branches or unions could decide to call their members out on strike. Power on the employee side was therefore local; local strike initiatives could force the entire union to become involved.

The beginning of the 1930s was marked by a deep recession with high unemployment. In 1932, the new Social Democratic government wished to initiate an expansionary, albeit cautious, policy partly by increasing public sector employment.

This was prevented for a long time by a strike called by the Building Workers' Union. In such circumstances, the government threatened to pass a Bill to introduce government power to impose mandatory control over the use of strike funds—for example, the rights of third parties would be protected and conflicts harming the national interest would be subject to tighter restrictions. It therefore became a joint interest of the labour market organisations to protect themselves against the government. Thus the Saltsjöbaden Agreement was concluded by SAF and the LO.

This agreement assumed that the LO would be able to discipline its member unions and that they in turn would be able to control their local organisations and members. It was not until the Congress in 1941 that the LO secretariat acquired this power, by which the LO secretariat's approval was needed for all strikes of any dimension if the strikers were to be able to enjoy any financial support from the central strike funds.

In this manner, the organisational base was created for the co-ordinated central negotiations that became the dominant pattern after the war. We can summarise the conditions as follows:

(1) a joint interest in being protected against the government;
(2) centralised control over conflict funds on both sides;
(3) a joint interest in maintaining the established order and hence the introduction of sanctions to punish rebels.

The last point is very important. As the control of conflict funds had been centralised, no threat could be directed against the organisations from below. The only way for any section within the whole of this organisational area to pursue a policy that deviated from that of the collective as a whole was to break away—which, in some instances, they did. However, these breakaway groups were never capable of effective functioning: they could not gain the right to negotiate because they were not recognised by SAF. SAF thus protected the centralised power of the LO, in order thereby to retain a counterpart capable of making effective decisions and with full control over the use of conflict funds.

Central, co-ordinated negotiations survived for a long time, from the 1950s into the 1980s. Fairly soon, a sophisticated justification for the system was formulated. According to this—the Rehn-Meidner model—the function of the state was to hold back demand by means of general economic policy, at the same time that the trade union movement adopted a tough pay policy. Some companies would be forced to cut back production or close plants. The labour thus forced out of work, with the aid of a labour market policy intended to increase the mobility of labour, would be channelled towards more efficient companies and industries.

Power over the Business Sector

One of the most often quoted formulations in the Social Democratic Party's programme, usually broadly expressed, is as follows: 'An underlying driving force for any socialist movement must be to transform society so that power over production and its distribution is placed in the hands of the people as a whole.' This is very traditional state socialism. This element of state socialism has always existed in the Social Democrats' debate about, and policy towards, organisations that are dependent on the free market, *viz.* business enterprises. However, very soon a different idea gained ground. In Sweden, this is normally called 'industrial democracy'. This concept was long associated with one of the most important Social Democratic politicians of this century, Ernst Wigforss.

In the Gothenburg programme drawn up by Wigforss, there is no denying an element of state socialism. However, government power was to be supplemented with the active participation of the workers via workers' councils.

In 1920, the first Social Democratic government appointed a commission to inquire into industrial democracy. In the directive to this commission, Wigforss made it clear that by giving the workers the right to determine working hours, working conditions and pay, industrial democracy was a purposeful means of restricting the omnipotence of the employer and therefore of the capitalist. The means of bringing about this change within business enterprises and thus within the capitalist system of production would be what he called 'operative councils'. However, the trade union movement—principally the LO—did not support the proposal. They felt that the party was interfering in areas that were the sole preserve of the unions, and within business enterprises the unions principally wanted to carry on their traditional fight for better pay.

The 1950s and 1960s

During the 1950s and 1960s, centrally co-ordinated negotiations and the government's economic policy were successful. During this time, the Swedish model also attracted considerable positive interest abroad.

At the same time, the Swedish social structure was changing considerably. The country was becoming urbanised. Growing numbers gained their livelihoods by working for central and local government bodies. The proportion of gainfully employed women increased steadily. Taxes took a growing proportion of the gross incomes of individuals and of Gross National Product. The labour market shifted in favour of salaried employees. The number of academically qualified groups grew dramatically. Both the latter phenomena were closely linked with the expansion of the public sector.

The 1950s and 1960s were the Swedish model's golden years. Swedish industry produced and competed efficiently, and there was full employment. Under these favourable conditions the system of centralised negotiations also functioned well. The old ideological conflicts concerning power over business enterprises appeared to have been forgotten.

However, beneath the surface tensions of various kinds were building up. The far-reaching restructuring in industry led to opposition from the disadvantaged areas in the country. Strong centralisation came to be regarded as counter-productive by the labour market, as workers saw the gradual erosion of earlier pay differentials.

New trade union organisations began to appear as competitors to the LO and its member unions. The principal value of centralisation was its co-ordinated, and therefore—from the point of view of the entire union movement—sensible action. But now the problem of free riders arose. The large LO groups could be forced to accept social responsibility for holding down inflation; at the same time, however, other groups could exploit the situation to pursue their own tougher demands.

Suddenly in December 1969, 8,000 workers at the iron mines in Kiruna were called out on strike by their radical local leaders in support of demands for substantial increases in wages and improvements in working conditions. The strike was unlawful and in breach of the statutes of the miners union and the LO, and it was in breach of the agreements with the employers. This strike received enormous publicity and set up a shock wave which reverberated throughout the country and threatened the stability of the Swedish industrial relations system. In this situation, the central LO executive found itself in a tight corner. Once again, the focus shifted towards winning power over business enterprises.

These changes were at the same time powerful forces directed against the established system. When the first major breach of the system occurred in the Kiruna strike, it marked a serious threat to the rules of the game as it had so far been played on the Swedish labour market. During the strike and its immediate aftermath, the action was interpreted in many ways. All these interpretations can certainly provide some element of the explanation. To a great extent, the strike was nevertheless a protest against the policy of incomes solidarity and against the centralisation of decision-making that had become established. The only way for a union organisation at national or local level within the LO to strike outside established negotiating procedures had to be by means of a 'wild cat' strike. The legal strike weapon was locked away in the hands of the LO's national executive.

By the beginning of the 1970s, stimulated by the Kiruna strike, a wave of 'wild cat' strikes spread across the country and the LO and the unions found themselves under growing and increasingly intractable pressure. They had inherited a centralised organisation designed for conducting centralised and co-ordinated negotiations, but these central negotiations were more and more coming under the sway of the policy of incomes solidarity that itself soon consisted of the simple equalisation of all pay, regardless of the type of work for which it was compensation. This approach met growing resistance. How would the LO be able to adapt without abandoning the organisation that had been built up in the 1930s and 1940s?

The solution adopted was to launch an offensive in the very area where the Wigforss commission had failed—industrial democracy, or what is now called corporate democracy. By this means, the LO could offer the unions more influence at the local level without needing to give away any of its own power over pay policy. Employee investment funds were brought on to the agenda for the same purpose. In this way the unions took over a question that they had not previously been able to discuss because they could not decide whether it was a decision that belonged to the sphere of the LO or the party.

The solution to the LO's dilemma was to promise more influence at local level at the expense of the employers and the capitalists.

Centralised Common Sense

Postwar economic policies, controlled for a uniquely long period by Social Democratic governments, in general depended very much on what can be called centralised common sense. There was a general belief in large-scale operations, long series production and centralised decision-making involving understanding and support from unions and employers' organisations.

As far as the labour market was concerned, this meant that full employment was the target. However, this was to be ensured for the labour market as a whole and not within the individual enterprise. Nobody could be guaranteed security at his or her own workplace, but all had to be prepared to move from declining sectors and regions to expanding ones. A further ground for a negotiating system was the policy of incomes solidarity and the idea of a national economic norm. The norm gradually came to be called the EFO model after the names of the economic research officers at the LO, TCO and SAF, but it had also been used earlier. According to this model, it was possible to decide what resources were available to pay higher wages and salaries on the basis of price changes in world markets and adding to these the expected increase in productivity in the sectors of business exposed to competition. The policy of incomes solidarity would in its turn spread the same pay increases through the economy—for instance, to employees in the public sector and building—and bring about an increase in charges and prices that would lead to a general increase in the price level. However, this could be accepted, it was thought, as it took place in a controlled way and did not jeopardise competitiveness.

The demand for mobility of labour determined the structure of the social security system. It came out most clearly in the pensions issue. As a main argument for ATP—the general supplementary pension scheme—it was put forward that the earned pension rights did not depend on where the employee had worked. The pension was determined by the number of years of gainful employment and—within certain limits—the income of the individual. The pension rights were guaranteed by the future production capacity of the entire economy and not by any individual insurance company.

What in actual fact decided the ATP question is unclear. For a long time SAF tried to interest the LO in a negotiated solution, but it seemed as if the LO had decided at an early stage in favour of a legislative solution. Perhaps this is the most important reason why the Social Democratic Party discovered the political value of making the earned pensions of employees a parliamentary issue. But even prior to the parliamentary debate various alternatives —three of them—were being proposed and became the subject of a referendum in 1957. The first was a premium reserve system that was almost in harmony with the proposal in which SAF had tried to interest the LO; the second was the expansion of the basic pension scheme; and the third was the proposal which, after having obtained most votes but not a decisive majority in the referendum, was adopted by Parliament by a majority of one. ATP came to be based on an allocation system where each year's disbursements had to be covered by the same year's income. This meant that the system could be quickly brought into effect, which was a political point and perhaps well suited to the highly expansionist economy of the 1950s and 1960s.

Both the security of the individual's employment on the labour market and his or her future pensions would thus be guaranteed by the entire economic system. The individual employee would have nó reason to become tied to a particular workplace or employer. This independence was regarded as a positive feature. 'The worker's principal means of power is his ability to tell his boss to go to hell and find himself a job somewhere else,' said Gosta Rehn, the LO economist, in a loose translation.

Economic affairs and politics were regarded as matters for the individual employee and voter and the power elite at the very highest level, 'the government and the LO national executive respectively'.

This attitude towards society and the social structure had many advantages. It was probably a condition for the very rapid economic progress that Sweden enjoyed during the first decade of the postwar period.

By safeguarding employment on the labour market and not within the firm, the local unions were weakened, as was the relationship between the individual employee and company management. The build-up of a company's specific expertise and stable relations between the company and individual employees were prejudiced.

To summarise, total national systems without links with the performance of individuals and without any guarantee for the assets of the individual may, in the long term, undermine the rights of the individual and his or her general position instead, as was intended, of offering protection against the full force of collective decisions and enforcement. The explanation is naturally that the central organisations and their representatives are not enlightened despots, but consist of several different groups with conflicting and competing interests.

The 1970s: Economic and Political Disintegration

During the 1970s, the disintegration of the old order continued. The forces bringing this disintegration about may be summarised as follows.

(1) Marginal taxes and progressive taxation increased sharply.
(2) The public sector continued to expand at an accelerating pace.
(3) The difficulties in increasing government revenue from income taxes led to attempts being made to finance the public

sector with the aid of higher payroll levies on employers. The result of this policy, supported by an agreement between government and unions, resulted in dramatic increases in labour costs.

(4) Despite the continuous tax increases, the government's budget deficit swelled—after the increase in incomes from the pay explosion in the middle of the decade had ebbed. The deficit was also a result of the automatic cost escalation and indexation forcing up the level of expenditure in various fields.

(5) Political life became increasingly unsettled. Factors contributing to this were the single-chamber Parliament, as well as the growing irresolution of Social Democracy when the difficulties encountered by the old model became increasingly apparent.

(6) Tax scales were brought into the pay negotiations. Members of SACO/SR were the first group to feel the difficulties, or rather the impossibility, involved in using pay policy—*viz.* increases in gross pay—as an instrument to combat the combined effects of inflation and high marginal taxes.

(7) Dissatisfaction with the policy of incomes solidarity continued and resulted in a wave of 'wild cat' strikes. These strikes, coupled with wage drift, brought added flexibility to the system. At the same time the strikes in themselves undermined the long-term stability of the system. Initially, local trade union representatives were able to express understanding of the 'wild cat' strikes. Gradually, there was also an adjustment at union and central level. The unions started to prefer confrontation rather than understanding and compromise, and this also paid off for some time.

(8) The EFO model ceased to be usable both because fixed exchange rates disappeared in an increasingly uncertain international environment and because the idea of 'the norm' was compatible with a shrinking industrial sector only so long as the public sector absorbed the labour released and thus held down visible unemployment.

(9) Leap-frogging of various groups of employees by each other has increased and methods of making pay and income comparisons have been improved. To some extent, this trend is due to the policy of incomes solidarity having led certain LO groups to feel disadvantaged *vis-à-vis* salaried employees (Metalworkers–PTK problem), and to some extent it is a result

of the continuing levelling process that had encouraged existing high-income groups to develop better yardsticks to argue their case (for example, SACO/SR's lifetime income calculations).

Throughout the entire postwar period, the public sector has been expanding sharply in Sweden. A great deal of the growth in the public sector has taken place under the auspices of bipartite organs.

One example is AMS, the labour market board, which consists of public sector salaried employees and representatives of the labour market organisations. AMS is an organ with a long history, but its present functions were formulated as part of what was called the Rehn-Meidner model. Its function was to increase mobility on the labour market and thus to further growth and minimise inflationary tendencies in the economy.

When the opposition to the mobility policy stiffened and the structural, long-term unemployment became a problem of growing severity, AMS began to take on more selective industrial policy functions. Consequently, the board came to be a corporate board with the function of watching over trends in the industrial sector (not to mention the labour market and sections of the educational field). The extent to which it also controlled them is difficult to estimate.

At certain periods during the postwar period, perhaps principally during the 1960s and 1970s, there was a willingness—on the part of the employers, too—to regard business enterprises as institutions. They were administered by professional corporate managements which had to achieve a balance between the demands the various interests made on the institutions (the interest model). This approach facilitated the growth of a viewpoint and practice concerning society that is known as corporatism.

This approach was destroyed by the persistent economic difficulties that followed in the wake of the first oil crisis. In fact, this crisis made it clear that business enterprises were not eternal institutions. They were organisations that could either change or die. They therefore had no possibility of handling any long-term responsibility *vis-à-vis* the government administration. Instead, their function was to assume responsibility for the changes that were necessary if the economy was to remain vital and dynamic during a period of sharply changing conditions.

The Current Situation

SAF Begins to Tire

The disintegration of norms that occurred during the 1970s, together with the growth of union power centres that competed with the LO, resulted in growing disturbances and persistent threats to labour market peace.

SAF, which had not only been the LO's negotiating counterpart, but also its ally in maintaining the system, began to tire. Instead of labour peace, SAF was faced first of all with 'wild cat' strikes and then by legally decided major conflicts. Instead of a common labour organisation front against the expansionist aims of the state, as in the 1930s, SAF saw itself beaten by the collaboration of the state and its supposed counterpart. In such circumstances, a decision was made to politicise the issues—that is, to seek to influence public opinion with the aid of various campaigns and information programmes.

Once more, a sort of symmetry had been created. The solution of the 1930s had been an agreement between the parties on the labour market to keep the government out. Dire straits had now forced the LO to seek the aid of the Social Democratic Party and, with its aid, establish a political platform that could be offered to the grassroots at the expense of the counterpart employers' organisation. In such circumstances, SAF adopted a similar strategy, but instead of allying itself with any one political party, it turned to the electorate direct.

This represented a deviation from a trend. The labour law offensive of the Social Democrats and the LO had resulted in a political—albeit not a party political—counter-offensive from SAF.

This was accepted by the public after a period of initial opposition. Suddenly, therefore, the employer and the capitalist camps had achieved a goal that had been beyond their reach since the Social Democratic breakthrough, namely legitimacy in the political arena. The general public, the voters, accepted SAF's right to formulate problems and to campaign for specific responses to these problems.

The best-known example yet of a political offensive by SAF is the campaign that has been, and is still being, waged against the employee investment funds that were forced through Parliament by the LO and the Social Democrats. During the gestation period many reasons were put forward for their creation. Their principal purpose, nevertheless, has been to give the LO room, or rather breathing space, to meet the demands of its member unions and individual members that would otherwise not be compatible with the LO's organisation and traditions.*

The unintentional result of the confrontation on this issue was the strengthening of SAF legitimacy on the political scene.

Crumbling Central Power

The economic policy strategy of the Social Democratic government means, *inter alia*, that the industrial sector will be permitted to expand, at least in terms of output. The heavy devaluation soon after the government took office marked the start of this policy.

The devaluation and the international economic recovery that started at roughly the same time resulted in high earnings and excellent scope for exporters to expand. Capacity was created for solid increases in centrally agreed pay increments and for wage drift. In order to benefit from this new potential private sector, employees had to break away from the co-ordinated negotiations —otherwise the restrictions on public sector employees would also be a hamstring on their claims.

The government's own actions, principally the devaluation, have built up solid pressure for change from below. The public sector labour market has been stagnating while the private sector labour market is suffering from shortages of key personnel.

As a result of this pressure for change, which built up just when the established negotiating arrangements were ready for change for other reasons, we can see a situation in the pay round where there is no longer a central power with access to natural sanctions.

The union and employer association negotiators have tasted the promise offered by free negotiations—and the power this devolves to them. And they seem satisfied.

---

* The Swedish 'Employee Investment Funds' are not funds owned by the employees through which they invest in the company where they are employed. They are five general funds that buy shares in any company they choose through the stock market. A majority of the members of the fund boards consists of trade union nominees. The capital for the funds is raised by the state in the form of payroll levies and profits taxes which are paid by the employers. No dividends are paid either out of the capital or from the income, to individual employees or enterprises.

The effective centralised power—the LO and SAF block—has already started to crumble away. Without their central authority, it will come down to the survival of the fittest. The two main organisations have to some extent abdicated voluntarily. SAF and the LO no longer possess the mandate of their members to negotiate on their behalf.

Conflicts between Private and Public Sector

Even before this, the centralised power of the LO and SAF was threatened. New, strong groups had sprung up with interests of a different type. They could principally be found in the public sector employees' unions. Throughout the 1970s, employees saw their purchasing power failing to increase. The employers' labour costs, on the other hand, continued to rise. The difference was the continuing rise in payroll levies that were intended to finance the expansion of the public sector.

Gradually, it became clearer that the public sector employees had interests that are by no means the same as those of private sector employees. This picture has clarified further now that public sector expansion has come to a halt. Whatever crumbs are devoted to one purpose have to be taken from somebody else's cake. In these circumstances, the lastest conflicts between public sector and private sector employees—so long hidden by strong economic growth and the increase in government borrowing—come to light. Public sector employees, therefore, feel themselves threatened and stick together. They wish to retain their negotiating cartel and other joint organs.

Public sector employers never gained the right to function as a counterpart to what SAF once was. This was mainly due to their principal, the government, always being inclined to value the political benefit of labour market peace higher than the long-term benefits of a moderate pay agreement. Governments also have a natural inclination to regard the people who work for them as voters and not merely as employees.

The Future

The Brakes. Trade unions in the modern sense are the child of industrialism. It was only with the creation of a developed labour market that trade unions could be formed. It can equally truly be claimed that the unions are the child of the market.

Nowadays, we can see the dependence of the unions on the market most clearly when unemployment is rising. It weakens the unions, even if the initial disturbances on the market lead to stepped-up enlistment of new members.

The objective of the unions is to raise wages. Despite all the widening of union activities that has occurred, pay negotiations still make up the backbone of union activities. This is reflected, for instance, in the internal power structure within trade union organisations. The negotiators always have the highest status. They are engaged in 'producing the goods' for the organisation.

In these two respects—market dependence and simple goals—unions are similar to business enterprises. The differences arise principally as the result of the unions being democratic organisations, *viz.* the rule 'one man, one vote' applies. Decisions are made collectively, the majority decides, while the minority loses. The constant tendency towards narrower pay differentials is explained by the unchanging need to create a majority and the capacity to maintain it at the expense of the minority.

Collective decision-making is difficult. If they are to function effectively, organisations above a certain size have to create an executive elite. Without this elite, the organisation will not be capable of surviving. Once national organisations have been created, the attraction to many of accepting a free ride becomes irresistible. The contribution of the individual member, however willingly and enthusiastically it is made, means very little to the organisation. The same applies to those who are passive. Collective agreements will go on being made anyway. So what are the dynamic forces that keep the organisation going? It is the private interests of the elite. They can build up their own positions: a professional career, and one that is well rewarded in terms of money, power and reputation. Thus are oligarchies created. And organisations become trapped in the 'iron law of oligarchy' formulated by Michels, the German sociologist.

*The Iron Law of Oligarchy.** In 1911, Robert Michels published an analysis of the development of the German Labour Party in which he expressed his disillusionment. The name of the book, which has become one of the world's classics of sociology, is *Zur Soziologie des Parteiwesens in der modernen Demokratie—uber die Oligarchischen Tendenzen des Gruppenlebens.* Although Michels based his thesis on observations of the Labour Party, he argues, quite sensibly, that the same tendencies apply in all organisations.

Michels's theme is very simple. He argues that all representative

* This and the following section are based on an essay by Patrik Engellau, 'Samhallsradet'.

organisations exhibit an irresistible tendency to develop a professionalised and elitist leadership increasingly divorced from the rank-and-file membership and that the elitist leadership will become increasingly conservative, in the sense that it will be mainly concerned with protecting its organisation. 'From having been a means to an end, the organisation will turn into the end itself.'

The effect of Michels's iron law of oligarchy on a mass movement, such as a party or a trade union which can only operate efficiently with a hierarchical system of government, means that with time the leadership of the organisation will rise above the masses and become part of the elite of a society.

The Swedish Law of Oligarchy. Robert Michels's notion of the relationship between the state and the organisation whose development he describes reflects the historical circumstances during which he lived and observed society. At that time, the state was almost by nature hostile to socialist movements and this, Michels argues, set the tone of their relationship.

The existence of the party is constantly threatened by the state which gives it the possibility to exist, and this means that the party, after having reached a certain level of development, is careful to abstain from activities that could irritate the state too much.

Michels's iron law of oligarchy therefore had a built-in force which stopped it from developing beyond a certain point. As the oligarchy became divorced from the grassroots, it increasingly lost the power which could provide it with the force to vanquish its adversary (the state).

Looking at the Swedish situation at the end of the 1960s and in the early 1970s, we find that the situation postulated by Michels does not apply. The Social Democratic state governed by a party which shared a common ideology with the workers did not repel the upward movement of the oligarchy. On the contrary, the state quite willingly let itself be invaded by radical forces. There was room for the oligarchy to continue its movement upwards and into the welfare state.

In Sweden, the iron law of oligarchy operated more freely than Michels himself expected. We may therefore introduce a Swedish law of oligarchy, which is an extension of the iron law and which can be summarised as follows: when threatened by its grassroots, a Swedish oligarchical organisation will continue its march in an attempt to form an alliance with the state and with the intention of using the state to achieve its purposes, rather than relying solely on its membership.

Michels's thesis of the iron law of oligarchy is a telling illustration of the conditions under which mass organisations and the process of collective decision-making evolve. Trade unions are a classic case of mass organisations for collective decision-making and they are subject to all the general conditions which determine the evolution of organisations of this kind.

The trade union organisations are faced with a serious dilemma. They must, if they are to remain of interest to their members, decentralise their activities. They must be able to deal with a great many issues that can only be grouped locally: work environment, work organisation, influence. They must also be able to appear as the legal representative of the individual employee when his or her long-term investment in expertise specific to an individual enterprise and in personal relations at work is threatened, *viz.* when the tacit contract is breached.

If the union organisations can decentralise their organisations in this way, then, on the other hand, they have every chance of continuing to function effectively and of surviving. They will earn their keep by providing increasingly individualised services.

However, their historically inherited, centralised structure makes it very difficult for them to change their organisation. The structure reflects Michels's thesis concerning the iron law of oligarchy, and they are trapped by the government's desire for centralised negotiations. The state can influence only central negotiations. Now, as in the 1930s, the state would like to see labour market organisations that are strictly controlled from the centre so that it can discipline the labour market, but the organisations no longer have the same opportunity to discipline their member associations/unions and individual members.

Conclusion

In the 1930s, a spirit of compromise built up between unions and employers, expressed in the Saltsjöbaden agreement, through the common interest of the LO and SAF in protecting themselves against the power of the state and the scope for increased influence for the senior executives of the organisations that this opened up. Today, further centralisation is no longer possible, although the state is still demanding it. The top executives of the organisations could attempt to comply with the wishes of the state, in order thereby to preserve their own influence—but they would fail.

This is the principal conclusion that can be drawn from the foregoing analysis. The picture is complicated by the interests of public sector employees and employers and their standpoint *vis-à-vis* the representatives of the state. They have every reason to seek to preserve centralisation as long as the public sector is organised in the way to which we have become accustomed. In the next few years, most conflicts on the labour market will originate in clashes between the differing interests and power structures of the private and public sectors. These conflicts will be played out in a political environment of growing volatility. The political parties will no longer group themselves solely along a right–left scale. New groups include environmentalists and representatives of a type of 'new moralism' (the name is not used in any derogatory sense). Class voting will decline in favour of conviction voting. Overall, this means that the voters will have a richer panorama from which to make their choice. This is in harmony with long-term socio-economic trends. A higher standard of living will add to this picture.

In such a situation, the Social Democratic Party will find itself in a difficult position. It must make a response to these political currents, by an appeal to the new middle-class voters, while remaining for financial and other reasons tied to the LO. The LO is, as we have seen, highly conservative. In some sense it must also remain so. It organises the wage-earners, a dwindling group in the labour market.

But the labour market is becoming increasingly dominated by salaried employees. Employees will prefer to have trade union organisations that can support them on the spot, at their work-place. They will want organisations that are effective locally. The game being played at the central level will gradually lose its interest. If the unions are to survive, they must become decentralised. Otherwise, the employees will become more interested in individual agreements with their employers.

9 TRADE UNION TRENDS IN WESTERN EUROPE: A EUROPEAN PERSPECTIVE

Roland Tavitian

This chapter is not presented by a specialist in industrial relations, but by an economist who has progressively become aware of the importance of industrial relations and of so-called consensus in the smooth and effective operation of a modern economy, especially from the standpoint of international competitiveness. To be more explicit, one could suggest that there are three different ways of looking at unions in an industrial society.

(1) They may be considered as representing the interests of their members—both in the sharing of income and in the organisation of work. This is the traditional view of economists.
(2) In a broader sense, they may be considered as representing the values and aspirations of their members and the social groups they represent in a complex and diversified society.
(3) Finally, and as a projection of the preceding from the standpoint of society at large, they can be looked upon as one set of institutions having a number of specific roles in the overall functioning of the social fabric—not only to transmit claims or signals from the bottom to the top, but also to ensure arbitrations between conflicting claims from their members and to transmit some important signals (such as economic data) from the top to the bottom.

This last function is probably the most difficult to elicit. It is also particularly difficult to build upon in a period of rapid change, where the basic traditions and assumptions of the trade union movement (and of industrial relations) have to be questioned. It seems to me, however, that it is an intrinsic part of any policy discussions on our subject-matter.

Bearing this in mind, this chapter will first attempt a summary interpretation of the basic changes going on in the economic environment and the challenges they imply for unions and for

222

industrial relations. It will then sketch out a tentative synthesis of trade union trends in Western Europe—based partly on the highly interesting national reports presented, partly on personal experience. It will finally present some thoughts on the development of trade union and industrial relations activity at the EEC level.

A New Context for Industrial Relations in Western Europe

Industrial relations—as we have known them in the postwar period—have been an intrinsic part of a successful economic system that enabled most Western Europeans to more than double their real income *per capita*, to close up a good part of the income gap compared to the USA, to ensure full employment and to establish model welfare policies. Internal class struggles were resolved and even traditionally fearful and protectionist populations were convinced of the virtues of open trade and international solidarity.

Yet over more than ten years, this economic context has completely changed. Growth rates for OECD countries as a whole have come down from an average of 4.5 per cent to between 2.5 and 3 per cent. Most experts expect medium-term average rates of the order or 1.6–2 per cent for Western Europe, and around 3–3.5 per cent for the USA and Japan.

For Western Europe at least, full employment is no longer an achievable target, social protection systems have to be substantially overhauled, the traditional yearly increase in real wages has to be forgone for some time.

This slowing-down coincides with a number of deep changes which will require substantial adjustments in personal and collective behaviour:

(a) Substantial changes have appeared in the international economic equilibrium and in the international division of labour; the emergence of Japan and the newly industrialised countries, and also the partial catching-up by most European countries with US standards of living and productivity.

(b) International economic interdependence has strengthened considerably and so it becomes increasingly difficult to regulate it from the economic and monetary standpoints.

(c) The rapid evolution of technologies, especially in the field of information technologies, has a profound effect on production and employment conditions, and frees a labour force whose reallocation cannot be ensured without substantial efforts requiring new approaches.

(d) Social demands and individual attitudes have evolved extensively, often as a result of the very success of the period of prosperity. The need for personal fulfilment, the search for other forms of solidarity, the transformation of attitudes to work, are important features to which traditional private and public economies have some difficulty in adapting.

Substantial adjustments are required: they are particularly difficult to achieve especially in Europe, because of the growing frictions between the production system, on the one hand, and its physical and human environment, on the other. Enterprises are burdened with increasing constraints not only in terms of costs, but also in terms of rules and regulations. These rules express to a large extent the efforts of the public authorities to reduce the costs (unquantified) of growth in terms of environment or living and working conditions.

Many of the basic tenets by which we have been living in Western Europe are thus challenged—even the belief in European (or white supremacy in research and innovation.

Yet the prospect is not for stagnation. The contrast between needs to be satisfied and resources that remain idle points to the key issues: they are related to the reallocation of resources, both people and capital, and to the need for more flexibility and responsiveness to new demands.

Such a process of reallocation relies mainly on innovation, investment and work organisation; it is bound to take place on a decentralised level; the enterprise is the best judge of the choices to be made and of the risks it will take. Economic considerations and social trends thus converge to emphasise the need for decentralised approaches.

This is being felt by an increasing part of public opinion in Western Europe. It is striking that in so many countries, past emphasis on the responsibilities of the state is losing ground in favour of an increasing reliance on industry and enterprise.

Many signs point to an encouraging response to the challenges ahead in terms of performance, competitiveness and return to a sound growth. But this positive response will not mean a return to the Golden Age of the 1960s, for it seems bound to imply at least two major casualties: the end of guaranteed full employment, and a marked decline in social solidarity *à la* Beveridge.

Challenges for Unions

Such a context challenges the unions on several grounds. As more diversified membership, especially with women and the young, makes it more difficult to define straightforward priorities in unions' claims, it also questions the traditional quest of union policies for uniform standards (e.g. a standard working time or a standard work status). The poor prospects in terms of yearly real wage increases weaken what has been for decades the unions' most immediate reward to their members. New tensions appear between categories of workers defending their relative status, which challenges the authority of central organisations. The centralised collective bargaining systems, where they exist, appear unable to cope with the diversified approaches required for wages, for working time, for work organisations. Unions have more difficulty in delivering their traditional goods. They undergo a double risk: less loyalty from their members, and less acceptance by the public. Yet, the weakening of unions also means the weakening of industrial relations.

Challenges for Industrial Relations

Traditional collective bargaining items are tending to dwindle. The pressure for decentralised wage settlements unleashed the strength of small professional groups within unions defending their narrow interests (corporatism).

The major risk of an all-out move towards decentralised responses is not only to forgo social solidarity, but also to lead to forms of social division or anarchy that would be counterproductive even in economic terms.

Social cohesion is, after all, a key asset in international competition. The USA does not have to worry about it since the size and the wealth of the country are such that one can hardly imagine a type of social tension which would disrupt the whole nation's economy. Japan seems also to be protected from such a risk, simply because of the strong collective identity of that country. On the other hand, West European countries seem exposed to such major disruptions (*vide* UK)—mainly because they have to question some of the basic tenets of the social systems they so successfully established 40 years ago.

Industrial relations were a major part of this compromise. What is suggested here is to look not only at how they might evolve, but also at how they might help the economy to evolve.

The Future of Trade Unions and Industrial Relations in Western Europe

Any attempt to forecast future trade union attitudes is a for-midable task—especially when one tries to do it from an overall European standpoint. Apart from the diversity of national situations, there are at least three major obstacles to this.

(1) Trade union policies and practices are, in all Western European countries, a unique combination of pragmatic responses and programmatic ideologies. To deduce their future attitudes from their programmes is often misleading—and even the French Communist-inspired CGT, as an extreme case, is renowned for its pragmatism at shopfloor level.

(2) Trade unions (and industrial relations) are—as said earlier—an intrinsic part of our social systems. Trade union attitudes and behaviour will be determined to a large extent by the way the other parts of the system behave.

(3) Whilst most trade union leaders are fully aware of the deep nature of the crisis, they still uncomfortably operate an apparatus run on longstanding and outmoded bases (cf. CFDT's warnings to the French Socialist government).

To sum up, trade unions have mainly a reactive function. Neither programmes, nor official statements can serve as a reliable analytical basis; and their main 'political' target (i.e. solidarity) cannot be achieved by simple, 'linear' means as was possible 20 years ago.

French unions are learning that nationalisation and state inter-vention will not resolve the conflicts between the 'general' interest and the workers' own interests. German unions are accepting a decentralised approach to working-time reduction which will be a far cry from the demand for a standard 35 (or 38) hours.

After these cautionary words, I shall jump in at the deep end and present an impressionistic view of present and possible future trends. The first (and already risky) step will be to compare, simply by pointing up their similarities and differences, the trade unions and industrial systems in Western Europe. Next it is worth looking at some of the major issues that are being dealt with —particularly in Germany, France and Italy. It will help us to understand the changes going on in trade union attitudes and in industrial relations. Finally, tentative answers will be given to some of the questions raised by the SAF memorandum at the outset of this investigation (see Introduction).

Differences and Similarities in European Trade Unionism: Different Forms, Different Backgrounds, Common Features

Any careful analysis of trade union activities in Western Europe must first stress the basic dissimilarities between countries. No two single countries have similar patterns. Trade unions have been shaped in their structures and in their life by different parallel histories, by different environments. It is worth illustrating this by a short summary.

Yet in spite of their diversity, they present some common traits to an outside observer, say from the USA or Japan. These common traits can be observed more basically at the level of their goals and the role they seem to play in our societies.

Differences in the Organisation and Operation of National Systems. Denmark, Norway and Sweden are accustomed to strong central confederations with central collective bargaining and strong links with the Social Democratic Party. The situation in other West European countries is substantially different, especially as regards trade union structure, since most South European and Benelux countries have 'plural' unionism. Neither Germany nor Britain operates central bargaining, and in France it is very limited. Plural unionism entails a different sort of political link (very complex in the case of France and Italy); the political link in Germany is of a very different nature from the Nordic ones.

Another significant source of difference—perhaps of special importance today—is in the degree of union participation in the management of social security. Scandinavia and Britain have, broadly speaking, a 'universal' system of social security essentially run by the state; Central and South European countries have historically shared the responsibility of social security management between the state and the two sides of industry—unions are involved as partners, to a variable extent, in managing boards.

Sharp contrasts thus emerge between national trade union organisations and bargaining systems. Yet it will be suggested that behind these differences, there are some basic similarities.

Similarities in Broad Goals and Values. These are more difficult to identify, but I suppose an informed (and impartial) observer could present the following assessment.

In the first place, all West European unions pursue a goal of solidarity, which generally started from class solidarity but which has moved towards a broader concept of social solidarity. The welfare state, in its British or its German version, was an outcome of this concept and excused unions for some time from looking at the cost of transfers. Its crisis now forces unions to take a hard look at social security, much more so in those countries where they participate in its management. Several of them participate today in the search for 'new solidarities' of a more decentralised sort at the local level.

Secondly, most West European unions have, through their central organisations, an arbitration function which has proved, and may remain, crucial to the working of our societies. One aspect of this arbitration is obviously related to wage claims. Even in countries without central collective bargaining, central executives exert an advisory influence on sectoral unions' positions —for example Germany and France. If one looks beyond that, one encounters many other aspects of this role of arbitration. One of them is the choice between the varying, and often conflicting, claims of their members; even at sectoral or company level, each union has to harmonise the claims of various levels of skills or competence and various categories of individuals. For that matter, women and young people considerably broaden the range of possible choices; they make arbitration considerably harder, while at the same time questioning some of the traditional union values—attitudes to part-time work, for instance. Finally, even their political or ideological leanings force them to arbitrate between far-reaching reforms and routine bargaining. More than anywhere else, European unions are concerned with societal issues which may lead them towards utopias or generous programmes, but they have to relate such programmes to hard day-to-day issues and experiences. In short, in all European countries, European trade unions have until now been one key element in the complex process of regulation, or 'steering', that contributes to the cohesion of our societies and to their evolution.

The third and last aspect that must be mentioned is the positive attitude of unions towards international issues, especially of an economic character. Trade union leadership, at least in the European continent, shares a fairly common positive view of international trade and developing countries. It is a combination of idealistic solidarity with the rest of the world, and especially the poor, and of practical understanding of the negative consequences of protectionistic policies supported both by prewar experiences and perhaps by participation in Brussels discussions.

Clearly, this last is not a neat doctrine: it often hides behind illusory shadows, as, for instance, the once fashionable demand for 'fair trade' and for social clauses in EEC agreements with developing countries. It cannot be clear-cut; here again unions have to arbitrate between the interests of the sectors directly affected by imports, such as textiles, and those of other sectors which benefit in terms of their own efficiency or welfare by those imports. Words and shadows are often of considerable help in achieving such arbitrations, but by and large both the European Trades Union Congress and most of its members support the open-trade policies of the EEC. There seems to be a sharp contrast here with US trade union attitudes.

Unions and the Management of Change

Under present circumstances, there is often a sharp contrast between public statements by unions and their actual behaviour in bargaining or negotiations. Brief reference will be made here to the way some of the important medium-term issues are being handled. It may give some insight into their attitudes to change. Three cases will be discussed, concerning Germany, Italy and France, respectively.

The recent German agreements are the first case of interest, illustrating as they do how entrenched positions on both sides can be modified step by step. The main union demand was a 35-hour week to be reached over five years. In fact, the actual agreements were fairly diversified. In the case of the metal industry, the final agreement was on the following basis:

(1) The normal weekly working time was brought down from 40 to 38½ hours, with the possibility of varying between 37 and 40 hours to take account of company requirements, to

be compensated over a period of two months. This will be implemented in 1985.

(2) Basic wage increases were set at 3.3 per cent as of 1 July 1984, and 2 per cent as of 1 April 1985 (less than the probable rate of inflation).

(3) Company working-time schedules can be arranged in a flexible manner within the above framework.

Two major points are worth nothing. Unions have accepted a differentiation of approaches from company to company. They have also accepted, within a plant, more flexible operating hours. This would appear to be a significant step towards a situation where the collective agreement sets an overall framework, whilst actual schedules or norms are set at company level.

Let us now turn to Italy, where an important framework agreement was signed on 22 January 1983 between unions, employers and the government. Two of the key issues at stake were the adjustment or possibly the withdrawal of cost-of-living clauses and the reduction of working time. After lengthy and difficult discussions, a framework agreement was signed, comprising four major elements:

(1) The cost-of-living adjustment factor in collective agreements would be reduced so as to limit it to about 20 per cent of its full previous impact.

(2) Employers agreed to a reduction of 50 hours on a yearly basis—staggered over three years.

(3) Wage increases for the two coming years were limited by an overall ceiling.

(4) The government agreed to increase family allowances.

The last example is the negotiation in France of social security benefits and financing. As has been said earlier, the management of the French social security system is tripartite and complex. On the basis of a presidential guideline aimed at putting a ceiling on social security contributions levied from enterprises, a number of negotiations were started in the course of 1983 on health, retirement and unemployment benefits. The agreements, concluded early in 1984, resulted in:

(1) Substantial downward readjustment of benefits.

(2) A basic reform of the unemployment benefit system.

The major feature here is that the unions for the first time accepted an agreement which reversed the traditional method of balancing social security expenditure by increasing government subsidies and employers' contributions.

Similar examples could be given for Holland, Belgium or Denmark. The necessary reversal of previous trends or habits will not take place without protest or complaint. Nor will it result in neat and unambiguous agreements.

Participation in Companies and 'Political' projects

While increased participation in company 'control' remains a major concern for several European unions, it seems that it does not receive top priority or manage to become embodied in legislation.

There is, of course, the special case in France of nationalisations (already referred to) and the recent legislation on workers' rights, but the latter was mainly a matter of adjusting French practices in line with the situation of advanced industrial countries (with some bits of French legalomania) and it seems to have been well accepted by the modern part of industry.

It might be appropriate here to suggest a generalisation, inspired by the French experience, but also valid in Southern Europe at least. Trade unions are realising that with the massive, and highly differentiated, changes under way, the enterprise level is the only one where bargaining, in the broadest sense, has a chance to develop substantially. They are also aware that issues related to work organisation, peculiar to each company, are the key ones as regards both the success of the firm and many of the workers' expectations. Both these considerations lead them to centre their attention at the enterprise level. A growing scepticism about the potential for legislation leads them to put emphasis on negotiation and on the search for dialogue.

Some Tentative Answers to the SAF Memorandum

The tendency towards decentralised bargaining seems inescapable. It is more difficult to accept in those countries, like Scandinavia, where centralisation was at its strongest. But, as Norbert Blum, the German Labour Minister has said, it is difficult to dismember tariff agreements altogether—there must be some common denominator, some common framework. The challenge here is to define this framework in a practicable way. It is also, then, to ensure the right links between company-level actions and their framework. It may prove as difficult for employers as for unions and needs innovative thinking.

The need to forgo the traditional yearly increase in real wages leads unions to look for other areas of legitimation. The pattern seems to vary from country to country, but it may take three different courses.

(1) Within the enterprise, unions may look for a more active presence which will oscillate between problem-oriented consultative, or participative, practices, and more dogmatic, centrally imposed legislation. The Benelux, French and Italian cases seem to contrast with the Swedish fears of radical projects. One might think that the increasing recognition of the importance of the enterprise would rather reduce the risk of radicalisation at that level. The experience of the French nationalisations, supported only by one part of French unions, shows in practice how difficult it is to reconcile the 'general interest' with the employees' concerns. The recent laws extending workers' rights do not seem to have basically worsened company relationships. Much will depend, however, on the ability to use existing arrangements to cope with the social aspects of technological change.

(2) Outside the undertaking, the unions' attitude towards legislation is mixed. Perhaps they share to an increasing extent the general scepticism in regard to government efficacy. At the same time their weakening might, at a later stage, result in increased calls for legislation. On the other hand, one must remember that the adjustment or overhaul of social security systems will involve a great deal of effort in bilateral or trilateral processes, especially in Central and Southern Europe.

(3) Unions are also responding in some countries to decentralisation trends by developing their participation in local development activities, in training, and in social security agencies. Some of the confederations are trying to reinforce their regional or local units for such purposes.

The question of the future strength of the unions is the most controversial. Clearly, many of the unions in Europe are registering a decline in membership and also in a much more differentiated way, in acceptance. At the same time, however, the increase in the pressures exerted by some sectional groups—civil servants, for instance—and the difficulty for governments to get a real grasp on events on the socio-economic front perhaps increase the role of the trade unions—both as arbitrating agents within their membership, and as spokesmen in private talks rather than in public statements.

This is a very hazardous guess. It first implies that the union leadership both understands the challenges it is facing and is responsive to its membership. In the second place, it is perhaps more applicable to unions operating in Latin-type societies where situations are often hazy and unstable and words often serve as screens, than to Nordic-type societies where there is an expectation both of a clear-cut framework and of words saying what they mean.

Prospects for Industrial Relations at Community Level

Moving now to the question of industrial relations at the EEC level, we enter on to even more controversial ground. The front of the stage is occupied by the battle on the Vredeling Directive, and to a lesser extent, by the discussions on working time. This is, however, only the tip of the iceberg and perhaps a misleading view of it.

Ever since the formation of the EEC, the question of some sort of industrial relations at Community level has been raised by some people within the context for social harmonisation, often from very divergent points of view. On the one hand, most of the trade unions of the founding members supported, though sometimes half-heartedly, the process of European integration and particularly the common market; but they were at the same time concerned that the market might reduce their own capacity for action. Similarly, industry in the same countries was keen on social harmonisation as a necessary condition for a single market, but could not see the ways and means to achieve it in an orderly way.

Discussions were quite lively both on the practitioners' side within unions and employers' organisations, and among theoreticians. The same questions reappear now, in a much more critical situation—and in a very different context.

Should the Community have any dealings with national industrial relations, or should it try to remain neutral towards them?
Should it try to develop its own level of industrial relations, or
should it abstain in this area?

It may indeed appear as a paradox to talk about industrial
relations at the European level at a time when: (1) there is a fairly
broad consensus in Western Europe about the need to decentralise
collective bargaining from the national level downwards; and
(2) unions have little to offer at European level. Yet the problem
is there, and the ETUC (European Trades Union Confederation),
UNICE (Union of Industries of the European Community) and
the Commission have to face it.

The first part of this section will be devoted to this major and
highly controversial issue, looking at some of its facets for the coming
years. The main thesis will be that Community-level industrial relations will appear both necessary in principle, but disappointing in
practice, as long as they consist of duplicating at Community level
methods and practices inspired (or copied) from national experiences. Community-level industrial relations will only develop if
they find their own, original ways, still to be invented.

The second part will argue that this invention cannot start
merely from the top (i.e. from the institutions downwards) and
that its development must rely on the ability of the major actors to
foster new patterns and new practices of a multinational, 'trans-
European' character. Examples of this decentralised, but
multinational, approach will be discussed first in relation to large
companies, and second around the concept of European
'networks' of affinity to be developed in due course.

The Debate on European-level Industrial Relations

Views on the prospects for the development of a European level of
industrial relations are radically divided on three distinct lines of
thought, which do not correspond to a simplistic opposition between both sides of industry.

The first line of thought is that offered by outright opponents to
any substantial development in this area. They rationalise their
opposition on several major grounds. Some of them simply deny
any positive role to unions. Others feel that national systems are
much too different from one another to be able to generate some
kind of common, practical ground for substantive agreement; or,
in a different and perhaps more subtle approach, that social issues

(and conflicts) are too sensitive and should be managed and solved responsibly within national boundaries. Finally, there are those who see that experience since the mid-1970s has merely resulted in attempts by unions to present claims at an additional level (*un 'troisième guichet'*) superimposed on those presented at national or sectoral level.

The second line of thought, almost as heterogeneous as the first one, is pursued by those who feel that economic integration (the common market) needs some sort of social 'regulation' which cannot rely simply on official, institutional, policies of the sort the European Council and the Commission are developing. The followers of this line fall mainly in the trade union camp, mostly in Benelux, Italy and France; but they also emerge among some policy-makers who feel that progress towards monetary integration will, sooner or later, call for a harmonisation in wage patterns which cannot simply rely on monetarist policies (these are sometimes incompatible allies).

Some time ago, this second group had also many followers on the employers side in the founding countries. Disappointing experience with the numerous meetings in Brussels have led them to turn towards a third line of thought which may be called sceptical pragmatism. Advocates of this approach do share the concerns of the second group, but don't see—in the fundamentally different situation of the economy, the successive enlargements and the inability of ETUC and UNICE to cope with present issues—any prospect for practical moves in the near future.

Rather than attempting to forecast what could actually happen, we shall concentrate here on some of the basic aspects of the issue, as it appears in 1984 from a prospective viewpoint.

An Embryonic Structure of Industrial Relations is at Hand

The question of the Community social dialogue, as it is usually called, has been under consideration since the 1960s. The Rome Treaty had defined one institutional aspect, by creating the Economic and Social Committee, wherein national social actors meet mainly to voice a concerted viewpoint on Community developments and initiatives. Very soon afterwards there appeared the need for the creation of representative structures at Community level for workers (European Trade Union), and for employers (Employers' Liaison Committee, Union of Industries of the European Community). This led to the prudent creation of the

Standing Committee on Employment (1969)—a forum for dialogue between these organisations—the Council (Employment Ministers) and the Commission and to several tripartite conferences (including also the Finance and Economic Ministers). Their achievements are generally regarded as disappointing.

The structures are there then, but nevertheless the dialogue limps along. The Standing Committee on Employment meets regularly but has failed to achieve one of its main objectives, which was to stimulate dialogue between the social partners and to ensure its follow-up. A dead-end has been reached, not due solely to the seriousness of the general economic situation—which has caused positions to harden—but also to certain special factors:

(1) The Community social dialogue cannot be a simple transposition of national practices; it must be based on needs perceived at Community level.

(2) The practice and purpose of intersectoral discussions vary widely from country to country. They are non-existent in some of the most advanced countries, except at a very informal level.

(3) While the aims of the discussions have broadened considerably in the last ten years they have at the same time become hazier. Views on diagnosis and remedies diverge not only between labour and management, but also within each side.

(4) These internal differences lead to a forced alignment of views within each camp, on the basis of the smallest common denominator. Dialogue is then engaged on the basis of abstract and extreme positions which tend to lead to polemics.

Overcoming Formidable Difficulties

As soon as these structures were established, in the early 1970s before the 1973 enlargement, they had to cope with major problems. The main one was their actual role. They tended, and still tend, to work mainly as a source of pressure on Community public policies in the social, economic and industrial areas, but were not able to develop their own authority towards their constituents as an autonomous source of norms for industrial relations. The latter direction would have implied a will and an ability to take joint commitments at the European level, which would be implemented by both sides of industry at national level. Some attempts were made in the social areas, for example for collective dismissals or for vocational preparation for the young. Others were hoped for in economic areas, in relation with the economic and monetary union plans—which pertinently raise the central issue of compatibility between union policies within countries and targets at Community level, for instance on the wage front.

These difficulties have been compounded both by the enlargement and by the complete change on the economic front occurring around 1973. British unions and employers had a great deal of difficulty in accepting the approach sketched out above, but perhaps more fundamentally, the crisis required a complete shift of emphasis on purposes.

The emerging Community system of industrial relations was still aimed (for the official union position) at restoring full employment, preserving expansionary policies, and establishing Community norms; employers, by contrast, pleaded for wage restraint and labour flexibility in terms so abstract as to become almost ideological. It was very difficult to incorporate the key issue of reallocating resources, for which the industrial relations semantic and tradition is not quite prepared, especially when communications are so complex between the centre and the periphery.

Two further issues poisoned the debate. First, there is the autonomy of social partners, sacrosanct in certain countries such as Germany, which is brandished by some in a systematic way. Second, there is the strange process by which the Community and its performance are solely identified with public decisions and expenses.

Some of the Achievements as Pointers to the Future

To some observers, the major problem is that Community industrial relations are part of its social policy, and that the achievements of its social policy are only measured by their 'visibility'—contrary, for instance, to what happens in competition or trade policy. However, the following paragraphs will give a few examples of what has been achieved.

The first example deals with the so-called reorganisation of working time (i.e. flexibility *and* reduction). Discussions on this issue have been going on in Brussels both in the Council and in the Standing Employment Committee since 1979. On the substance, reorganisation of working time, as formulated by the Commission, can be summarised as aiming at somewhat more flexibility in working-time rules, including the extension of part-time work, and at some reduction in standard working time, on a yearly rather than a weekly basis, taking due account of economic requirements in terms of wage compensation and larger-plant operating times if necessary. Unfortunately, the main difficulties lie in implementation: the need for a decentralised approach and the actual response of individual workers. The role of the Community is at least to provide the impetus for an overall framework.

Although no tangible decision has been taken, the last recommendation was accepted by nine countries (the UK being against). However, the most significant impact to date has perhaps been the contribution to an acceptance by unions of such elements as part-time work, or interim work—especially in France, Italy and Belgium where such issues were morally and politically taboo. The subject will still remain on the agenda but it is in the actual movements in member states rather than on spectacular Community decisions that the responses will take shape.

In two other areas—new technologies and collective bargaining, and the future of social protection—the Commission has tried to overcome the complexity of European-level discussion by organising tripartite round tables within each member state. In each case, its role has not been that of a decision-maker, nor even of a political body coming with a definite policy-line, but rather that of a middleman attempting to delineate the problem in all its complexity and to suggest some key issues. Participants generally admit that such discreet round tables have indeed contributed to a better understanding of the issues; a majority would like more of this type of operation, which is of a novel character and can only work in an informal way behind closed doors.

Dialogue is also taking place at sectoral level. Its role here is not only as a support to sectoral aspects of community activity, particularly restructuring or redeployment problems; it can also act as a useful support to the central organisations' discussions on broader issues, such as the social aspects of new technologies or the reorganisation of working time, by bringing the partners down from abstract generalisations to more specific issues and a more concrete language. It is perhaps the only currently active aspect of social relations which is to some extent independent of Community institutions, but it is also a fragile and, at times, temperamental creature.

Dialogue takes various forms. The institutionalised 'joint

sectoral committees' (steel, agriculture, transport, textiles) are only one form. In some very active sectors, such as construction or engineering, there is no official structure and everybody seems satisfied. Dialogues may take place in bilateral informal meetings or simply through contacts between secretariats.

The subject and aims of such meetings also vary. Although some sectors (e.g. agriculture, transport) seem to concentrate on the idea of European-level agreements or the formulation of opinions on Community policies, others tend to concentrate on questions of common interest, such as vocational training and working conditions, or on the co-ordination of union claims in the member states (engineering sector).

The intensity of the sectoral dialogue would seem to have little to do with the presence or absence of common policies, but rather depends on the degree of perception of common problems in the sector, which is quite another matter.

Although sectoral European union secretariats seem often to have a more realistic approach than the ETUC, sectoral dialogue seems hampered by three major obstacles: (1) the difficult and complex relationship between sectoral and central organisations at European level, on both sides; (2) the fear of a corporatist approach by a coalition of both sides towards protectionist pressures (textiles); and last but not least (3) the ambiguous attitude of the political institutions as regards the potential of sectoral dialogue, illustrated by the severe cuts in operating credits decided in 1983 by the European Parliament and automatically applied by the Commission. It must be added that recurrent policy statements by the Council for the development of formal sectoral committees do not constitute the sort of political support that would help.

Sectoral dialogue may bring a substantial contribution to Community-level industrial relations if it is given a chance to develop pragmatically, but with due concern for overall Community cohesion.

In short, it is not a too optimistic view to assert that the social partners and the Community institutions are engaged in a slow learning process, where they have to adjust.

(1) to the basic changes needed both in the content of industrial relations in a slow-growth period, and in the methods they require (more decentralisation);
(2) to the implications of any attempt at multinational indus-

trial relations: a cautious selection of the subject-matter, a special care for communication lines, the need to turn from rigid central norms towards leadership by guidelines.

Many things have to be invented here. Industrial relations are not a matter for blueprints, but rather for prepared responses to new challenges.

The Scope for other Initiatives

Part of the crisis of identitiy of the Community comes from the fact that it has been identified with its institutions, that its impact is measured by its expenses. Europe cannot be built by those institutions alone. It also needs the initiative of actors—not only on the economic front, but on the social front as well. Public opinion is only beginning to be aware of this, and the importance of such initiatives as those of the Gyllenhammer group.

This last section will deal with a short presentation of what is being or what could be done. I am thinking here of two broad areas. The first one—on which I shall not dwell at length—concerns labour relations within large multinationals in Europe.

It is not the content of the Vredeling Directive proposals that I want to deal with—this can be left for the discussion—but rather the substance of the matter with which it tries to cope, namely the broad issue of information and consultation within multinationals. This is important, not only in the immediate interests of employees, but also in order to promote a better understanding on their part of the complex way an international economy operates. Many multinational companies have played a pioneering role by making innovations in personnel policies and by promoting more exchange or contacts between personnel representatives of their various branches. In that way, they have made a sometimes substantial contribution towards the shaping of tomorrow's industrial relations (one may think of the attempts of Philipps or Saint-Gobain to establish group committees, to take the simplest examples). Taking for granted the strains such initiatives create, one may wonder whether more encouragement or more publicity could not be given to them.

In a broader approach, Europe is now the place where hundreds of initiatives are being taken by companies or unions to cope with the major challenges we are facing in areas related to work—for example, training or information on new technologies, youth employment, working time, etc. It is a fascinating and promising scene, even though its impact on total figures may be limited. Some of the measures are supported by the Community, although I am told that large companies are frowned on by their bankers or colleagues whenever they apply to the European Social Fund. I wonder whether the workers', the general public's and the politicians' awareness of the new world we are entering would not be heightened if such forms of innovation were more substantially publicised and supported?

Facilitating contacts between such actual or potential innovators of different countries might be a key element in tomorrow's Community policies. Free circulation of people and ideas in these areas is of special importance, but it has a cost, in terms of language barriers, time, etc. Trainers, personnel managers and union leaders could be priority targets for such a policy.

The problem here is to find the right way of supporting initiatives which rely on individual efforts and may be stifled by institutions. A recent report to the Commission tried both to stress the importance of the issue and to explore some of the areas and methods. It seems clear, however, that it can only take substance if the actors themselves—and their representative bodies—become aware that such an approach is not a marginal question, but one of the necessary supports to an integrated economic market. This is far from being the case as yet.

Suppose, however, that one (or several) European association(s) for social initiatives were to be created. Its (or their) purpose would be to bring together all persons of institutions convinced of the key role that exchanges of people and ideas *between* European countries should play in the shaping of tomorrow's social and industrial relations policies, and of what may be called a European identity. Its role would be basically to bring technical support or contact facilities to those wishing to establish contacts with their colleagues in other countries; it could also on occasion give useful advice to the Commission or even to the established organisations on technical issues. It would not compete with existing initiatives, but would rather try to encourage their emulation, and serve as a sort of exchange.

It is my belief that such an approach would greatly help to act as a catalyst on the forces of constructive change now operating in all our countries. More and more people in Brussels are concerned about the excessive focusing of attention on institutions and the omission of 'actors' (or agents) in the Community process. The question of Europe as an area for social initiatives is on the agenda.

10 TRADE UNION TRENDS IN WESTERN EUROPE: AN AMERICAN PERSPECTIVE

Malcom R. Lovell Jr

In providing an American perspective on the West European industrial relations scene it may be appropriate briefly to review economic and industrial relations developments in the USA over the past several years.

The US economy has been regarded by some as a 'job machine' creating over 20 million jobs over the past decade and over 5 million since the trough of the recent recession. Job growth, particularly in the last several years, has been in manufacturing as well as in services. Indeed, jobs in the service sector continued to grow even during the recession years of 1981–2. While there are many and frequently contradictory reasons given to explain this phenomenon, it stands in sharp contrast to the flat job growth seen in most European countries. While some say that the unimpressive US productivity figures have played a prominent part in job creation, others credit the relative lack of government and labour constraints (commonly seen in Europe) which protect existing jobs at the sacrifice of future employment.

A reasonable explanation would involve both reasons and others as well. Certainly the size and flexibility of the economy would have to be cited. The US market is so huge and diverse that even when leading industries are suffering a decline, others (often new ones) are beginning an upsurge. The more mobile US labour force must also be credited with an important role in job creation. While worker mobility *per se* does not create jobs, it does make possible a national employment strategy which strives for a net increase in *total* jobs rather than the maintenance of existing jobs. Young people particularly are not reluctant to leave the communities in which they grew up when jobs are in short supply. While middle-aged people are more reluctant to move, it is a far more common occurrence than in Europe. And while the USA has been tardy in fashioning sensitive programmes to help relieve the burden of our displaced workers, the emergence of the multiple-earner family has played some role in this regard. People are

242

mobile because industry has been mobile. Modern, more efficient plants are constantly being built in areas of the country seeking to attract new business with agreeable tax and regulatory treatment and frequently without the history of labour strife typical of the more heavily industrialised areas of the country.

And, finally, there is in the USA an overriding competitive spirit that thwarts efforts on the part of its big institutions to impose their will on the economy. Big companies, big labour organisations and influential governmental bureaus are not permitted to impose the dampening influence which great power held over time frequently produces. For example, there is no central employer organisation that speaks for all business and none which has any influence in establishing national wage patterns. The Chamber of Commerce, the largest business organisation in number of members, is as likely to be at odds with the Business Roundtable, representing the largest companies, as it is with the government or the American Federation of Labour – Confederation of Industrial Organisations (AFL–CIO). Both political parties have supported deregulation in recent years, with the Carter administration being almost as vigorous in this respect as is President Reagan. Since 1982, the reductions in government spending and influence in areas inhibiting the functioning of the marketplace have been widespread. Neither do the unions exercise the restraint on business growth and profitability seen in some West European countries. First of all, they do not operate under any social theory antipathetic to the success of the private enterprise system, and second, the low rate of organisation (approximately 20 per cent) and only moderate support from national labour laws[1] dilutes their power.

Perhaps one of the most dramatic differences between West European countries and the USA is in the nature of its labour organisations. Unions such as the Communications Workers of America and the United Automobile Workers have understood the competitive challenge facing the industries with which they work and have accepted the legitimacy of much of the tough cost-cutting activity that has occurred in recent years. These unions have co-operated with efforts to restrain cost increases and to improve quality and productivity at the same time as they have

[1] The AFL-CIO leadership believes current labour law and National Labour Relations Board (NLRB) interpretations have played an important part in the success of many companies to operate in 'a union free environment'.

argued for the companies to pursue these goals in the most humane fashion possible. The unions representing clothing workers, long sensitive to the highly competitive nature of the business, have recently worked to encourage research in the applications of new technology to preserve as many American jobs as possible in the face of foreign competition.

Industry and pattern bargaining long associated with industrial relations in transportation, manufacturing, and construction are slowly giving way to a more decentralised approach. Where it is still dominant, it has proved sensitive to wage developments in the non-unionised sector as well as to the competition from abroad.

Management in the USA has pursued a far more aggressive policy than most of its European counterparts in operating successfully without a union. As suggested above, there is disagreement whether this represents more sensitive managerial behaviour in the handling of their human relations problems or whether it reflects the influence of labour laws more favourable to management. The rapidly growing service industries in the private sector have remained particularly resistant to unionisation, which has further aggravated and complicated the tasks of America's labour chiefs.

To help halt the slide in trade union influence, the AFL–CIO has redoubled its political efforts and this year for the first time endorsed a candidate for the Democratic Presidential Nomination prior to the party's 1984 convention. Working for Mr Mondale, the union played a pivotal role in blocking the surprisingly strong showing of Mr Hart and had the unlikely event of a Mondale victory occurred it could have expected a position of considerable influence in his administration. It was interesting to note, however, that the Democratic Party platform was more moderate in its tone than one would have expected given the key role played by the AFL–CIO. For example, for the first time in recent memory the platform did not advocate a comprehensive health insurance programme, nor did it give unequivocal support to the domestic content legislation long sought by the United Auto Workers' Union (UAW).

The deregulation taking place in transportation and communications has placed additional competitive pressures on companies in these industries which have led to a further weakening in the bargaining position of the trade union representatives. It is interesting to note the willingness of the unions representing United

Air Lines workers to accept employee ownership of 20 per cent of the common stock and union membership on the board of directors in return for substantial pay cuts and work rule-changes. Unlike their European counterparts, these unions were not committed to a social theory that workers should own the companies, but rather made a business judgement that only by such a move could their jobs be salvaged with the added plus that were the company to be successful, workers would profit from the appreciation of their stock.

Perhaps the most significant difference between US and European trade unions is that in the USA unions are basically committed to the capitalist system. They are strongly anti-communist. Walter Reuther, one of the founders of the UAW, fought one of his most important battles with the communists of his day, finally removing them as an influence—a condition which still applies. Lane Kirkland, the current president of the AFL–CIO, opposed as he is to President Reagan, is one of the strongest supporters of a strong American role in combating international communism. Unions do strongly advocate public and private programmes which protect workers from bearing the full impact of market forces. They are frequently champions of civil and equal rights causes and supporters of programmes to relieve poverty and want. They have not followed some of their European brethren in supporting nationalisation of industry or other moves towards a socialist society. This, of course, could change if organised labour believed it was being forced out of the significant role it has long enjoyed in the USA as a major social and economic power. Despite its present slump in membership and influence, the American trade union movement remains a vigorous and resilient force which is not likely to be driven to extreme positions to maintain its vitality and popular support.

Americans viewing the world economic scene are apt to view Japan and the emerging Asian nations as providing greater economic leadership and competition than that provided by West European countries. It is not so much that Europe does not have the resources, technology, capital and managerial skills, but that as societies they have lost the ability—and perhaps the will—to adjust rapidly to changing economic demands. The trade union movement in Western Europe has played a major role in shaping the nature of society and the economies of the various countries, and it is therefore timely that a review of these trends be made. If the American view that Asia is slowly supplanting Europe as an economic power is correct, a study of trade union trends as they affect the competitiveness of European society is in order. Even if this American view is overly pessimistic, it is clear to a reader of these reports that most of the nations of Western Europe are uneasy about their economic future and that the various trade union movements will play an important role in setting the course in Europe over the years ahead.

The tremendous economic progress and rise in standards of living in Japan, Korea, Taiwan, Malaysia and Singapore have demonstrated the capacity of determined nations to improve substantially their lot through achieving greater international competitiveness. It is unimportant at this point whether the success of these nations is the result of a freer flow of capital and technology, shrewd industrial policy, or a determination to work harder and postpone immediate gratification for long-term goals. What is important is that an economic gauntlet has been thrown down with the option, on the one hand, of greater wealth for the nations which avail themselves of the burdens and fruits of international competitiveness and, on the other hand, of slower growth and a reduced standard of living for those who choose not to play.

The West European nations are thus viewed by many Americans as being in the position to choose between a variety of futures. They may choose to rest upon their economic laurels and put the achievement of non-competitive social goals above policies designed to foster the production and sale of goods and services in the world marketplace: a form of 'genteel socialistic poverty'.

In contrast, however, the nations of Western Europe have the opportunity and the capacity once again to become leading economic contenders in the international arena. The human and technological resources of each of these countries are capable of blazing the way on paths of growth and prosperity if it is decided to pursue such goals. In this chapter I will attempt to illustrate the nature of this continuum from bleak to prosperous futures by citing the experiences and trends of the several West European countries as reported in the Swedish Employers' Confederation study.

Finally, it is important to emphasise that when I say European nations have a choice I am not saying that there is one 'correct' and one 'incorrect' path. Once a nation decides in its collective wisdom that it wants to be competitive, there are a wide variety of policies which arguably could produce the desired results—and no one nation (and this includes the USA and Japan) has all the answers. What I am suggesting from 'an American perspective', after reviewing these eight national studies, is that a national consensus must be formed regarding the *primary* objectives of a society at a particular point in time. If, at the end, these objectives have a closer relation to dividing the pie rather than baking it, there is apt to be a smaller pie! If, however, there is general agreement among the major elements (or social partners) in a society that economic growth is necessary for full employment and a rising standard of living, it is far more likely that the economic and governance decisions made over time will lead to a more competitive and therefore prosperous society.

It also needs to be recognised that the human state is neither all social nor all economic. Levels of economic growth which are achieved only at high social costs are generally rejected by reasonable people. Democratic societies, therefore, are engaged in a constant search for 'the right mix' which puts into proper balance for each society policies to achieve economic goals and policies to achieve social goals so that the most highly valued of each can be attained. As a matter of fact, in a free society it is not possible to gain a national commitment to achieving a respectable place in the competitiveness struggle unless the distributive and governance systems are acceptable to a majority of the citizens. One could say, then, that the West European nations are at a crossroads in deciding what level of economic competitiveness is consistent with their priority requirements for corporate governance, economic democracy, and immediate over long-term rewards.

The post-Second World War period in Western Europe has produced not only unprecedented economic growth, but vast social change. Workers and trade unions have in every country achieved a degree of power and influence over political and economic events surpassing that held by their counterparts in the USA. In this regard, the Scandinavian countries, the UK and Holland have witnessed workers and their unions playing the most dominant roles, with those in West Germany, France, and Italy playing important but somewhat lesser parts in the governance of their countries. There have been rises and diminutions of influence within each nation as well. In the UK today, for instance, the influence of trade unions is less than it has been in several decades. Perhaps because of this influence and perhaps because of the general postwar affluence, West European nations have focused a great deal of attention and have accorded high priority to questions of wealth and power distribution. The Scandinavian nations, Holland and West Germany throughout most (though not all) of the postwar period were able to reach a national consensus on the social issues which contributed to a 'harmony' in these countries, now being shaken by the new economic challenges of increased international competition.

The Swedish Employers' Confederation study outlines the course of action being taken or considered by eight European countries in order to deal with the new economic challenges, as well as discussing the historic trends in trade union roles leading up to the present time. In varying degrees in the different countries, the trade union movement and the forces which influence it are coming to grips with the new challenges. Focus is beginning to shift from those measures aimed at dividing the pie to those geared to enlarging it.

Trade union willingness to function in a manner supportive of achieving economic growth varies from country to country; in many instances, union leadership itself is divided as to the most desirable course of action. Unions which historically have taken the initiative in securing social change now find themselves on the defensive with economic forces, a more highly resolved employer community, and a changing public opinion forcing their hand. In Norway, Denmark and Holland, the trade union movement is now recognising the need for greater competitiveness and is becoming a partner in the process. In France and Italy, a somewhat weaker group of unions is seeking new roles (sometimes reluctantly) in a new industrial environment. The UK and Germany have trade unions which are divided as to the priority between economic and social goals, while in Sweden one sees the greatest reluctance on the part of the union movement to abandon its plans for a changed society to assure a more secure economic future.

A review of the SAF reports leads to the following comments regarding trade union behaviour in choosing between economic and social goals.

In France, where the freedom to manage has been seriously eroded, there appears to be a growing realisation that jobs will be best protected through the competitive power of its industry and that private initiatives must be encouraged to regain economic prominence. The Mitterrand government appears to be taking the bit between its teeth most dramatically in regard to the steel industry, but also in regard to becoming generally more competitive. It is not clear whether the French trade union movement recognises the need to pursue these new goals or whether it is politically and organisationally unable to mount effective opposition.

In Italy, where unions enjoyed limited power in the 1950s and enhanced status in the 1970s, they appear to be weakened and divided as they face the 1980s. It is suggested by Mr Butera that, as part of the ongoing transformation of the industrial relations system, one can observe a 'weakening of rigidly egalitarian and solidaristic policies and the strengthening of interest in the individual contribution to overall performance'. He also suggests that 'the challenge to management prerogatives [on these bases] will probably disappear'. The trend today is towards greater worker and union participation in the design and experimentation of the innovative process on a decentralised basis. With rapid technological development and more imaginative labour–management systems, Italy is moving rapidly towards becoming a major contender in the international marketplace.

West Germany appears to be a case where economic pressures have caused trade unions to change their strategy but not their goals. DGB and its affiliated unions, according to Mr Müller-Vogg, have not redefined their role or mission in view of the changed economic situation. The union ideology, which has always carried traditional Marxist baggage, is now gaining some support outside the labour movement from youth organisations and the environmentalists.

It is somewhat ironic that the DGB strategy during the 1960s and most of the 1970s resulted in a fairly co-operative labour–management relationship with the union taking positions basically supportive of management's goals for the industries involved. Mr Müller-Vogg argues that the West German trade unions, rather than constructively rationalising social and economic goals, are tending to address the more general political questions of peace, ecology, basic democratic rights, the liberation movement, etc. In addition, by its strike for a 35-hour week, the metalworkers' union apparently sought a palliative (of dubious long-term worth) for the lack of job formation that clearly underplayed the importance of competitiveness. Whether the agreement that ended the strike —which somewhat expanded management's ability to improve manpower utilisation—helps or retards West Germany's ability to compete, remains to be seen.

Swedish unions appear to be attempting to rationalise economic goals by assuming that achievement of their social goals will produce a more competitive economic society, all arguments to the contrary notwithstanding. By pressing for collective ownership (employee investment funds) as the first order of business, they are staking all on the concept that managers sharing trade union ideology will produce a more competitive enterprise over time than those currently charged with achieving success in the marketplace—a questionable assumption at best! The 1982 agreement on efficiency and participation concluded by SAF, the LO and PTK may be helpful at the local level, although an observer might come to the conclusion that the agreement was heavier on participation than on efficiency. From the reports reviewed from the eight countries, one would have to view Sweden's LO as contributing less to achieving a more competitive society than the trade union movement in many of the other countries.

In Norway, the reaction to the economic shocks of the late 1970s and early 1980s was less confrontational. Labour, management and government in major industries seem to be working problems out together. For example, reforms regarding the organisation of work and employee involvement in management seem to have been worked out jointly. Although Norway evidently has a way to go to become a lower-cost country and to develop its knowledge-based industries, it appears that the trade union movement will represent more of an asset than a liability.

Denmark appears to be closer to Norway than to Sweden in the willingness of its trade unions to function in a manner supportive of economic growth. This is a fairly recent development, however. In the early 1970s, both the LO and the Social Democratic Party were slow in assessing the adverse effect of the 'solidarity' wage policies and the liberal social programmes on inflation and the state of the economy. Since 1979, measures to control inflation and contain social costs, coupled with a more receptive attitude towards technological development and innovation, became more prominent. The establishment of the Danish Business Investment Fund, with the unions putting up one-third of the funds and the banks two-thirds, along with the formation by the LO of a micro-economic research unit, are fairly dramatic examples of moves to a more decentralised co-operative and innovative mode. Also illustrative of Denmark's LO's reorientation is the very moderate programme developed at its 1983 Congress supporting a

competitive free enterprise society with the twin goals of competitiveness and equality.

In the Netherlands, the traditional conflict between capital and
labour appears to be overshadowed by the painful readjustment
process enforced by stagnating economic growth. Concern for an
economy which is delivering a poor performance compared with
other industrialised nations is requiring both managers and unions
to seek ways to work together to improve the nation's competitive
posture. Seeking some control on how this process will develop,
the new FNV leadership has expressed its support for a joint
reindustrialisation scheme in which both management and unions
would share important roles. A possible result might be agreement
on co-determination and worker participation in work
organisation, investment planning, personnel policies and profit-
sharing. Mr Van Zweeden believes unions will have to sacrifice
many of the 'gains and securities' they obtained in a century of
battle if the Netherlands is to re-emerge as an important economic
power. This is perhaps expecting too much of the trade union
movement.

In the UK, there is little evidence that the radical elements in
the TUC are prepared to function in a manner supportive of
achieving economic growth. The more moderate union powers,
however, are more receptive to this point of view. As with the
AFL–CIO in the USA, the TUC would favour a formal industrial
policy over a free market approach in order to achieve a more
competitive economic system. The lack of general political support
for the Labour Party, coupled with rank-and-file recognition of the
need to increase productivity, curb the TUC's power to block
management initiatives as effectively as it did in the past.

A recent OECD study concludes that 'nothing has
fundamentally changed in West European industrial relations and
as soon as economic circumstances change for the better, workers
will flock into unions and with a return to militancy inflation will
again soar'. While this view certainly represents one possibility in
assessing the future, it is too pessimistic to be accepted as the most
likely outcome. First of all, economic circumstances are unlikely to
return to the pattern prevailing in the 1950s and 1960s. International trade has become too important to the free world to be
ignored, and international competitive forces have changed
dramatically in favour of new systems of work organisation and
new technology, as well as in favour of nations more firmly com-

mitted to prevailing economically in world competition. While Western Europe may revert to its old habits during periods of temporary economic respite, it is more likely that the new economic pressures and incentives will force trade unions to a more supportive role in improving the performance of West European business and industries.

One cannot review the SAF reports without being struck by a challenge to the West European trade union movement similar to that which also confronts American labour organisations. This challenge goes to the heart of the function and purpose of trade unions in today's democratic society. Are trade unions primarily the representatives of their members in the collective bargaining and political process, or do they represent a larger political constituency? West European unions have generally acted as if the latter role were controlling, whereas unions in the USA more consistently adhered to the former. There is some evidence that the European trade unions are now moving in the direction previously charted by the American unions and that the American unions are moving towards the European model. While it is most unlikely that the change in direction of the American unions will be more than marginal, the European unions may well move significantly towards the US model.

Sweden's LO long one of Europe's most powerful trade union federations (and perhaps for this reason) shows the least inclination to re-examine its role. Seeking responsibility for capital as well as for labour, the LO remains a dominant political as well as economic force. It has been said that, 'whereas companies typically operate in the international marketplace and are sensitive to its disciplines, actors on the Swedish political stage dance to their own music'. Over the long term, such dancing will have to take place in less sumptuous surroundings if the ability of Swedish business to compete in the more competitive international marketplace declines. But at the moment SAF has its work cut out for it to bring both the body politic and the LO to face economic reality more squarely.

Norway's trade unions are an example of a movement in evolution from its more traditional Scandinavian base towards a more decentralised co-operative relationship with management. The LO and other large unions in Norway, according to Mr Thorsrud, are gradually becoming more conservative, and changes in social and economic patterns are taking shape. Shifts in cultural

values and attitudes regarding work, learning and new technologies, are gathering currency. The growth of new unions in
service industries and the professions are prodding the older
organisations to 'catch up' with their membership. Nor has
Norway followed Sweden's example of the unions seeking to take
over the ownership of the nation's enterprises. Representation on
boards of directors and participation with management on
questions regarding the organisation of work are being worked out
at both the political and local levels.

Denmark's labour movement prior to the late 1960s was committed to the dual goals of representing the 'opposite interests' of
the workers and collaboration with management. Towards the end
of the 1960s, with the rapid increase in real wages evening out, the
LO and its member unions proposed a revolutionary new policy
aiming at a complete structural change of influence and distribution of income and ownership in the private sector. This
objective of structural change of the existing society marked a
departure from the LO's past. Although the wage-earner fund, the
cornerstone of the new push for 'economic democracy', was not
introduced after 1973, the decade of the 1970s set the LO and its
member unions on a course with more emphasis on changing the
nature of society than on achieving economic gains for its
membership.

According to Mr Tarp, in 1979 the LO president stated that the
LO had moved into fields other than the traditional industrial
relations and labour market tasks since it was now up to the trade
union movement to shape the course for the future development
of society. The failure of this effort can be attributed not only to
the firm opposition from private business, but to its lack of support
from the overwhelming majority of the rank-and-file voters. Since
1980, however, the LO has once again reconsidered its goals,
policies, and perhaps philosophy and ideology.

The programmes that the LO envisages for the 1984–9 period
include improvement of the competitive strength of private enterprises, a fairer distribution of the tax burden and a changed,
more efficient, public sector. While maintaining a keen interest in
the nature of Danish society, the trade unions now appear to be
abandoning the concept of 'counter-power' and donning once
again the mantle of 'co-operative partner'.

In the Netherlands, unions throughout most of the postwar
period developed from battle organisations into instruments for

maintaining industrial peace. They also played a major role in the restructuring of Dutch society. Today, the trade unions are losing much of their clout on socio-economic policy. The current, more conservative government offers fewer opportunities for the unions to exert influence. Unions are now turning towards freer, more de-centralised bargaining. This is illustrated by the 1982 agreement in which the central organisations of management and labour concurred on recommendations aimed at collective bargaining at the industrial and company level. These understandings are aimed at encouraging economic growth, improving profitability and the sharing of existing employment. Unions now appear to favour promotion of the im-mediate interests of their members and affirm their position as responsible partners on the economic scene rather than full-fledged political and social opponents on the national scene.

Unions in Italy have never experienced the political influence enjoyed by their counterparts in the Scandinavian countries or in the UK. Collective bargaining takes place at industry, company and plant levels. This may account for the greater flexibility ex-hibited by Italian unions in dealing with the very substantial work-place changes now taking place. The somewhat chaotic industrial relations system in Italy in which, according to Mr Butera, 'what is codified only vaguely corresponds with what happens', may now give way to the unions' search for a 'new legitimacy' within a more structured, centralised political exchange. But more likely, be-lieves Mr Butera, is a transformation of the industrial relations system with more formalisation, a greater variety of represen-tation, and major changes in bargaining strategy with new opportunities to participate in the design and experimentation of the innovative process.

Mr Butera sums up the changes he sees in Italy's industrial relations structure by predicting a combination of the following:

(1) institutional participation—unions taking part in the de-cision-making process through political influence (lobbying) and formal procedures;
(2) bargaining—decentralised;
(3) design/participative pattern—move from antagonistic to a collaborative mode.

Italian trade unions thus appear to be following a pragmatic course—perhaps out of necessity rather than design. Italian unions appear interested in the grand designs of society, but are clearly addressing themselves first to their members' interests.

In France, economic pressures may be tending to separate the unions from the state. President Mitterrand's apparent determination to achieve a more competitive economy may convince employers and unions to rely on each other rather than on the state. Certainly unions will not neglect the use of their political power to further their economic and social aspirations, but there appear to be signs that union leadership appreciates that a more immediate priority lies in demonstrating greater sensitivity to the day-to-day workplace problems of the men and women in the workforce. Trade unions in France are experiencing a weakening of the revolutionary forces as compared with the more pragmatic reformists.

West Germany is perhaps one of the clearest examples of the union movement being torn between its role as a political force for change and that of the workers' representatives within a capitalist society. Mr Müller-Vogg refers to the conflict as being between the union acting as a 'counter-power' or as a 'regulative factor'. While acknowledging that unions are 'always both things', he clearly believes that in West Germany the trend is in the direction of a political 'counter-power'. This is the opposite course from that perceived taking place in France and Italy, but somewhat similar to the position of the left wing in the UK's TUC.

In the UK, the TUC with its intimate ties to the Labour Party and its long history of active involvement in government, has now lost influence and power. In the past, unions cowed managements with their strong base in law, solid worker support, the nationalisation of key industries and a dominant influence in many pre-Thatcher governments. All of these forces have changed and, while still an important power to be reckoned with, the TUC is not the giant-killer of old.

To add to its troubles, the TUC is being confronted with the fact that the majority of its members probably do not support the Labour Party. Perhaps most illustrative of TUC mainstream thinking is the paper on *Strategy and the Future Role of the Unions* developed by the General Council of TUC. This 1984 document:

(1) recognised past responsibility and the need for a more positive future union role;
(2) recognised that unions have been out of touch with their membership;

    (3) expressed a need to come to terms with workplace-centred
       trade unionism;

    (4) accepted the need for future collective bargaining to accom-
       modate to industrial change.

In the USA, the status of unionism has some similarities with
Europe, but marked differences as well. Trade unions have
typically eschewed a 'management role'; labour representatives on
the Chrysler and Eastern Airlines boards are the exception rather
than the rule. And even under the most liberal Democratic
administrations, the influence of organised labour in government
has never approached that seen by almost all the European nations
at one time or another in the postwar period. The American trade
union movement, on the other hand, has generally been
supportive of technological change and, until quite recently, has
supported a 'free trade' rather than a highly protectionist set of
policies. Management in the USA has been much freer to make
both workplace and policy judgements. But in spite of the 'milder
US labour climate', many US companies have vigorously sought
what is euphemistically called 'a union-free environment' and in
some instances have succeeded beyond their wildest dreams.

It is not surprising, therefore, that the American labour
movement is now becoming even more closely identified with the
Democratic Party and that it is seeking its salvation by achieving
greater political influence rather than by renewed emphasis on the
collective bargaining process. It is possible that the pendulum
having swung rather far to the left in the European labour community is now moving to the right, while that in the USA is
swinging in the opposite direction.

The pendulum in Europe, however, has a long way to swing
before its trade union movement is in a position to play the
basically constructive (though adversarial) role seen in the USA.
The highly complex and cumbersome government and union constraints on European management could be crucially responsible
for the slow (to negative) job growth and its resulting high unemployment. Whereas the signs of change are evident in almost
every nation reported on, the rate at which the change is taking
place has not gathered much steam.

One of the interesting differences between Europe and the USA
can be observed in the behaviour of the employer community. In
the US, vigour in both the collective bargaining and the political

arena is the rule. This has not been historically true in Europe, although signs of change are emerging. Certainly Swedish employers and SAF are now playing a leadership role in an effort to counter the power of the LO and the governmental constraints built up over the postwar period.

It may be that in the years when the emphasis was on consensus that consensus itself became a goal rather than as a means to achieve a goal. Clearly, consensus remains a vital ingredient in a rational process of adjustment to social and economic change, but in a democratic society there is a time and a place—both in the political process as well as in the collective bargaining process—for more adversarial behaviour. Perhaps in the USA it is time for more consensus and less conflict. Europe's economic problems, however, may well require a more determined business community.

A Scenario for Western Europe

This chapter has discussed two related challenges currently confronting West European trade unions and indirectly facing the body politic of these countries. The first is whether the union movement is prepared to give priority to the goal of economic competitiveness and the opportunities for job and wealth creation associated with successful international specialisation, even when this requires a lower priority for its historic social agenda. The second is whether the trade union movement will best serve the society of which it is a part by acting, in Mr Müller-Vogg's words, as a 'regulative factor' or as a 'counter-power'. Are trade unions primarily the representatives of their members in the collective bargaining and political process, or do they represent a larger political constituency? These challenges are related because the way the second issue is resolved ('regulative factor' or 'counter-power') will influence a trade union's ability to respond to the first (competitiveness versus a social agenda).

It is clear from studying the SAF reports that in regard to both questions the term 'choice' may be inappropriate. The 'choice' in every instance is being heavily influenced by political trends, worker perceptions of self-interest and employer determination. The trade unions in the countries reviewed are adopting disparate responses, however, and one may expect the economic and social institutions in each country to be influenced by the judgements rendered.

Far wiser viewers of the West European scene have offered judgements on the area's economic future with greater insight and wisdom than this chapter can produce. Nevertheless, the purpose of our overview is to look ahead to the final decade of this century, and so some speculation regarding what lies ahead may be appropriate.

The nations of Western Europe are all democracies and all have the capability of making whatever long-term adjustment they may choose to the economic forces of the free world to which they are vulnerable. They are not, like their neighbours to the East, cast into a system from which they may not free themselves. They can ignore international economic forces, but at the peril of substantially reduced standards of living. Economic and political judgements which make 'sharing the misery' more equitable are apt, over time, to be rejected in favour of those which are more likely to create wealth. The 'reality test' is irrefutable, but it does take time. Those societies which correctly anticipate what economic behaviour will best serve them are most likely to experience a higher standard of living sooner than those whose judgements prove more fallible.

While it is clear (at least to this writer) that it is in the long-term best interest of the West European nations to commit themselves to the goal of competitiveness, it is not so clear—given the various cultures, histories and expectations—how best to go about its achievement. Those nations which are still arguing about whether or not competitiveness is important (i.e. Sweden) are apt to be overshadowed by those who are doing something about it (i.e. Italy, Norway and Denmark).

While most West European countries in the EEC are competing with each other on what might be described as a 'level playing-field', the disparate *national* policies affecting corporate governance, labour laws, cost of social programmes, wage structures and industrial policies make each country unique in its competitive potential. It would not be a useful exercise, therefore, to prescribe a regimen appropriate for all countries for each must pursue its own route, picking from its own experience and that of others those approaches considered most suitable. In addition, as suggested earlier in this paper, it is not a matter of a nation choosing between two mutually exclusive objectives. The question is not to choose between a just and humane society and a competitive one, but of assuring the economic discipline required by a competitive society within a democratic and socially sensitive framework of economic and political governance.

Based on the American experience, it is believed that one way to achieve this balance is by trade unions, employers and governments adhering to the following concepts.

Governments. The guidelines here are that governments should:

(1) Allow market forces to pick corporate winners and losers, but accept a responsibility for cushioning the impact of economic change on the men and women adversely affected. (Encourage labour force mobility through comprehensive programmes of retraining, placement, and relocation assistance.)

(2) Assume primary responsibility for maintaining monetary and fiscal policies designed to encourage economic growth.

(3) Structure industrial relations legislation which encourages the parties to resolve their differences in a decentralised fashion based on their common interests rather than on a national pattern.

(4) Encourage job growth by not penalising job creation and by recognising that 'job' security does not lead to 'employment' security.

(5) Adopt policies based on the recognition that the wealth gained by a more competitive society should be managed and distributed in a fashion which both encourages continued economic growth *and* is sensitive to the society's sense of equity and fairness.

Trade Unions. The guidelines here are that trade unions should:

(1) Accept the competitiveness of each industry as vital to job growth and increases in the standard of living of their members.

(2) Recognise that a trade union's primary goal is to represent the best interests of its members and that efforts to achieve social change at the political level should not jeopardise the realisation of this objective.

(3) Give equal attention at the enterprise level to 'expanding the size of the pie' as is given to its division.

Employers. The guidelines here are that employers should:

(1) Accept the responsibility for the success or failure of their enterprise. This would include introduction of new technology and the allocation of capital and labour resources to research and development along with other qualities of competent management found in a competitive society.

(2) Accept responsibility for articulation of points of view amenable to the preservation of the democratic capitalist system and vigorously pursue such goals within the political system.

(3) Carry out programmes designed to meet the perceived needs of the men and women in their employ which are consistent within a democratic system with the long-term competitiveness of the enterprise.

(4) Recognise that the employer has a responsibility for the employment security of the workforce second only to the long-term economic health of the enterprise.

On the basis of adhering to these concepts, a somewhat reckless observer might hazard a guess as to which European countries are most likely to adapt to a more competitive mode and to the required shift in the nature of work. First, I am somewhat optimistic after reading the reports contained in this book that Western Europe will indeed survive and remain a viable, though not necessarily pre-eminent, competitor in the free world's economic order. Italy, as a result of its confused industrial relations system, the vigour of its entrepreneurial spirit and its greater concern for economic progress in preference to achieving a revised social order, appears to be making the most impressive progress. Next, Norway and Denmark, both because of the behaviour of their trade union movements and a growing political will to maintain their standard of living, seem to be taking useful steps to achieve their goals.

In France, the government, to everyone's surprise (particularly that of the Communists, but probably of the right-wing parties as well), has set a vigorous course towards achieving a more competitive society. Employers do not have a rosy path ahead of them, but there is more to be optimistic about than one would have expected. The Netherlands stands to improve its economic performance with a government determined to achieve more vigorous economic growth and with employers taking heart from a more supportive public and a somewhat subdued union movement.

The Federal Republic of Germany has surprised many observers by not maintaining its strong competitive position in the international economic arena. With a trade union movement more dissatisfied and looking leftwards with an emphasis on 'counterpower', one might view the immediate future with some concern.

The UK, while making major strides under the Thatcher government to redress the abuses of the past, has a long way to go to regain its former economic pre-eminence and still carries the baggage of social division. If the moderate trade union forces prevail over their more radical brothers and sisters, and if the employers abandon their 'strength through joy strategy', as they appear to be doing, there is still hope.

Sweden is placed last in this litany of speculation because neither its governments nor its powerful trade union movement has placed competitiveness high on the list of things to be achieved. The employer community's keen interest in changing the rules of the game is an encouraging feature, but there are impressive obstacles to overcome. It is unlikely that the trade union intellectual leadership will abandon full employment and equality as its primary goals. Although these may well be highly desirable objectives, their achievement does not necessarily lead to a vibrant economy and their vigorous pursuit may well, under today's circumstances, lead to a stagnant one. The people of Sweden, through the political process, and the employers through collective bargaining, will have to articulate more clearly the long-term advantages to the country of a more competitive society. As a consequence, the nation may have to suffer through a period of internal dissention which, in the long term, will be a small price for a more prosperous society. Ironically, achieving and maintaining competitiveness may also prove to be the most effective route to reaching the trade union goals of full employment and equality!

A SUMMARY CONCLUSION

B.C. Roberts

The studies commissioned by the Swedish Employers' Confederation for this project clearly confirm that major changes in the patterns of trade unions and industrial relations are taking place in Western Europe. They are also taking place in the USA, Japan and other democracies which have trade unions and industrial relations systems which in essentials are similar to those in Western Europe. In all the countries examined in this study, trade union membership has declined in the past five years, though perhaps least in Sweden. The power of the unions to secure improvements in levels of pay, conditions of employment and the maintenance of jobs for their members has also to some extent diminished. So too has the political influence of the trade unions on governments as socialist parties have been defeated at the polls, or have had to adjust their policies when in power under the pressures generated by economic recession and the advent of post-industrialism. All the authors see this weakening in economic and political power of the unions as an important development, but most are cautious in interpreting the changes which have occurred.

Whether the 1980s will prove to be a watershed for the trade unions, it is impossible yet to say; but it is a theoretical possibility that the social democracies of Western Europe, after a century of increasing trade union power, which reached its pinnacle at the end of the last decade, have entered a period of trade union decline which may prove to be of lasting significance. However, the right to form unions, to bargain collectively, to strike and to exercise political pressure through party affiliations and demonstrations of protest against, and support for, particular policies have not been fundamentally challenged.

What is at issue are two questions. First: will the membership power and influence of the unions continue to decline, as has happened in the USA? Second: will there be a recovery in the strength of the unions which will be associated with a shift to more radical policies that will threaten the maintenance of social democracy? The contributors to this book have not given specific answers to these questions, although they were in the mind of SAF when it launched this inquiry. In analysing the changes that have

262

been taking place, however, they have tentatively suggested that a new *modus vivendi* may be arrived at which would be compatible with the maintenance of democratic social market economies.

Factors Determining the Role and Power of Unions

The future role and power of the unions will be determined by six factors:

(1) technological change;
(2) structure of the labour force;
(3) economic environment;
(4) style of management;
(5) dominant ideology;
(6) the role of government.

In looking ahead it is necessary to ask whether the changes in the structures and processes of industrial relations, brought about by changes in these factors and chronicled in this book, will continue to change in a direction that will permanently weaken or bring about a dramatic recovery in union power. It is unlikely in the foreseeable future that unions will simply wither away. We have not yet entered into a post-trade-union society in Europe, but some believe that the threshold has already been crossed in the USA. Many others believe that acceptance by the unions in the USA of the need to adjust to the demands of the market by agreeing to reductions in real wages is a demonstration of their resilience and will to survive that is likely to ensure that they have a significant future role to play. Malcolm Lovell Jr is of the opinion that the unions in Europe are, to a varying degree, showing signs of a similar response to realism.

In Europe, as in the USA and elsewhere, the effects of technological advance and changes in the economic environment have brought about a dramatic decline in the traditional manual worker constituency of the unions. The growing areas of employment have long been for non-manual workers in the service sector. The unions have had some success in organising white-collar office workers and low-skilled service workers in the public sector, but as in the USA their achievement in these areas in the private sector has been limited with the exception of Scandinavia. The new generation of high-technology-skilled workers have been largely indifferent to the attractions of union membership, seeing this as an outdated and unnecessary institutional restriction upon their career mobility and offering a dubious asset to their status and achievement in the fast-moving and open labour market which currently exists. It is possible, if future employment became totally bleak and technological advance gave way to stagnation, that these employees would turn to organisation; but it is a moot point whether they would turn to traditional unions. The image which the new generation of skilled workers seem to have of the unions is that of bureaucratic, restrictive, old-fashioned organisations rooted in outdated technology; these ideas may be further reinforced if the unions in Western Europe follow the trend in the USA by becoming largely limited to workers employed in traditional manual skills and the more lowly paid employees in the public and private sectors, such as janitors, laundry, catering, warehouse, retail trade and other types of the lesser-skilled general workers. Though many of these workers belong to unions, they are frequently difficult and costly to organise and their bargaining power is weak.

There has been a significant increase in the number of women workers joining unions, but proportionately much less than males. They are often in occupations difficult to organise and many of them have doubts about the image of unions which they perceive as male-dominated and the methods they use as more to the advantage of male workers than women. Part-time workers have become a more significant element in the labour force and this is likely to grow futher; but they, too, are often difficult to organise. In most countries the unions have not found a way of easily retaining unemployed workers in membership, and though unions actively urge policies to increase employment they are dominated in practice by the interests of their members who are in jobs. Unions also stress the needs of older workers, but the increasing number of older workers who have taken early retirement, or been made redundant, depletes the strength of the unions. As with many women and younger workers, this group tends to look to other organisations for help and assistance rather than to unions. The division between those workers in jobs, whom the unions look after, and those out of work, who depend on social security rather than wages and suffer from price increases brought about by wage inflation, shows no signs of diminishing and may well get worse.

Structural and Social Change

In addition to losing membership from structural change, the unions have less to do in protecting members' interests in a number of areas. The extension of social security provided by the state has made traditional benefits supplied by the unions largely redundant. The growth of health and safety protection, job security provisions against unfair dismissal, and legislation against discrimination on the basis of age, sex and ethnic origin, though supported by the unions, has reduced their role. Moreover, under threat from legislation, employers have extended and improved their personnel services to meet the needs of employees. Thus, while the unions continue to provide help and assistance to their members in all of these areas, their role is marginal in the minds of many workers.

The decline in employment in traditional industries brought about by technological change, shifts in demand and the growth of the service sector has called for reforms in company organisation and management policies. Large-scale organisational structures are giving way to decentralisation and the growth of small-scale units. With this development, and partly a cause of it, there has been a resurgence of liberal trade policies, within and across national frontiers. Competition and deregulation are in the ascendancy and economic efficiency is the dominant requirement of rising prosperity.

Alongside the changes in the structure of employment, technology and corporate organisation, there have been significant social changes brought about by rising standards of living, increased educational provision, mass communication and consumption and leisure patterns which have broken down traditional class barriers. These changes have been reflected within the enterprise by significant changes in managerial philosophy and style. Channels of communication are more open; there are greater opportunities through training and experience for upward mobility into the ranks of management and into self-employment. The differences in the employment conditions between white-collar and blue-collar employees in the provision of fringe benefits, such as holidays, sick pay and pensions, dining-room and parking facilities, have been greatly diminished and in many cases have entirely disappeared.

These social changes, together with the pressing need to raise levels of efficiency through advanced technology, have encouraged a natural spread of involvement in the processes of decision-making in the workplace. The growth of works councils, briefing groups, autonomous work groups and quality circles outside of the also greatly expanded degree of union representation and formal union–management relations, has emphasised common concerns and consensus solutions.

Emerging Attitudes

There are still many cases in all countries of management remaining authoritarian and decisions being made in an arbitrary style; similarly, there are many issues that give rise to conflict. Nevertheless, there is also a trend towards a more harmonious pattern of autonomous management–worker relations at the workplace. This development has created considerable tension within the unions, widening the gap between the workplace and the national levels of union organisation.

As unions have grown larger and the workplace has become more autonomous, union organisation has grown more bureaucratic. Composed of professional elites, union leadership has tended to become more concerned with national economic and political issues and more remote from the rank-and-file membership. Opinion poll evidence shows that union leaders are frequently distrusted by ordinary members who blame them for pursuing ideological and sectarian goals which many ordinary members do not share. Rank-and-file members complain that their 'bread and butter' interests are sacrificed to the political interests of union leaders who attach great significance to supporting socialist parties and making alliances with socialist governments when in office.

As a consequence of the increase in their bargaining power since the Second World War, unions have been under pressure to exercise restraint in their demands as a means of curbing inflation brought about by excessive wage increases. When socialist and communist parties have achieved power or shared it in a coalition with centre parties, this pressure on the unions to enter into a restrictive wage policy has been difficult to resist; but support has generally been less than wholehearted, and after a year or two has broken down.

The collapse of union support for incomes restraint has generally been due to the emergence of radical rank-and-file leaders who have seized the opportunity to exploit the resentment of ordinary union members at the holding down of their pay. Under this kind of pressure, union leaders have found it expedient to make demands that have inevitably wrecked the policy of constraint and unleashed the forces of inflation. Although in Sweden and the Netherlands the unions and employers' organisations managed for many years to make and police a central agreement that gave some protection from excessive union pressures, the system eventually broke down, as explained in this book by Leion and van Zweeden. With conservative governments in power unions have generally felt less obligation to follow a policy of constraint, but they have been forced in practice by the realities of the economic and political situation prevailing, especially the level of unemployment, to moderate to some extent the extreme demands they have shown an inclination to make. Although the unions blame governments for the increase of unemployment since 1979, this increase has been to a large extent due to the bargaining pressures they have been able to exert on pay levels which, though less than under the economic and political conditions of the 1960s and 1970s, have produced the unfortunate results of stagflation. The fall in the level of inflation since 1982 in West European countries has been significantly influenced by the lower levels of pay forced upon the unions by adverse economic circumstances and by a considerable improvement in productivity achieved, again, by compelling unions to accept new technology and a more efficient use of manpower. Unfortunately, by comparison with the USA, where the power of the unions has declined much further than in Europe, economic recovery has been much slower. There can be no doubt that the superior economic performance of the USA, especially high rates of growth and levels of employment, owes a great deal to the slower rise in wages and less resistance to economic change.

Looking to the Future

In looking to the future most of the contributors to this book are cautiously optimistic that, in the countries covered, employers and governments are moving towards adjustments in the industrial relations patterns that will bring about a new and more positive relationship. For this to be achieved, it will require governments and employers to place the unions under such pressures that they come to terms with the changes in economic and organisational structures and collective behaviour required to establish a stable equilibrium.

At the heart of the unions' problem in adjusting their objectives and methods are fundamental ambiguities that must be resolved. Though the unions proclaim the virtues of pluralism, they are also committed to the achievement of goals which involve the destruction of private enterprise and the replacement of a market economy with a unitary socialist system of public ownership. It is true that the determination of unions to achieve their ideological aims is generally qualified by the necessity to respond to the immediate practical needs of their members; but, as in the case of Germany, they also wish to achieve control of industry through co-determination or, in the case of Sweden, through union-controlled investment funds or, in Britain, France and Italy, through public ownership of industry.

Notions of industrial democracy have a long and varied history. Demands for control through co-determination of wage-earner funds have, in conditions of decline, been put on ice; but for those who see the evolution of the unions moving from an adversary role to a controlling power, this setback is only a temporary halt. Whether or not there is a new impetus towards the syndicalist society will depend, in the long run, on whether unions can demonstrate that they can overcome the problems which have led to their decline. In the mid-1980s this prospect does not look like one they could achieve in the foreseeable future in any of the countries examined in the study.

These ideological objectives, though seemingly remote from realisation, provide a justification and a powerful incentive for those who wish to see a unitary socialist state created to campaign ceaselessly and to organise to secure control of the unions. There have been many examples of strikes in the European countries primarily motivated by political objectives, though plausibly justified by reference to some more immediate economic or social grievance. The most dramatic of such events has been the twelve months' miners' strike in Britain, which was aimed not only at preventing the closure of uneconomic mines but also at the downfall of the government.

The survival of free trade unionism is dependent on the survival of a democratic political system which, in turn, is dependent on the existence of a predominantly privately owned enterprise system operating in the context of a market economy under the rule of law. If the trade unions become so powerful as to threaten the existence of private enterprise through a monopoly of bargaining power, or to secure control of companies through the right of representation on, and the right of veto over, boards of directors; or are able to bring down liberal and conservative governments by strikes in order to replace them with socialist or communist governments, pluralism, and free trade unionism with it, will itself be endangered. There is no guarantee that it will never happen, except through a clear recognition that it might if unions fall under the control of those who wish to abolish private enterprise and to create a unitary state based upon public ownership of the means of production and distribution, or if such elements are not effectively constrained by their members, public opinion and voluntary and legal rules which impose limits on their power.

The trade unions of Europe—and with them labour relations in general—stand today at a crossroads. They have been severely battered by the shocks of structural change brought about by technological and economic forces. Everywhere they are in decline and they have been compelled, in some cases, to retreat from long-established positions of power and influence. There is widespread uncertainty and disagreement within the trade union movement about which way the unions should be going and how they should respond to what is becoming a fundamental crisis. The central institutions of the unions have lost their prestige and status and can no longer meet the expectations of their members. Locked into bureaucratic structures and hampered by rigid concepts of organisation and behaviour, unions face a challenge which, in the long run, could become a question of their survival as is already happening in the United States.

Unions are not likely to disappear overnight, they are still powerful sectional organisations capable of doing great damage or of making a significant contribution to the stability and welfare of society. The trends analysed in this book suggest, though there are important variations between countries, that in spite of some growth of radical left-wing influence, in this period ahead, the political and economic power of the trade unions is more likely to get weaker than to grow in strength. This provides an opportunity to develop as Roland Tavitian suggests, a new approach to social cohesion, which is likely to be found in the evolution of a more responsible consensus between employers and employees and the organisations which represent their interests.

The basis of such a consensus must start from the mutual recognition and acceptance that in pluralist social democracies it is in the interest of all sections of society that employers and unions follow constructive and responsible policies. It is necesary if collective bargaining is to continue as a primary method of determining substantive conditions of employment that unions come to terms with employers on the need to prevent increases in labour costs from generating inflation and increases in unemployment. This requires that under conditions of advanced technology and volatile economic circumstances the role of the unions must be reconciled with decentralisation, adaptation, flexibility, mobility, involvement and low-cost conflict resolution which are essential means to the achievement of the more efficient use of resources and improvement in the quality of working life.

The social democracies which most effectively restructure their industrial relations systems so as to satisfy these imperatives are likely to be those in which employers and unions respond positively to the social values which are essential to societies which wish to remain free, dynamic and protect the welfare of all their citizens.

NOTES ON CONTRIBUTORS

Federico Butera is head of RSO, a consulting group that is engaged in organisational development and management training. Previously he worked for ILO and EEC, and lectured at Italian universities and internationally. Between 1962 and 1973 he was head of the Italian Centre for Sociological and Organisational Studies. Federico Butera has published ten books and around 50 magazine articles in his special field.

Anders Leion is a graduate economist. Has worked in various fields in the public sector. Between 1968 and 1975 he was employed at LO, Swedish Trade Union Confederation, and between 1981 and 1983 at SACO/SR. At present he is working with the Swedish Institute of Public Opinion. Anders Leion has written several books on the Swedish industrial relations system.

Malcolm R. Lovell, Jr, MBA, is a graduate economist of Harvard and is now distinguished Visiting Professor at George Washington University. He has previously been Secretary of State at the Department of Labor and President of the American Rubber and Tire Manufacturers' Trade Association. Malcolm R. Lovell, Jr, has published books on labour market legislation in the USA and on immigration.

Hugo Müller-Vogg is a DPhil and *Frankfurter Allgemeine Zeitung's* US correspondent since 1984. Previously he was financial editor of the same newspaper in Düsseldorf. Hugo Müller-Vogg was awarded his doctorate for a thesis on relations between labour market organisations in West Germany during the 1966–74 period.

Jean Nousbaum was, until his untimely death, a consultant who worked for a large number of employers' associations and was chairman of an executive recruitment body (APEC). Jean Nousbaum published reports from OECD seminars on labour mobility and on negotiation of collective agreements and a report for the ILO on the possible entry of Portugal into the EEC.

Benjamin Roberts is Emeritus Professor of industrial relations at the London School of Economics; and Visiting Professor at MIT, Princeton, Berkeley, and UCLA. He has also lectured at universities in Europe, the Far East and Australia. Benjamin Roberts is editor of the *British Journal of Industrial Relations* and has written a great many books and articles on trade union organisations, negotiating systems and co-determination in Western Europe, North America and Japan.

Aage Tarp, BA (economics) is a lecturer and research fellow at Copenhagen School of Economics. From 1958 to 1983, Aage Tarp was employed by the Danish Employers' Confederation, his positions including head of the long-term structural change department. Since 1961 he has also been principal lecturer in business economics and administration at the Danish Institute of Technology.

Roland Tavitian is a consultant and lecturer in economics at the University of Paris-Nanterre. He has also been head of the Department of Employment at the EEC Commission and worked for the French Planning Secretariat and the World Bank.

Einar Thorsrud was professor and research fellow at the Labour Research Institute in Oslo, and Professor in Social Psychology at the University of Oslo. From 1962 to 1972 Einar Thorsrud was head of the Industrial Democracy Project, and from 1975 to 1981 Chairman of the International Council for Quality of Working Life. Until recently, Einar Thorsrud was engaged in research in management and organisations, a subject on which he had published several articles.

Antonius Fredrik van Zweeden is a journalist and since 1966 member of the editorial board of *Niewe Rotterdamse Courant NRC/Handelsblad*. A. F. van Zweeden has published several books on labour market organisations in various countries, including Holland, Western Europe and the USA. He has also described the Swedish negotiating model in a book.

INDEX

Note: Sub-entries are in alphabetical order except where chronological order is more significant. Major trade unions and employers' organisations are included. These are entered under their acronyms. Their full names are not indexed but can be found by consulting the first page reference for each one. The following abbreviations are used: FRG = Federal Republic of Germany; GB = Great Britain.

access to company control (France)
   53–63
   to means external to enterprise
      61–3
   to property 53–61
   see also democracy; property
AFL-CIO (American labour
   federations) 243–5, 251
aims see goals
American perspectives on European
   trade unions 242–61
   employers 260–1
   governments 259
   trade unions 259–60
   see also United States

Bain, G. S. 101, 102–3
bargaining in 1980s and 1990s
   (Norway) 194–5
BDA (German employers'
   organisation) 76
Blum, N. 231
board representation (Italy) 149–52
   see also democracy
Booth, A. 101
Borchgrevink, T. 190
Britain see Great Britain
Brown, W. 107
Bullock, Lord 108–10
Butera, F. 137, 249, 254, 271

Callaghan, J. 108
capital
   and labour, equivalence of 166–7
   participation in (France) 55–6
Catlin, S. 101
CBI (British employers' organisation)
   108, 128–30
centralisation (Sweden) 206–7,
   210–11
CFDT (French union) 44, 48, 51,
   53–4, 56–7, 59–67, 226
CFTC (French union) 45, 48, 52, 57,
   67

CGC (French union) 45, 47, 48, 53,
   56, 64–7
CGIL (Italian union) 138, 142, 150,
   152, 156
CGPME (French employers'
   organisation) 46, 49, 70–1
CGT (French union) 44, 45, 48–9,
   51–2, 54–67, 226
Churchill, W. 114
CISL (Italian union) 138, 142, 150–2,
   155–6
CNPF (French employers'
   organisation) 46, 49, 70–1
CNV (Netherlands union) 161–3, 167,
   175–6, 177
community level industrial relations
   (France) 54–5
company control see access
'Confindustria' (Italian employers'
   organisation) 138, 152
conflict
   in Netherlands 160–1, 176–9
   in Sweden 217
consensus in Netherlands 176–9
counter-power (FRG) 78–82
crisis
   energy (Norway) 185–7
   phase 1969–73 (Italy) 143

DA (Danish employers' organisation)
   6, 19–20, 22, 26, 35, 40, 43–4
de Gaulle, C. 45
democracy, industrial participation
   in France 55–6
   in GB 108–10, 128–30
   in Italy 149–52
   in Norway 197–9
   see also access; property
Den Uyl, J. 176–7
Denmark, trade unions in 5–44, 227,
   231, 248, 250, 253, 258
   background 6–8
   full employment and creation of
      welfare society 8–12

273

policy, targets and ideology 14–20
policy, reactions to crisis since 1974
    20–4
policy, internal reactions to 24–30
in 1980s and 1990s 30–42
employers and DA's future role
    and function 43–4
DGB (German confederation of
    unions) 75–8, 80–3, 86–9, 249
differences, national 227–8
disharmony *see* conflict
diversity of enterprises (France)
    69–70

economic
    disintegration (Sweden) 212–14
    planning (GB) 128–30
    trends (France) 65–6
Elshaikh, F. 101
Emery, F. 189
employers and employers'
    organisations
    American perspectives on 260–1
    in Denmark 6, 19–20, 22, 26, 35,
        40, 43–4
    in France 46, 49–50, 70–1
    in FRG 76
    in GB 100, 108, 128–30
    in Italy 138, 152
    in Netherlands 159–60, 169–70
    in Norway 181, 193–4, 200–1
    in Sweden 204–5; *see also* SAF
employment, full (Denmark) 8–12
energy crisis (Norway) 185–7
Engellau, P. 204
Englestad, P. H. 200
equilibrium prospect for GB 130–6
ETUC (European Trades Union
    Congress) 234–5, 239
European perspectives on trade union
    trends 222–42
    new context for industrial relations
        223–6
    future 226–33
    community level industrial
        relations, prospects for 233–41
exports
    Denmark 5
    France 45
    FRG 75
    GB 100
    Italy 137
    Netherlands 159
    Norway 180
    Sweden 204

Federal Republic of Germany, unions
    in 75–99, 226–30, 247–9, 255, 261
    trends and demands 76–8
    ideology 78–82
    regulative policy 82–7
    trade union practice 87–92
    organisational policy 92–6
FNV (Netherlands union) 159, 161–3,
    167–8, 172, 175–6, 251
FO (French union) 46, 47, 48, 52–3,
    60–1, 65, 67
France, unions in 45–76, 226–35
    passim, 255, 260
    participants in industrial relations
        46–50
    aims of unions and management
        50–2
    routes of access to company control
        53–63
    future prospects 63–7
FTF (Danish union) 6, 36
future 226–33, 267–70
    in Denmark 43–4
    in France 63–7
    in GB 119–24
    in Italy 155–8
    in Netherlands 170–5
    in Norway 188–91
    in Sweden 217–20

Germany *see* Federal Republic of
    Germany
Giscard d'Estaing, V. 45
goals
    national similarities in 228–9
    of unions in Netherlands 161–4
governments
    American perspective on 259
    in Denmark 5
    in France 45
    in FRG 75
    in GB 100
    in Italy 137, 152–4
    in Netherlands 159
    in Norway 180
    in Sweden 204
    see also political
Grafstrom, L. 252
Great Britain, unions in 100–36,
    227–8, 237–8, 247–8, 250, 255, 261
    decade of growth (1969–79) 101–3
    Royal Commission on 103–5;
        failure of 107–8
    Heath government and industrial
        relations reforın attempt 105

legal support 105–7
industrial democracy committee
  proposals 108–10
future 19–28; Labour government,
  next 124–8
recession and legal reform 110–13
Labour Party and 113–19, 124–8
employers, economic planning and
  industrial democracy 128–30
new equilibrium, prospect for
  130–6
Gross National Product per capita
Denmark 5
France 45
FRG 75
GB 100
Italy 137
Netherlands 159
Norway 180
Sweden 204

Hart, G. 244
Healey, D. 108
Heath, E. 105, 107
history of unions
  in Italy 140–3
  in Norway 181–4
  in Sweden 205–14

ideology in FRG 78–82
industrial democracy *see* democracy
industrial relations
  community, prospects for 233–41
  new context for 223–6
  reform attempts (GB) 105
industrialisation phase 1945–60 (Italy)
  141–2
Italy, unions in 137–58, 227–32
  passim, 235, 247–9, 254, 258
  historical context 140–3
  organisational mutation in large
    enterprises 143–6
  industrial relations in 1970s 146–54
  present and visible trends 155–8

Japan 222, 224, 227, 245–7

KAD (Danish union) 7, 37
Kinnock, N. 120
Kirkland, L. 245
Kok, W. 176

labour and capital, equivalence of
  166–7
Labour Party (GB) 113–19, 124–8

large companies
  Denmark 5
  France 45
  FRG 75
  GB 100
  Italy, 137, 143–6
  Netherlands 159
  Norway 180
  Sweden 204
leadership of unions (Netherlands)
  168
legal reform and support for unions
  (GB) 105–7, 110–13
Leion, A. 204, 271
LO (Danish federation of unions) 6,
  7, 10–44 *passim*, 250, 253
LO (Norwegian federation of unions)
  180, 192–202, 250
LO (Swedish federation of unions)
  204–7, 209–13, 215–17, 220–1, 250,
  252, 257
Lovell Jr, M. R. 242, 263, 271

management (France) 50–2, 57–8
  see also democracy
Melhuus, M. 190
MHP (Netherlands union) 159, 161
Michels, R. 218–19
Mitterand, F. 45, 248, 255
Mondale, W. 244
Müller-Vogg, H. 75, 249, 255, 257,
  271

NAF (Norwegian employers'
  organisation) 181,193–4, 200–1
nationalisation (France) 53–4
NCW (Netherlands employers'
  organisation) 160, 169
Netherlands, unions in 159–79, 247–8,
  251, 253–4, 261
  disharmony and conflict
    (1960s–70s) 160–1
  structure and aims of unions 161–4
  'big trade-off' 164–6
  equivalence of labour and capital
    166–7
  leadership of unions 168
  employers' organisations 169–70
  present and future developments
    170–5
  union power 175–6
  consensus or conflict 176–9
NKV (Netherlands union) 159, 161–2
Norway, unions in 180–203, 227, 248,
  252–3, 258, 260

historical background 181–4
societal change after energy crisis
    184–7
transition phases 187–8
future 188–91
challenges and strategies for 1980s
    and 1990s 192–202
Nousbaum, J. 45, 271
NVV (Netherlands union) 159, 161–2,
    177

oligarchy (Sweden) 218–20
organisational
    changes (Italy) 143–6
    policy (FRG) 92–6

participation *see* democracy
planning, economic (GB) 128–30
pluralism (France) 46–7
policy, union
    Denmark 20–30
    organisational (FRG) 92–6
political
    crisis (Denmark) 20–4
    disintegration (Sweden) 212–14
    parties (France) 48–9
    projects and participation 231
    trends (France) 64–5
    see also governments
population
    Denmark 5
    France 45
    FRG 75
    GB 100
    Italy 137
    Netherlands 159
    Norway 180
    Sweden 204
power of unions 263–4
    in Netherlands 175–6
    in Sweden 207–8
Price, R. 102–3
property, access to (France) 53–61
    co-operative production societies
        54–5
    management, supervision of 58
    management role 57–8
    nationalisation 53–4
    participation in capital and
        shareholdings 55–6
    wage funds 56–7
    workers' right of expression 60–1
    works councils 58–60
    see also access; democracy
public sector

Denmark 6
France 45, 69–70
FRG 75
GB 100
Italy 138
Netherlands 159
Norway 180
Sweden 204, 217

Qvale, T. U. 200

rationalisation phase in Italy
    (1960–68) 142
Reagan, R. 245
recession and legal reform (GB)
    110–13
recruitment in 1980s and 1990s
    (Norway) 192–4
reform of industrial relations, attempt
    (GB) 105
'reformist' unions (France) 52–3
regulative policy (FRG) 78–87
Rehn, G. 212
representativity (France) 46–7
Reuther, W. 245
'revolutionary' union organisation
    (France) 51–2
Richardson, G. R. 101
Roberts, B. C. 100, 272
role and power of unions, factors
    determining 263–4
Royal Commission on Trade Unions
    and Employers' Organisations
    (GB) 103–5
    failure of 107–8

SACO/SR (Swedish union) 204,
    213–14
SAF (Swedish employers'
    organisation) 204–7, 211, 215–17,
    220, 248, 250, 252, 257
    memorandum 1–2, 227, 231–2
Saltsjöbaden Agreement (Sweden)
    206–7
Schön, D. 189
shareholdings, participation in
    (France) 55–6
SID (Danish union) 7, 28, 37–8, 42
similarities, national 228–9
SNPMI (French employers'
    organisation) 46, 49, 70–1
social change 265–6
    Norway 185–7
social welfare (Norway) 195–6
strategic change (Norway) 199–202

structural change 265–6
structural crisis (Denmark) 20–4
structure of unions (Netherlands) 161–4
Sweden, unions in 204–21, 227, 231–3, 248, 250, 252, 258, 261
historical background 205–14; origin and dependence of institutions 205–6; Saltsjöbaden Agreement 206–7; power over business sector 207–8; 1950s and 1960s 208–10; centralised common sense 210–11; economic and political disintegration (1970s) 212–14
current situation 215–20; SAF tires 215–16; central power, crumbling 216; conflict in private and public sector 217; future 217–20

Tarp, A. 5, 253, 272
Tavitian, R. 222, 272
technological change (Italy) 145
Thatcher, M. 114–15
Thorsrud, E. 180, 201, 252, 272
'trade-off, big' (Netherlands) 164–6
trade unions *see* American perspectives; Denmark; European perspectives; Federal Republic of Germany; France; Great Britain; Italy; Netherlands; Norway; Sweden
transition phase (Norway) 187–8
TUC (British Trade Union Congress) 100, 104, 107–9, 112–19, 123–31 *passim*, 134–5, 251, 255

UIL (Italian union) 138, 142, 150, 156
United States 222, 224, 227
see also American

values, similarities in 228–9
van Zweeden, A. F. 159, 251, 272
Vickers, G. 186
VNO (Netherlands employers' organisation) 159–60, 169

wage funds (France) 56–7
Wagner, G. 169
welfare *see* social welfare
Wigforss, E. 208
Williams, T. A. 189
Windmuller, J. P. 160
work councils (France) 58–60

YS (Norwegian federation of unions) 181, 193–5

*For Product Safety Concerns and Information please contact
our EU representative GPSR@taylorandfrancis.com Taylor & Francis
Verlag GmbH, Kaufingerstraße 24, 80331 München, Germany*

T - #0008 - 230425 - C0 - 234/156/17 [19] - CB - 9781032370934 - Gloss Lamination